White Settlers

Charles Jedrej and Mark Nuttall

White Settlers
The Impact of Rural Repopulation in Scotland

harwood academic publishers
Australia • China • France • Germany • India • Japan
Luxembourg • Malaysia • The Netherlands • Russia • Singapore
Switzerland • Thailand • United Kingdom • United States

3 Boulevard Royal
L-2449 Luxembourg

British Library Cataloguing in Publication Data

Nuttall, Mark
   White Settlers: Impact of Rural
   Repopulation in Scotland
   I. Title   II. Jedrej, Charles
   304.809411

   ISBN 3-7186-5752-X (Hardcover)
   ISBN 3-7186-5753-8 (Softcover)

Contents

Acknowledgements

Our research in Scotland was funded by the Economic and Social Research Council between 1990 and 1993. Throughout the research many people gave generously of their time and hospitality. It would be impossible to name everyone in print (both for reasons of space and for personal preferences for anonymity), but those who deserve mention include Tom Forsyth, Gavin and Kaye Lockhart, Marion and Fraser Whyte, Margaret and Robert Harvey, Sandy Macrae, Alan Macrae, John Macrae, Bill Ritchie, Roy Wentworth, Ken Macleod, Rick and Hilary Rhode, Janette Crosley, and Martin and Zara Wheeler. During the period of writing we also received valuable feedback and advice on various aspects of the research from many colleagues and associates at Edinburgh University, Brunel University, University of Wales, University of Alaska–Fairbanks, and the Centre for North Atlantic Studies at Aarhus University. In particular, we would also like to thank Richard Jenkins for his comments on an earlier version of the entire manuscript.

Introduction

In the late sixties and early seventies there occurred first in France, West Germany, and East Germany, and then in other industrialised countries what came to be called by demographers urban-rural, or counterstream migration. After over a hundred years of growth of urban populations and the decline in rural populations, that pattern began to reverse. What is variously called rural rejuvenation in Britain and America, or the renaissance of the countryside in France (Kayser 1988) is closely associated with counterstream migration. The change had not been anticipated or predicted by demographers, and indeed the first reports were met with scepticism (Zelinsky 1977, Vining and Kontuly 1978, Brown and Wardell 1980, Champion 1981). Among larger countries with remote rural regions two patterns of deconcentration have been noted: the repopulation of remote rural regions and the deconcentration of large urban cores into adjacent territory of lower density (Campbell and Johnson, 1976:127–145; Champion 1989). This book is concerned with the former as it has affected rural Scotland.

Subsequent demographic research suggests that after an initial surge the growth of population in non-metropolitan areas slowed down in the late seventies, and that metropolitan regions are recovering. Nevertheless, according to Champion, in Britain 'the recovery of the big cities has taken place alongside a renewed upsurge in some remoter and more rural parts of the country' (Champion 1987: 388). The reverse in the decline of the rural population of Scotland occurred during the decade 1971–81 when almost all rural Districts experienced a period of rapid population growth, a growth which has continued during the subsequent intercensal period (Scottish Office 1992:23). Only Caithness, Cumnock & Doon Valley, and, very narrowly, Roxburgh, Districts did not register an increase in their population during 1971–81. An inspection of the extreme cases, the largest increase and the largest decrease, point to changes in the energy industry in Scot-

1

land. In Cumnock & Doon Valley coal mining, a rural rather than urban industry, was coming to an end while Shetland was involved in the growth of the North Sea oil industry. The role of natural change diminished during the two decades to become a subsidiary influence as a component of net change. As before, when the rural population decline slowed or stabilised in the nineteen thirties, it is likely that the growth in population in rural areas will comprise a greater number of people moving into the towns in these areas rather than into the countryside.

Beyond securing the demographic facts, empirical research has been pre-occupied with detecting the causes of counterstream migration. This has generally consisted of sample surveys of immigrants into rural areas where the questionnaires seek to discover the migrants' motives. They are then analysed to disclose the distribution of these reasons among the kinds of people who emerge in the survey sample. Migrants are usually, on the basis of their motives, classified into three categories: one, those for whom employment is not a factor but who find living in a rural area more congenial than a large town; two, those who have had to move into the rural area because of their employment; and, three, those who have tried to meet a preference for living in the countryside with a need to earn a living. These findings are then compared with reports of similar research in other parts of the country with respect to the different proportions in each category, and this leads to debates about the relative validity of voluntarist theories (counterstream migrants choose to live in the countryside as a 'lifestyle' option), the consequences of state intervention through various development agencies, grants and tax incentives, and structural changes in industrial production (see, for example, Jones, Ford, Caird, and Berry 1984; for an English study, see Bolton and Chalkley 1990).

Yet there are problems in attempting to distinguish between the effects and the causes of counterstream migration and locating the motivations of the counterstream migrants themselves. The economic and social consequences of repopulation in any particular locality need to be carefully distinguished from the extension of social and economic development from the metropolitan centres to the rural peripheries which created the conditions for counterstream migration. As far as Britain is concerned it seems to be generally accepted that since the beginning of the 1920s, and with increasing pace since the end of the second world war, urban and rural parts of the UK have converged upon a common employment structure, real income level and style of living. Rural localities and their residents have been inducted into the wider social structure. The rural community, according to Littlejohn, 'becomes less an area of common life than an area within which the individual chooses his associations subject to such barriers as are imposed by social class or physical distance' (1963: 155). This theory is contradicted by explanations offered by and attributed to some counterstream migrants. These accounts appeal to the differences between town and country not merely as physical environments, but also as 'ways of life' to explain migration.

In Scotland there is also a vigorous public debate about the social and cultural impact of migration into Scotland, especially into rural areas. Expressions of concern range from the editorial launching a new magazine, *Wester Ross Life* (1994: 26), which declares, rather anxiously, that it will not 'shy away' from 'controversy', which turns out to be discussing in a balanced way the 'influx' of incomers, to the wilder activities, declarations, and publications of various individuals describing themselves as 'Settler Watch', and 'Scottish Watch'. These two groups attracted considerable press coverage in the late summer and autumn of 1993, and not only in Scotland: both John Hancox (1993) in *The Guardian ,* and Neal Ascherson (1993) in *The Independent* took up considerable space to address themselves to the meaning of these events. Scottish Watch (1994) have used Census data in one of their pamphlets to support their claim that repopulation amounts to the English 'flooding' into Scotland, that the Scottish people are the victims of a new wave of clearances which are being carried out by the cheque book rather than the torch, and that the indigenous culture is being eradicated. There is an 'Englishing of Scotland' underway. However, Dickson (1994) has carried out a detailed analysis of survey data relating to Scotland in general rather than rural Scotland alone, and concluded that 'there is more evidence to support the idea that the English born people have in many respects assimilated themselves into many aspects of Scottish life . . . it could be argued that the broader English population in Scotland has experienced some form of 'Scottishing' effect' (1994:131).

Such investigations into the attributes and impact of migrants seem obvious and natural enough. The rather abstract demographic concept of 'counterstream migration' is recognised in practice, in situations, for example, where the researchers are explaining the nature of their enquiries, as the 'problem of incomers'. The matter of 'incomers' is an issue in which everyone has an interest, and people soon, and with enthusiasm, recount incidents from their own experience, or those of other people, in terms of relationships between locals and incomers. It is presumed that academic research would also take for granted the existential reality of 'incomers' and set about answering, using scientific methods, such worrying questions as 'what kind of people are they?' 'how many of them are there?' 'why do they do it?' Clearly for some people there are important questions to be raised about incomers.

The existence, in general terms, of locals and incomers is, to all concerned, so obviously a feature of the rural social setting that it seems that the only meaningful questions that can be raised concern the empirical attributes of locals and incomers. Ordinary people in their everyday lives manage adequately with vaguely defined words since in practice 'everyone knows who the locals/incomers are'. Scientific investigation, however, needs objectively defined terms. The presumption is that the scientific vocabulary is no more than an accurate version of the everyday vernacular, and that therefore through objective and accurate investigation the 'problem' of incomers will be clarified, this being the necessary first step towards identifying a 'solution'.

The approach we adopted for this research was, from the beginning, focused on the conflicts and ambiguities surrounding the matter of rural repopulation: repopulation is a good thing but incomers are a problem, incomers rejuvenate the local economy, but the indigenous people are marginalised. We recognise that, while representations such as 'locals', 'incomers', 'lairds', 'crofters', 'white settlers', 'the English', 'absentee property holders', 'Highland culture', and so on, are agreed upon, the reality to which they refer is elusive and contested. Everyone agrees that there are 'locals' and 'incomers', but it is not easy to find a consensus about who they are or what is 'Highland culture' and the 'ancient way of life' that incomers threaten. There are some relatively stable points, but crude reality alone cannot underwrite the significance of the representations. There are sociological and cultural processes at work which amplify some features and mute others, thereby endowing what may be called 'key concepts' with a salient and compelling quality. We believe and hope to show in the following pages, that the situation is not of a kind that can be resolved one way or the other by appealing to accurate scientific investigation, and more and more research, until at last we know what exactly is the truth of the matter. These matters are essentially contested. In this book we have tried to sustain both a detached analysis and at the same time an involved but critical concern to promote institutions and policies which are likely to contribute to a rich and viable rural dimension of the Scottish landscape. After all it is ours.

We have made use of a variety of sources. Both of us have travelled extensively throughout the southwest, the north, and northwest of Scotland, and have stayed for varying lengths of time in several places enjoying the hospitality of people willing to share their experiences and thoughts about the topics of this book. This is not a community study. Indeed to have adopted such a method would have presumed the reality of something that was in question. Instead it might be more accurate to describe the field work method employed here as 'a network study' rather than community study, though even this might be misleading since the research was not directly concerned with the properties of such networks. In other words, studying in networks, not studying networks.

As an intellectual project, we have also explored themes central to much of our previous research. Jedrej's work in Africa had alerted him to the complicated meanings and overtones of the figure of 'the stranger', while Nuttall had been concerned with, among other things, the attempts of Greenlanders to construct a new yet authentic personal and collective identity on their journey to nationhood within the context of an evolving subordinate relationship to Denmark and even Europe. Indeed parallels between Greenland and Scotland are from time to time drawn by those campaigning for Scottish independence from Britain (England). So there was also a coincidence of personal academic interests. Yet the differences and distances remain crucial: in the matter of trying to understand human affairs anthropologists claim a positive virtue in coming at social phenomena from an angle, tangentially as it were. When we embarked on this research, the Arctic and the tropics should, we thought, give us an obtuse enough angle.

The situation confronting anthropologists enquiring into aspects of urban-rural migration in a literate culture and industrial society is one where the usual method of participant observation as a means of generating a corpus of texts and documents is almost redundant. Novels, poetry, official documents, books, newspapers, biographies, magazine articles, pamphlets, histories, programmes, advertisements, brochures, guides, academic dissertations, surveys, manifestos, to identify only the most obvious, are without number and are continually being produced. In this research we have made use of all such texts, and others, and have cited them where appropriate. Given the wealth of what is called 'secondary material', what then is the additional benefit of generating even more texts through participant observation?

Participant observation is not just about generating documents, as the intractable nature of such material to anthropologists other than the field worker who actually wrote the notebooks and journals testifies. Though anthropologists interrogate their notebooks and other records while subsequently writing their accounts they do so in the context of an intimate personal experience of the circumstances in which these documents were produced, or in more general terms, the discourse from which the texts were abstracted. These circumstances are not simply a matter of having lived with the people whose society and culture is being described, but of having also deliberately and persistently sought to understand and experience social life in their terms. Participant observation in this investigation of urban-rural migration is in part about returning to the origins and circumstances, and to the authors, of the varied texts which already exist. So much, then, for the origins of the work which resulted in the present book. It may now be helpful to chart out the themes and subject matter the reader will encounter in the chapters which follow.

The first two chapters provide what might be called a conceptual and a historical background respectively to the phenomenon of rural repopulation in Scotland and attention is drawn to both the particularities of the Scottish experience and to what is common to other parts of the United Kingdom and Europe. The conceptual background comprises a critical examination of the common sense terms 'local' and 'incomer', 'town' and 'country' and their relationship to such scientific abstractions as 'counterstream migration'. The historical background is not a demographic history of rural Scotland but a review of the commentary which accompanied the depopulation of the countryside, which is a very different thing. A comparison with contemporary controversy accompanying repopulation reveals remarkably similar concerns although the two phenomena provoking the reactions are in direct contrast. Evidently people are more sensitive to and disturbed by changes in the population in the countryside than to absolute levels of population, no matter how stable.

Chapter three describes the local experience of recent population changes in Nithsdale and in Gairloch. At this less general level, it becomes evident that there are subtle differences between the Southwest and the Northwest of Scotland as regards the experience of counterstream migration. It seems that in the Northwest people tend to talk about 'incomers' in connection with changes to 'ways of life' and 'tradition', that is, to matters of culture, but in the south west the presence of 'incomers' seems to be associated with a feeling of loss of 'community', that is, to changes in social structure.

It is against a background of decades of alarm about the consequences of rural depopulation that chapter four returns to the matter of locals and incomers raised in the first chapter. The analysis reveals how the apparently incompatible relationship between, on the one hand, tourists, sojourners, and permanent settlers, and on the other, tradition and community, is actually dialogical so that the former also bring into existence the latter. The tourist induces the tradition but in circumstances in which it seems as if tradition is being eroded, and a sense of the presence of community is the product of a perspective which is largely objective, and objectivity is, above all, a quality of the outsider.

Chapter five also returns to the first chapter to take up again the spatial dimension and examines how a sense of place as an attribute of identity becomes amplified in the presence of 'strangers', while at the same time the identity, meanings, and history of places is challenged and defended. Particular attention is given to the conflict between those who seek to appropriate the landscape as scenery, as a view, as a heritage, and as sites to be objectively and scientifically researched, and those who seek to engage with the land in a personal relationship, as a means of livelihood as well as a source of personal identity. In this respect crofting, as a practice and an institution, receives considerable attention from governmental and other policy making quarters. A 'real local' is a 'real crofter', and yet crofting is also attracting the 'white settlers', and 'new ruralists'.

Chapter six discusses in general terms the institution of crofting as a model for sustainable rural development, and considers the argument that the croft ('a small piece of land surrounded by regulations'), and the practice of crofting, though usually perceived and valued as preserving a 'traditional way of life', is also a vehicle for promoting rural repopulation, innovation, and change. Finally, following on from this, chapter seven considers how definitions of local and incomer are contested with regard to conflict over resources and community empowerment. While the consistent focus in this book is on the Scottish situation, we hope that we have drawn attention to some of the theoretical and indeed social and political implications of counterstream migration generally.

Chapter 1

The Meanings of Counterstream Migration in Scotland

Locals and Incomers

As the various chapters of this book illustrate, assessing the impact of counterstream migration in Scotland is not immediately feasible. Previous research has also pointed to some of the difficulties. For example, Lumb's survey of seven localities throughout the Highlands and Islands revealed little correlation between the proportion of incomers in a population and their apparent impact upon it. Incomers may be numerically significant but socially insignificant, or numerically insignificant but socially significant (Lumb 1980: 53). Moreover, Lumb found that the dualistic notion of an indigenous population receiving incomers is also untenable as a representation of objective reality (1982: 62). Jones *et al*, in their examination of counterstream migration in the Highlands slide from a discussion of 'peripheral counter-urbanisation', by way of 'long distance migration', to 'the English'. They justify this operational definition of counterstream migration partly on the grounds that 'the indigenous population make a clear distinction between Scots incomers and "the English"' (1986:16). However, without any insight into why and in what circumstances people make such a distinction, and what it means, there is no way of assessing the relevance of this observation to the demographic analysis of counterstream migration.

In this chapter it is argued that the apparently simple shift from the vernacular vocabulary of locals and incomers, of town and country, to the technical terms and definitions of demography (urban-rural migration) is

9

not a move from a set of loosely defined inexact terms to some clearly defined scientific terms, from inaccurate to accurate representations of reality. Rather, there is a quite radical change of language from a vocabulary which is fundamentally metaphorical to an account which strives to represent the objective reality of migration in a literal way. Moving between these two modes of representation is not a simple matter of tightening up on definitions. Consider the following three cases.

First of all there is the experience of an American author of a sociological study of an Argyllshire community. He had, after several months residence among the people, come to accept, like the residents themselves, the pervasive sense of the settlement being divided into 'locals' and 'incomers' since these concepts underpinned the peoples' understanding of their own history and that of the events which constituted the history of the locality. So he was surprised, and that is the important fact, to discover after he had carried out an objective statistical survey that the settlement had been almost entirely repopulated by in-migration. Out of fifty nine household heads, only seven had been born in the locality (Stephenson 1984:124–7). Similarly, only 25% of the population of Lumb's survey localities were 'locals' who had never resided outside the locality, while one third of the population in 1979 were not resident in 1971 (Lumb 1982: *ibid.*).

Secondly, the irrelevance of objective considerations in the definition of locals and of incomers is manifest in attempts to use the terms in a way which discounts their symbolic, or metaphorical, value and takes them at their face value. Highland Regional Council, which is considered to be the most advanced of all Scottish Local Authorities in its concern to establish planning regulations and controls which will promote low cost housing for local people, arrives at a definition, as it must, of a local person as one who has been 'ordinarily resident for at least three years in a specified area', and Dumbarton District Council has defined a local person for the purposes of controlling housing in the Loch Lomond area as someone who has been continuously resident in the area for eighteen months (Scottish Homes 1991:45, 53–6). The notion that someone might become a 'local' a year and a half after moving into a locality is quite incompatible with the rhetorical sense of the term.

Thirdly, that the vocabulary of 'locals' and 'incomers' is not a literal description of reality is also evident in the way the terms are used. Rather than indicating a puzzling and problematic experience requiring explanation, they are deployed in making sense of otherwise abnormal events and experiences in the locality. As a consequence of their compelling obviousness, these concepts function as terminal points in explanatory accounts, and in the interpretation of controversial events. For example, a sense of the lack of availability of housing in a rural locality is often accounted for in terms of the relationship between locals and incomers. Such accounts have a long history which is more or less independent of general demographic trends in rural-urban or urban-rural migration, whether in England, or in Scotland. There are reports from before the First World War of an insufficiency of housing for local people in the English countryside being aggravated by the competition of townspeople 'turning cottages into villas and to the increasing tendency, fostered by bicycles, of urban workers living in rural districts' (Board of Agriculture and Fisheries 1913: 4). Forty years or so later and another Government report notes the 'antagonism' between 'townspeople' and 'country people', and remarks that incomers have acquired cottages that would 'ordinarily have been available for the countryman' (Ministry of Works and Planning 1942: 27). Fifty years on again and Scottish Homes reports the commonly held view that 'one of the major difficulties in developing owner-occupation was the influence from outside housing markets with people moving into rural areas and buying houses for significantly above the local market value' (Scottish Homes 1990: 9).

What is striking is the notion that 'incomers' are somehow out of place and disturbing what would 'ordinarily' be the case. The discrepancy between expectations, such as 'a local market value', and reality, the price houses are actually bought and sold for, is accounted for by the presence of incomers. This suggests that as the number and variety of incidents departing from what is considered by some people as normal or ordinary, including, perhaps, rural repopulation after generations of depopulation, increases so will their sense of the presence of increasing numbers of incomers. It follows also that when those who consider themselves to be 'locals' wish to bring about changes in their community it is strategically effective to use people identified as 'incomers', as Frankenberg (1957) showed in his study of a Welsh village. This study is also one of the few post war British 'community studies' to go beyond reproducing the rhetoric of community and to show instead how it is produced and deployed by the actors themselves (See also Bell and Newby 1974).

In this rhetoric a normal community is a community of 'locals', one with out 'incomers' and, as the term 'incomer' itself suggests, there was, in the life of a community, a time in the past when this was true, and, if there are presently incomers, will be true in the future when the incomers have been assimilated. This feeling is well exemplified in Norman MacCaig's poem 'A man in Assynt' which concludes wistfully imagining the repopulation of Scottish shores and glens (MacCaig 1985). The poet remembers the depopulation of the Highlands as he watches the tide withdraw, baring the rocks and sand, and then he thinks and hopes that as the tide will eventually return so that other 'sad withdrawal of people, may too reverse itself and flood the bays and sheltered glens with new generations'. The unstated assumption, which is virtually universal in all expressions of concern about Scottish rural depopulation, is that repopulation will be achieved by 'locals'. The 'dying landscape belongs to the dead, the crofters and fighters and fishermen' and the implication is that it will come alive again only after some kind of mass resurrection.

In fact, shortly after MacCaig published his poem in 1969, young men and women did appear on the deserted shores of the sea lochs and in the silent glens where they set about with great effort and considerable ingenuity rebuilding crofts and farms abandoned a generation ago. They had been abandoned because of the displacement of the old sea routes by roads, and by the introduction of public utilities such as electricity which also introduced differences and relative deprivations which rendered some holdings unlettable. However, such differences were in part precisely what was attractive to the kind of young people who had travelled in places such as India and South America, who came not only from urban Scotland but also from North America, South Africa, and other continents, as well as Yorkshire, or Derbyshire, and elsewhere, and many had attended prestigious universities. Ironically they were relearning, sometimes deliberately sometimes by accident, the old crofting and fishing skills, and raising families in circumstances that other people consider to be no longer acceptable to present generations.

Therefore, to the extent that the topic of counterstream migration resolves itself into discourse about 'locals' and 'incomers', it supplies explanatory concepts, rather than defines the beginning of a researchable problem into which an objective investigation might be carried out. In short, the vocabulary of 'locals' and 'incomers' is a complex and deeply embedded metaphor providing the terms through which people express and give meaning to the experiences which constitute their lives. The social anthropological interest lies in the metaphorical and symbolic attributes of the vernacular concepts and the ways in which they structure experience. Given the metaphorical force of the notions of local and incomer, in the sense that their obviousness is such a matter of common sense that they can be appealed to in order to interpret and bring meaning to events and experiences, what then is the source of the obviousness of these ideas? In other words, as Elias and Scotston (1965:172) in an early and insightful study of

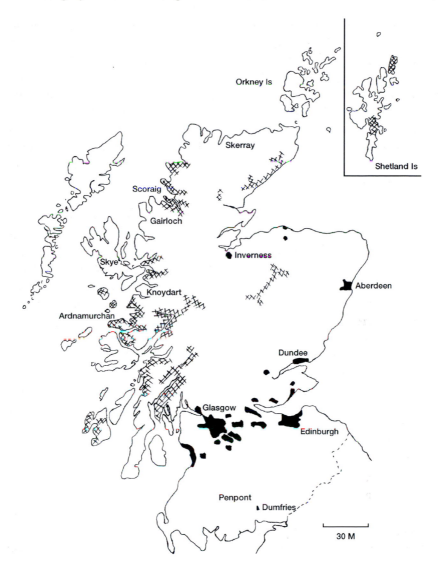

❂ Areas showing an increase in population
★ Urban areas

Map 1. Scotland, the beginning of rural re-population. Rural areas in Scotland more than twenty miles from urban areas and showing an increase in population during the decade 1961–1971. Based on Scottish Development Department Planning Map Series, No 14, 1972.

a community of 'old families' and 'newcomers' recognised, their compelling quality has to be accounted for in ways other than by looking for the empirical attributes of such entities in some objective reality, since that effect, trying to identify incomers and locals, is a possibility which is suggested only by and through the configuration of the usages of the words themselves.

Similar considerations apply to the contrast between town and country which is so intimately linked to that between incomers and locals. Nowadays there is little material difference between rural society and urban society except the feeling that there is something different about rural life. This feeling arises, firstly, from what might be called the amplification of systematic features of social structure, features which are muted in the urban setting and, secondly, because in the construction of national identities the rural landscape and its inhabitants are resorted to as a treasury of images. A number of studies have explored how in the discourse of the dominant and metropolitan culture, subordinate and marginal cultures are despised and yet simultaneously enter into the construction of the identity of the dominant culture (e.g. Said 1978; Stalybrass and White 1986; Herzfeld 1987). These asymmetrical structures are such as to give rise to a persisting ambivalence in the meaning of the term 'local' or 'native' as it is used by those who do not consider themselves to be either native or local. Those who identify themselves as local, or indigenous, are presented with perplexing problems of rejecting parts or all of these imposed constructions while at the same time recognising the historical reality of the social relationships which generate them. The rest of this chapter will examine how the vocabulary of locals and incomers, and of town and countryside, is informed by such systematic relationships of inequality of very general occurrence.

In Scotland the dimensions of meaning involved in the use of terms such as 'local' and 'incomer' are a function of the inescapable experience of asymmetries in social relationships. The relationship between local and incomer borrows from the richly ambiguous and asymmetrical national (or inter-national) relationship between Scotland and England, or Scotland and Britain. It is debatable whether the phrase 'white settlers', which is heard as often as 'incomers', borrows from the image of Scotland as a colonial subordinate of England/Britain to express the meaning of the relationships at the local level between incomers and locals, where the thwarted expectations of those who 'belong' are seen as having been usurped by those who do not, or whether the movement of people from England into rural areas of Scotland who then take over properties which 'ordinarily' would have been inhabited by local Scots is being used to elaborate the ideology of national subordination to England/Britain. It probably works both ways. The use of the expression 'white settlers' to describe usurping incomers is also an ironic but pointed self-reference by those who deliberately identify themselves not just as 'locals' but particularly as 'black natives', all of which is part of the imaging of a Scotland whose traditions and identity are threatened by a colonial relationship to a metropolitan England, or cosmopolitan Britain, clinging to the remains of an empire. Scottish Watch articulates these feelings when it writes that 'the Scots are most likely to be found in decaying urban labour camps — our cities and industrial towns. The English are most likely to be found enjoying the good life in the country — our country' (1984:6).

At another level the expression 'white settlers' resonates as a response from those who have been described as 'locals' by those who consider themselves to be cosmopolitan, and therefore non-local. While accepting the designation 'local' they reject the outsider's cosmopolitan meaning of the term which is essentially ambivalent (Nadel-Klein 1991). 'Locals' in this usage are either romantic heroes and heroines, a people of integrity, courage, loyalty, and hard work (in other words, 'noble savages'), or they are sly rustics, backward and degenerate roughs ('barbarians'). Sometimes they may even appear to be both at once, so that one may hear it said of 'locals' that they are polite and civil in one's presence, but behind one's back, while among themselves, they are treacherous and deceitful, given to drinking and fighting. Such a view is, however, basically the local as treacherous barbarian rather than as bold romantic. This ambivalence pervades the perspective and experience of the middle-class outsider and contributes to the feeling of an overt and a covert quality to the social life of a rural locality, of secrecy and talk of 'mafias', and mystery behind appearances, but it is largely a product of a particular perspective.

This view is reproduced by scholars such as Tylor who, in his influential *Primitive Culture*, first published in 1871, projected the ambivalence onto the locals, or 'natives', and then described them as 'unstable'. 'So when we read descriptions of the hospitality, the gentleness, the bravery, the deep religious feeling of the North American Indians, we admit their claims to our sincere admiration; but we must not forget that they were hospitable literally to a fault, that their gentleness would pass with a flash of anger into a frenzy, that their bravery was stained with cruel and treacherous malignity, that their religion expressed itself in absurd belief and useless ceremony' (Tylor 1929:31). Notice how it is possible to substitute 'Scottish Highlanders', 'Greek Mountain Shepheards', 'Corsican Goat-herders',

'Vosges Peasants', or any other marginalised people with which you are (un)familiar, for 'North American Indians' in this passage and still apparently make sense as a matter of fact. Tylor could not make up his mind whether what he called the 'low civilisations' of Europe, such as those of the Hebrides and Ireland, were to be accounted for by degeneration from a previously civilised state, or whether they were the 'relics of unchanged barbarism'. That it is the metropolitan duality of meanings of the term 'local' which is 'unstable' rather than the 'locals' is well exemplified by the writings of Alastair Alpin MacGregor who, after a series of hopelessly romantic books in the nineteen thirties with titles such as *Behold the Hebrides*, *Summer Days among the Western Isles*, where the inhabitants are portrayed as spiritual, other worldly figures, turned these representations up side down in *The Western Isles* (1941) with a description of Hebrideans as idle, drunken louts, which not only caused offence to the inhabitants but scandalised sections of the Scottish literary establishment (*The Scots Magazine* September 1975). Those so described, when they respond by characterising locally resident cosmopolitans as 'white settlers', deliberately call attention to, and thereby reject, these ambivalent meanings of the identity 'local' in favour of a sense which alludes to the objective inequalities of class stratification.

The claims of those describing themselves as 'locals' are premised on the notion of the natural, yet ancestral, and enduring rights of an indigenous population. For those for whom the locals are either romantic figures or examples of uncivilised humans, there can be no question of them being anything other than survivors from either a glorious past carrying with them the remnants of a once great culture, or an ancient population which has hardly yet been touched by the extension of civilisation. In this respect all these perceptions, share a presumption of a kind of historical longevity and a continuity, however attenuated, of a local population, indeed a community, which supposedly stretches back into the 'mists of time'. It is largely because of this consensus that 'locals', a community with a culture, are defined and investigated historically by themselves and by others, while 'incomers', a temporary aggregate of individuals, are the objects of social and psychological surveys. The historical research accumulates more and more concrete information as local histories are piled up, and so the subject, 'locals', is substantiated and realised, while the social surveys are condemned to repeat themselves endlessly, the results of the last survey fading even before the next one comes along to replace it, and thereby in the methods, rather than the results, constituting the transient nature of the incomer population.

The romantic view of the history of the Scottish local prevails so that it becomes a kind of orthodoxy and yet in its fashioning ironically contributes to an amplification of the impact of the presence of migrants from England, and the Lowlands of Scotland, even Germany and France, who in this respect are simply aggregated with 'the English'. Even as the 'local' culture is being recreated and promoted, so is it accompanied by anxious alarms about the 'Englishing of Scotland'. First of all, the majority of cosmopolitans who visit or dwell in rural Scotland are attracted by their experience of the scenery as romantic, and they will, naturally enough, not wish their 'view' to be spoiled by rustic louts, and so they will be more likely to people the scenery with romantic figures. There is also an obvious link between the expansion of popular tourism in the sixties bringing people on holiday from England, but also from continental European countries, and the growth in facilities catering for tourists. The first of the present craft shops on Skye opened in 1950, according to the Craft Shop at Hungladder, Kilmuir. The expansion of this sector must also be considered alongside the decline in fishing and agriculture as employers. It is a short step from being a consumer of tourism looking for facilities to becoming a producer for other tourists. So guest houses, hotels, restaurants, inns, craft shops, boat charter businesses, and the like, come to be owned by people who previously used them, that is, tourists and holiday makers.

However, those involved in tourist related business, the 'incomers', are likely to concern themselves with cultivating the distinctiveness of the locality, promoting 'local scenery' and making visible 'local' craft fairs, 'local' folk festivals, and other events which will encourage trading and business. Even agricultural shows which are more likely to be of interest to 'locals' than 'incomers' will, because of their potential as an event of interest to holiday makers, come to involve 'incomers'. At the Sunart Agricultural Show in 1988 the biggest number of entries, and largest audience, for any single competition category was for the 'Dog with the Waggiest Tail'. The first four places, unsurprisingly, all went to the dogs of holiday makers, though this was not, of course, reported in *The Oban Times,* the local paper, where the headline was 'Mull man takes the honours at the Sunart show'. This was for some stirks. The dog competition was mentioned later in the report as an 'innovation' along with the traditional but 'newly formed Sunart Pipe Band' (*The Oban Times* 1988: 2).

These are areas of high visibility for urban Scots who have experienced a degree of upward social mobility and are travelling on sentimental journeys to scenes of childhood in rural Scotland and for whom the Highlands especially are a well spring of images from which is constructed a personal and national identity. It is rather disturbing for them, therefore, as they move from one bed and breakfast to the next, from one restaurant to another, from hotel to inn, and browse in traditional Scottish craft shops, attend local music festivals, to discover that the people they have to deal with are not only from migrants from Edinburgh or Glasgow but, more often than not, from Nottingham, Leeds, even Berlin, Toulouse, Toronto, and elsewhere. On the other hand, this may be a continuation and elaboration of a tradition of Highland innkeeping by other means. Burt in 1730 observed that innkeepers in the then largely monoglot Gaelic speaking Highlands invariably spoke English and were therefore useful interpreters (Burt 1818 312). And in *Kidnapped,* David Balfour encounters an innkeeper on Mull who not only spoke English but French and Latin as well. Such experiences may also be perplexing because emulating the middle class means coming to identify with the cosmopolitan view, and therefore of confronting the possibility that what one thought to be the reality of one's past, as a 'local', is revealed through the romantic constructions of 'incomers' to be an aspect of an essentially ambivalent image. Rather than recovering their roots, they are floundering in a quicksand of uncertainty, a predicament which contributes to the prominent and continual search for identity. Who are the Gaels? What is a real Highlander?

The metaphorical force of the notion of local, and by implication, incomer, is also a product of the structure of feeling referred to as 'belonging'. If there are locals there must be a locality, and the sense of a rural locality, whether a discrete nucleated settlement, a village, as in England, or a named area of dispersed settlement as is more common in rural Scotland, is a necessary concomitant of the feeling of 'belonging', in so far as this is considered to be a defining attribute of personal identity. In an expression such as 'my family belongs to Applecross' there must be some more or less understood boundary to the territory identified as Applecross, and my family is defined as part of the totality which is the territory and all those who belong to it. Exactly where the boundary line might be drawn could be a contested matter in so far as the implication of such an announcement is that in some way an individual who is part of Applecross has certain expectations in Applecross which they do not have elsewhere, for example, and especially, as regards claims to residence which in practice means housing, and perhaps also employment. 'Incomers' do not belong, and are therefore not a part of the totality despite their presence in the territory. Such exclusive expectations, and the identities which are being defined metaphorically, are officially acknowledged when local authorities and official agencies attempt to define objectively the attributes of a local person for the purposes of privileged access to low cost housing. Highland Region also include in their definition of a local person someone who has 'a strong local connection with, through family association, a specified area' (Scottish Homes 1991: 56). In other words, the bounded nature of a locality, 'a specified area', is translated into a defining attribute of personal identity, and is a function of the part -whole relationship which is at the core of the structure of feeling called 'belonging'.

But the security of identity which is achieved in the appeal to locality by claiming to be a 'local' is only apparent. 'Belonging' is not simply to a portion of the surface of the earth, to an abstract address which can be expressed in terms of latitude and longitude, but to the concrete historical reality of a particular place. Though the local community may be, in some objective sense, stationary relative to the surface of the earth, the historically constituted and therefore changing meaning of the landscape is continually threatening to subvert that sense of attachment which constitutes the local community. And the embodiment of the major threat to community in this sense is perceived as the 'incomer', the stranger who, in Simmel's phrase, is not 'the wanderer who comes today and goes tomorrow, but rather . . . the person who comes today and stays tomorrow. He is, so to speak, the potential wanderer; although he has not moved on, he has not quite overcome the freedom of coming and going' (Simmel 1950:402). Yet, paradoxically, at the same time the figure of 'the stranger' in this sense is one which calls into existence a heightened awareness of community. The stranger confronts the population in such a way as to provoke both a sense of community and a sense of belonging. But this drawing of boundaries, especially in a spatial idiom, has the effect of transforming personal relationships, perceived as a network, into a bounded community, and results in highlighting some who are included but who should not be, 'strangers', and in marking the exclusion of others, childhood friends and relatives, who are living elsewhere, 'exiles' (Mewett 1982).

Such a sense of the rural locality being populated by those who belong and those who do not, incomers, is amplified by the experience of a quality of 'remoteness' which pervades certain rural regions. Edwin Ardener has pointed out that remote areas are not simply physically removed so that their remoteness is a function of geography (Ardener 1987). The experience of remoteness is phenomenologically complex. The defining attribute of a remote area is the paradox of both a sense of the difficulty of travelling to the area, and, at the same time, a sense of the vulnerability of the area to penetration by agents and agencies from elsewhere. The communities in such localities are invariably described as 'fragile', which description is intended to convey the need for intervention to sustain them, and an understanding that such intervention is likely to destroy them. The paradox is evident in the ambivalent feelings surrounding the building and improvement of roads to such areas (See, for example, Darling 1955:322–3). And therefore alongside the image of tranquillity, peace, and an ancient way of life, is the experience of rapid change and innovation amidst the ruins of previous projects and development schemes. Ardener goes on to argue that this quality of remoteness clarifies the experience of social interaction and awareness of social structures. Claud Cockburn, when he lived in rural Ireland, had also noticed this amplifying effect which he described as 'an awareness one continually had there of what may be called the presence of the past . . . This crowding in of history serves to intensify a consciousness of the pressures and contradictions of life and society in the present . . . The point is not that they exist uniquely in Ireland but that they are muffled by nothing' (1967:290–1). For instance, and of particular relevance here, the presence of strangers is notably evident in, and therefore indicative of, remote areas, so that regardless of actual numbers, assuming that some objective definition of 'stranger' could be arrived at, there would always appear to be lots of them. And the strangers are, of course, perceived as the innovating agents of change.

In this section we have drawn attention to a powerful metaphorical dimension of meaning in the paired terms 'local' and 'incomer'. These terms are not literal descriptions of a demographic reality, the folk term equivalents of the demographers' concepts. As metaphors they draw their compelling obviousness and ambivalence from the inescapable experience of the asymmetries of social class. At the same time there are a number of reflexive processes which amplify the experience of a duality of locals and incomers, such as those associated with the phenomenon of 'remoteness', and with the paradox of strangers both inducing and subverting the structure of feeling called 'belonging. All of which means that objective investigations which seek to substantiate, for example, the reality of the impact of incomers are bound to fail since by definition they ignore precisely those cognitive features of the situation which constitute the reality of the relationship between locals and incomers. The next section examines the complexity of such apparently simple terms as urban and rural which seem so obviously transparent in their meaning when used in such phrases as 'urban-rural migration'.

The Urban and the Rural

Rather like the distinction between night and day, the distinction between the rural and urban is not only a common experience but also one where it is peculiarly difficult to identify the point of transition from one to the other. Correspondingly, scholarly thinking about the rural-urban distinction has either stressed the opposition and contrast between the rural and the urban, or has concentrated on the continuities between them.[1]

The former position has two main subtypes, the first of which is epitomised by Marx in *The German Ideology* where town and country are opposed as the spatial dimension of the great division of labour between the mental and the manual where, as in late feudal society, the country was not only the site of pastoral and agricultural production but also of industrial production: iron smelting and metallurgy, spinning and weaving, mining, lime burning, grain milling and so on. The towns concerned themselves with the distribution and ownership claims of these products and the means of their production, with trade and markets, with legal and administrative affairs. One consequence of the industrial revolution was not only the growth of urban populations but also the urbanisation of industrial production, and therefore the close identification of rural life with agricultural production, thereby bringing about a great transformation in the division of labour between town and country. With the exception of mining which is always a rural industry, the countryside specialises in agricultural and pastoral production.

The second opposition between the rural and the urban is rhetorical rather than historical and is informed by a sense of contrast between two qualities of social life or social interaction. On the one hand, an image of people in close knit social relationships where 'everybody knows everybody', and where distinctions of class and rank are unambiguously recognised, is associated with rural scenes. On the other, a setting where individuals are strangers to each other but linked through impersonal instrumental relations, is identified with the city. Though, as has been pointed out, there is a phenomenological or subjective sense whereby strangers appear to be more in evidence in remote rural areas while they are muted in the urban setting. In an urban setting the individual imagines himself or herself to be linked to other individuals in a unique network of dyadic relationships which the individual has constructed and continually modifies. It is virtually unbounded and a high proportion of the individuals in the network will be unknown to each other. In a rural setting the individual imagines himself as belonging to, in the sense of being a part of, a bounded society and the experience of belonging will be all the more vivid to the extent that he or she participates in social interaction with others who likewise interact among themselves. These images are mutually exclusive and yet all of us are familiar with the experiences they represent. Such contradictory experiences may threaten our own personal integrity and this perhaps explains why they are so easily projected onto the dichotomy between the urban setting and rural setting, and there is little more to this analogical ordering than a feeling that the objective discreteness of the rural settlement or village must correspond to an equally bounded close knit little society.

More or less aware of the rhetorical nature of the rural-urban dichotomy, a more recently formulated position argues instead for a real continuum, rather than a contrast or opposition, between the rural and the urban . Between the metropolis and the cottage in the country there is no abyss but rather a gradient of provincial cities, regional towns, sub regional centres, market towns, large villages, small villages, hamlets, isolated houses, where there is a gradual movement from a preponderance of social life experienced as networks to one experienced as belonging to a community. However, it is nowadays difficult to maintain even this difference. Association in the country is no longer the outcome of circumstances but of individual choice. Moreover, in contemporary British society indices of consumption and life style reveal few disparities between the rural and the urban dwelling population, however defined, and certainly far less than that existing between social classes. Particularly significant here have been successive reorganisations and redefinitions of the statutory obligations of local government, the organisation of public services, including broadcasting, and utilities on a national basis, and the enormous expansion in the use of private cars. It is important to remember how comparatively recent are much of these now taken for granted features of everyday life, especially in rural areas. The material reality of rural communities for those dwelling in them was severely attenuated by the abolition of the parish as a unit of local government in 1929, although its responsibilities had already been reduced by Education Acts, particularly that of 1918, and the changes in the Poor Law brought about by the introduction of old age pensions in 1909 and, in 1911, of a national unemployment insurance scheme. The administration of the Poor Law by the Parish Council contributed enormously to the capacity of the school master, minister, factor, and farmers, to exercise social control and in turn to foster a sense of dependence or 'knowing where you belong' among the rest of the residents in the parish.[2]

This process of convergence between the rural and the urban refers not only to the extension of the infra-structure from the town to the country but also to the relocation of some industrial production back into the country-side as well as the industrialisation of agriculture. An important aspect of these developments has been the remarkable population movements which may be listed as; daily commuting between town and country, weekly com-muting, seasonal movements between summer residences in the country and winter in the towns, and finally the reversal in the decline of the rural populations even in the remotest regions. All of which would be expected to contribute to a blurring and even dissolution of the rural urban dichotomy.

Yet it is evidently the case that it would be premature to consign the distinction to the history of ideas. The rural and the urban, though trans-forming, are as distinct and vital as they ever were. As before deeply con-trasting values and images are clustering around town and countryside, as are a variety of material interests. Though it may be difficult to characterise the distinction between the rural and the urban in objective and socially significant terms, it seems clear that the experiences of such a distinction are both real and important for the population. A study of the images of the countryside held by urban dwellers takes it for granted that there is a radi-cal distinction between town and country, and the research showed that though, as might be expected, different people are attracted to different kinds of places in the countryside, their accounts for their preferences were expressed in remarkably similar terms (Palmer, Robinson, and Thomas 1977). The daily, weekly, seasonal, and permanent movements of urban populations into the countryside have actually amplified the contrast be-tween the city and the country.

The distinction between the urban and the rural has been transformed from an unintended spatial expression of a division of labour or social dif-ferentiation, to a continuum of scenes before which an individual conducts his or her life at different times, and, as scenes, these various settings are deliberately elaborated as cultural productions. The appearance of the coun-tryside is no longer the contingent outcome of its economic relationship to the rest of, the largely urban, political economy. Not only is the appearance of the countryside now a matter of deliberate concern, a concern which may, and often does, provoke conflict with 'traditional' economic rural interests, notably farming, forestry, and hunting, but there are also interests competing to describe and represent the countryside as a landscape.

Indications of such conflicts appear in the 1940s when concern began to be expressed in official quarters about the building of 'unsightly' collec-tions of houses in rural areas. A Scottish Office Report in 1943 urges con-trol over the design of new houses in rural areas and the extension of planning regulations over the whole country (Scottish Office 1943:4). The current

Scottish Office Planning Advice Note for new housing in the countryside, for which, it remarks, there is a growing demand, favours villages and discourages a dispersed pattern of isolated houses. It is critical of what it sees as 'the introduction of suburban house types which, by virtue of the shape, low roof pitch, overhanging eaves and verges, window proportions, and general detailing, including site layout, are out of character with traditional rural building styles' (Scottish Office 1991). The appeal to history is, typically, rhetorical. If there is a 'traditional rural building style' then it exists as much in the future, as something that the Scottish Office planners are trying bring about, as it does in the past.[3] The nineteenth century rural and vernacular dwellings of the Scottish regions display little difference between town and country, so that certain streets of houses in towns look like the farm houses of the surrounding countryside set in rows, gable end to gable end. Arguably building late twentieth century 'Country and Western' bungalows in the town and countryside is a continuation by other means of a popular culture practice.[4] However, according to the Director of Legal Services of Kincardine District Council, though planning law and regulations 'have total control over the placing of a small caravan in an area of countryside' they have 'very little influence on the planting of a thousand hectares of Sitka spruce'. Here the land owning interest prevails (Jones 1992).

The upland landscape in particular is especially subject to conflicting representations. On the one hand there is the lyricism and sentimentality of the Romance of the Scottish Highlands, a landscape of majestic glens, tremendous mountains, awesome cliffs, enchanting sea lochs, magical movements of light and shade, all infused with melancholy memories and ancient legends of dark deeds and tragic heroism, and inhabited by a deeply spiritual people moved by the landscape to create poetry in which 'Nature sees herself reflected in a magic mirror; and though many a various show passes processionally along its lustre, displaying the scenery of "lands and seas, whatever clime the sun's bright circle warms", among them all there are none more delightful or elevating to behold than those which genius, inspired by love, has framed of the imagery, which, in all her pomp and prodigality, Heaven has pleased to shower through all seasons, on our own beautiful land' (Wilson 1875). Wilson, a poet and philosopher who also wrote under the pseudonym of 'Christopher North', was a contemporary and promoter of Horatio McCulloch, the great Romantic landscape artist of Scotland. The currently popular photographs and text of C. Baxter and J Crumley (1989) are in the same genre. This image has been, since the middle of the nineteenth century, the prevailing or 'normal' image of the uplands and, to the extent that it is now virtually a 'folk' image, is not easily attributable to particular authors, though a good case can be made for The Rev John Thomson of Duddingston, together with Wilson, and McCulloch.

For others, such an image is not only a misrepresentation but also part of the problem afflicting the uplands which, in their account, are hardly to be distinguished from industrial slag heaps, such has been the ecological devastation, degradation, and deterioration. Moreover, this destruction of the ecosystem has, over time, 'a subtle interaction with the consciousness of the destroyer and it is reasonable to suggest that to inhabit a severely damaged one is spiritually debilitating, even depressing' (Planterose 1992). Any prospect of a deeply rewarding encounter with 'Nature' is ruled out. This sharply diverging view can be traced to Frank Fraser Darling's *Natural History of the Highlands and Islands* published in 1947, and informs the view of the Green Party in the Highlands. Nevertheless there enters into this scientific view a folk element in so far as the ecological devastation is presented as the work of outsiders, notably the Vikings and then, in the seventeenth and eighteenth centuries, especially as regards extensive deforestation, English iron masters and their need for charcoal. Regeneration of woodlands was prevented by the creation of deer 'forests' to satisfy the sporting pursuits of outsiders and by the introduction of the sheep of lowland graziers. Smout has criticised this view and argued that deforestation was already well advanced before the seventeenth century. Regeneration was inhibited by indigenous pastoralism, especially the prevalence of goats, ironically, an animal that is nowadays symbolic of 'white settlers' in the uplands, and by the decline in the usefulness and profitability of maintaining woodland in the face of cheap imported timber, the manufacture of chemical tanning agents, and the increasing use of coal as a fuel (Smout 1991).

Although the ecological challenge is relatively recent, it is curiously reminiscent of Dr Johnson's account, in vocabulary and structure, of the Highland landscape written two hundred and twenty years ago, before the Industrial Revolution and the intellectual revolution of Darwinian natural history. It is perhaps another example of a prefiguring of scientific understanding. For both Johnson and the ecologists the contrast to be drawn is not between a material urban civilisation and the spirituality of a rural Nature but between different kinds of rural landscape, specifically a barren landscape and a richly diversified one. Johnson contrasted the 'flowery pastures and waving harvests' of the lowlands of his own time with the 'hopeless sterility' of the Highlands. 'An eye accustomed to flowery pastures and waving harvests is astonished and repelled by this wide extent of hopeless sterility . . . It will very readily occur, that this uniformity of barrenness can afford very little amusement to the traveller; that it is easy to sit at home and conceive rocks and heath, and waterfalls; and that these journeys are useless labours, which neither impregnate the imagination, nor enlarge the understanding.' Nevertheless, Johnson goes on to argue that experience is necessary to qualify what we can otherwise only know imperfectly by analogy, and so the journey to 'regions mountainous and wild, . . . one of the great scenes of human existence' is in the end necessary (Johnson 1984: 60).

However, today's ecologists contrast the 'devastated terrain' that is the Highlands with a species rich and diversified ecosystem which is supposed to have existed in the past and which might exist again if their policies are implemented. In Johnson's personification, 'nature' has abandoned the Highlands, while for the ecologists relationships between humans and their impoverished environment have become so attenuated that understanding of, and contact with, 'Nature' is severely curtailed (Planterose 1992:15). Fraser Darling (1968) was later to concede the commercial value of scenery in the Highlands, and a current member of the Scottish Hill Farming Advisory Committee argues that 'Government aid for any form of monoculture (Sitka spruce, hill sheep) must be phased out and payments geared to integrated forms of land use containing a high employment element. Why not 'scenery production', enhancing the landscape and the habitats?'.[5]

However, though there may be general agreement that 'scenery' is no longer the simple outcome of either natural history or the unintended consequences of social history, and that now scenery must be intentionally produced, it has yet to be settled what that rural scenery should be. Such architectonic shifts may only be detectable as tremors at the local level but nevertheless the sense of the ground moving, the ground in which individuals feel themselves to be, metaphorically, rooted, threatens that taken for granted certainty of identity arising from a notion of belonging, and that threat is embodied in the figure of the 'incomer'.

Such an overview of the principal vernacular or common sense terms in which the experience of rural repopulation is articulated indicate the subject matter of subsequent chapters. They will analyse in detail the paradoxes, ironies, and ambiguities, which weave together a complex figure much of which is only partially visible at any one time. But if feelings about the demographics of remote rural areas are nowadays expressed in rather alarming terms, so that 'the filling of empty glens with people, regardless of origin, is dangerous . . . because it can destroy the ancient culture which is so precious',[6] then it is remarkable that the depopulation which was typical of the previous hundred years was greeted with virtually the same response. That there may be deep similarities in the meanings of, and structure of feeling aroused by, both emigration and immigration in rural Scotland is explored in the next chapter which examines the nature and history of this widespread consensus about the likely consequences of the decades of rural depopulation which precede the present phase of repopulation.

Concern about depopulation is a quite separate matter from that of reactions to the injustices and atrocities of the eviction of families from their holdings, and it expressed itself in terms of an idea about the rural population as a source of life, in the most general sense, for the nation as a whole. People could, and did, defend evictions and at the same time express alarm about the 'drift to the towns'. The alarming prospects for the nation were considered serious enough for Parliament, though not without opposition from the great landlords, not only to pass the Crofters Holdings (Scotland) Act in 1886 but in 1911 to extend much of its provisions to the rest of Scotland in the Small Land Holders (Scotland) Act. Nowadays official policy, if there is such a thing as regards rural depopulation, no longer assumes that it is something which must be prevented for its own sake. Of course, migrating to the town is not a problem but a solution for the migrant and the next chapter, using a variety of sources will also examine how the 'problem of rural depopulation' is mediated by perspectives of class and gender.

Notes

[1] Debating and updating definitions of the rural and the urban is a major industry. Particularly useful in this survey of developments have been French social scientists, especially Bernard Kayser (1988); Chamboredon (1985); Mendras (1984). Above all there is, of course, Raymond Williams (1973).

[2] See T. H. Marshall (1950) for an analysis of the implications of changes in State administration. For an account of the working and practical development of the 1845 Poor Law in relation to the provision of health care in a remote rural area during the latter half of the nineteenth century which brings out the solidarity of people setting up 'medical associations' in the face of the hostility of their land owners because of 'the burden on the rates' see Taylor (1981).

[3] The Planning Advice Note 36 acknowledges as a valuable source of analysis and advice a book actually subtitled *Tomorrow's Architectural Heritage*.

[4] The style, in all its unrestrained eclectic exuberance, is best seen in the Republic of Ireland. Memorably, a letter to *The Irish Times* 10th July 1990, began 'Writing as an English-

man of eight years residence in Ireland, I must protest about the lack of planning controls on house design which is ruining the Irish countryside'.

[5] Reported in *Scenes Scottish Environment News* April 1993, p. 3.

[6] Sir Iain Noble, a landowner in Skye, quoted in *The Glasgow Herald* 11th May 1989.

Chapter 2

The Problem of Rural Depopulation

Rural depopulation is a gradual process and in Scotland it is generally reckoned that the rural population as a whole, having increased during the nineteenth century, was beginning to decline by the turn of the century. However some rural counties had reached their maximum population by the middle of the nineteenth century and by 1891 had lost more than a fifth of their maximum population.

	Date of maximum population	% decrease 1891
Argyll	1841	35
Kinross	1851	35
Perth	1841	27
Kirkcudbright	1851	23
Inverness	1841	22
Wigton	1851	21

Table 1. Rank order of rural counties affected by depopulation by 1891.[1]

From the turn of the century until the 1930s the rural counties show a net decline of population with the north west the highest at around 24% of the 1901 population. However the loss by emigration from the rural counties over the same period is much the same for the north west and the south at about 68% of the mean population. It is actually highest for the north east (excluding the cities of Aberdeen and Dundee) at about 84%. As the Department of Health for Scotland observed 'the drift from the crofting counties is common knowledge but the correspondingly large emigration figures from the southern counties and the north east are not generally appreciated'.[2] Rural depopulation and migration from the land are not the same thing, although, as will become evident, they are often confused. Around 1931 the population of the rural counties stabilised but this was entirely due to the growth of the towns within these regions. The non-urban dwelling population continued to decline. It would be about forty years before demographers detected an increase in the rural population.

These demographic changes have been accompanied by a considerable amount of commentary, and it is the purpose of this chapter to examine the nature of this commentary and how it has evolved. In general the overwhelming view has been to deplore the decline of the rural population. Indeed such was the general level of concern that various UK Governments felt it necessary at least to appear to be addressing what was called 'the problem of rural depopulation' and often misleadingly described as 'the drift to the towns'. Reading contemporary material suggests that the problem of rural depopulation was then something like the current 'problem of global warming' where all kinds of disasters are supposed to come to pass unless 'the Government does something'. There appears to have been almost universal agreement that there was a problem of rural depopulation but what was the nature of the problem is often obscure, and always construed by different people in different ways. There are two aspects to the matter; the movement of people into towns and the movement of people out of the countryside. The strongest expression is of a generalised anxiety that rural depopulation is somehow bad both physically and morally for the nation as a whole and this view highlights the former aspect. Rather less evident but nonetheless there, at least by implication, is a concern with the latter aspect, that depopulation is inextricably and regrettably linked, sometimes as cause, sometimes as effect, to the loss of a special kind of virtuous rural way of life, of a kind of social life found only in a rural community.

That the problem of rural depopulation is refracted by perspectives is especially evident in the social history of the Northwest of Scotland in the nineteenth century where, for example, for the class of landowners, the problem of rural depopulation swings violently from how to prevent depopulation to how to bring it about. Controversy about the evictions and clearances in the Highlands and Islands during the nineteenth century contributed to the general debate about rural depopulation and at the same time perhaps the debate itself served to amplify the feelings aroused, feelings which have persisted and are inextricably entangled with the present day.[3]

However, the memorable Highland clearances had been prefigured by the much less memorable Levellers Revolt in Galloway in the summer of

1724. As Chambers writing in 1874 noted of the circumstances of the up-rising, 'it was a state of things very like what our advanced age has been fated strangely to see prevalent over large tracts of Ireland and the High-lands' (Chambers 1873:492). The Rev R Woodrow remarked at the time that 'it's certain great depopulations have been made in the South, and multitudes of familys turned out of their tacks, and sent a wandering' (Woodrow 1843:153). The small holdings of sub-tenants, which they had used for subsistence crops, were enclosed by the landlords and turned over to grazing cattle. The timing was prompted by a series of poor corn har-vests and the accumulation of several years of rent arrears. The potato, so much more suited to the environment and able to support a higher popula-tion density than corn, did not appear in Galloway until after the Levellers revolt.

Resistance took the form of throwing down the enclosing dykes and re-claiming the land. A band of thirty Levellers 'as they were ominously called' (Chambers 1874:493), declared themselves the government of the country and asserted their jurisdiction by refusing to recognise the courts and in-stead instituted their own. The land owners called in the military and six-teen levellers were arrested. While escorting the prisoners to Kircudbright tolbooth the troops were attacked at Balmaclellan, in a scene which was to be repeated in the Battle of the Braes on Skye one hundred and fifty years later, by a 'mob of women'. However, the more interesting question is, as Smout notes following Cobbett, the rarity of such events as compared with England. According to Smout in the north east and south east of Scotland the agrarian changes were not accompanied by land use changes from ar-able to grazing, which was less labour intensive, and so the class of small tenants in due course became landless agricultural labourers on reorgan-ised but still arable lands and they 'were materially better off in 1790 and 1830 than they were in 1720 or 1770' (Smout 1971:328). Moreover in the south west the leadership and organisation of the ministers of the subver-sive Covenanting tradition of Galloway played a part in articulating the discontent. In the north and west meanwhile, the consequences of the col-lapse of the Jacobite rebellion of 1745 had yet to be felt, and in any case the appearance in the latter part of the century of sheep graziers from the south of Scotland paying commercial rents was to coincide with the introduction of the potato as a subsistence crop and the beginning of the labour inten-sive kelp industry.

By the end of the eighteenth century Highland landowners who had prof-ited enormously from the labour intensive kelp industry sought to increase the number of kelpers, and thereby their rental income, by reorganising their estates into a large number of small holdings adjacent to the coast and therefore the seaweed (kelp), and a few extensive sheep farms in the landward areas. The prospective victims of these 'improvements', the estate tenants, generally refused to play their part and resumed their emigration, especially to North America, a movement which had been interrupted by the Napoleonic wars. In landlocked estates the situation was obviously rather different and such land owners were quite happy to see their tenantry leave the land. The anxiety of the land owners with an interest in kelp, however, expressed itself in a special investigation into emigration by the Highland Society, which was largely their own association, and shortly afterwards by a Government enquiry in 1803. All of which was ironically in concert with those such as Alexander Campbell who, after the manner of Goldsmith's *Deserted Village* but without the literary merit, lamented the loss of the Highland peasantry in a poem, *The Grampian's Desolate* which described how a 'train of national calamities' would follow 'stern Depopulation's ruthless rage' (Campbell 1804). The landowners sought to blame the activities of the agents of the emigration ships who were active in the Northwest, but disinterested observers saw the 'improvements' as the main cause. Parliament acted promptly by passing the Passengers Vessels Act of 1804 which was directed at improving the health and safety of emigration vessels but indirectly, and quite intentionally, curtailed emigration by raising the cost of passages. Telford, who had conducted the enquiry for the Government, recommended public works, such as the Caledonian Canal, and various roads. These were also undertaken. In 1827 the price of kelp collapsed, the land owners faced bankruptcy, and the kelpers were suddenly redundant. For the land owners the only way out was the creation of more sheep farms and that meant the eviction of the small holders or crofters who were no longer needed as kelpers. The same people who had been campaigning against emigration were now actively urging its necessity. Parliament again responded and in the same year removed the health and safety requirements which the Passengers Vessel Act of 1804 had imposed. Some landlords contributed to the expenses of emigration of their tenants, an outlay which was quickly recovered by the increase in rental from sheep farming tenants. In 1887 the then Duke of Argyll explained how he and his father had responded to the pleas for assistance to emigrate from his tentantry on Tiree. 'At great cost we enabled upwards of a thousand people to go' (Argyll 1887:437).

Though presented by the landlords as a problem of over population, it was really a problem of land shortage since those evicted to make way for extensive sheep farms were crowded onto increasingly meagre plots of land, or sometimes simply plots of rock. The destitution caused by the failure of the potato crop in the 1840s together with the financial consequences of the Poor Law Act of 1846 for rate payers, in this case the land owners and the sheep farmers as the major rate payers, only served to reinforce their conviction in the benefits of emigration. The Highland problem would be solved by encouraging emigration and to this end Parliament obliged with the Emigration Advances Act 1851.

Of course, emigration would only solve the problem if the land vacated by the migrants was taken over by those who remained and consolidated into larger land holdings for each household. This is not the same thing as using the vacated land to extend the sheep farms as was intended and carried out by the land owners. The residual population received little benefit from the emigration because most migrants holdings were incorporated into sheep farms rather than allocated to the crofters.

The complete removal of the crofting population was eventually prevented simply by the marginal quality of the land even for sheep which those who remained occupied, together with falling profits from sheep farming towards the end of the nineteenth century. Interest had moved on to the profits to be made from hunting deer. The sporting estates indeed required staff, women as indoor servants and men as stalkers and outdoor servants. And there was always casual labour required by the sheep farms. Nevertheless some estates, especially on the mainland were almost entirely cleared of population, e.g. Knoydart, and some islands e.g. Rhum. The land holding structure of Highland estates shows up well in an analysis of rents by the Napier Commission. It found that less than one per cent of the population, sheep farmers and deer forest tenants, some of whom were not even resident in the localities, paid 63% of the total rental and 99% of the population paid the remaining 27% of rental (See Hunter 1976:122–3). In short emigration may have reduced the absolute number of destitute people but the destitution was unaffected.

Country People: 'A Source of Life'

Contemporary commentary from those without vested interests reveals other concerns about the state of the rural population. Donald Macleod from Sutherland had published in a series of articles in the *Edinburgh Weekly Chronicle* in 1840–1 his famous eyewitness reports of the evictions carried out by the Duke of Sutherland's factor, and which were later republished as a book. A second edition was published in 1856 by four Greenock merchants who contributed an introductory address. Besides documenting the atrocities that were the actual evictions of the tenants and the injustices that resulted, Macleod was also returning to Alexander Campbell's theme of rural deso-lation and to what he called 'the extirpation of the Celtic race'; 'the expul-sion of the natives and the substitution of strange adventurers, sheep farmers, generally from England and from the English border' (1856:6), a theme which particularly concerned the publishers. 'One of the greatest evils which can afflict a land [is] the systematic expatriation of its peasantry' and they contrast the time when the land 'teemed with a stalwart and happy peas-antry' with the desolation that now confronts 'the traveller who may wan-der for days over extensive districts of the Highlands and see no evidence of human existence, except such as are inscribed on the face of the land by the ploughshares of the past'. The people have been driven to the shore or sterile moors, 'reduced to objects of poverty, and then stigmatised as igno-rant, filthy and incapable' (Macleod 1856:3). Here is a rather different moral argument which needs to be distinguished from the outrages of the evic-tions or the special pleading of the land owners about estate 'improvements'. It is one which is not difficult to trace in writing about rural depopulation for the next hundred years.

About twenty years after the publication of the second edition of Macleod's book in 1880, at a time of heightened agitation about land tenure reform especially in Ireland, J S Blackie, the Professor of Greek at Edinburgh Uni-versity, in an article in *The Scotsman* later reprinted in his published inau-gural address to the Perth Gaelic Society argued for some limited land reform in the Highlands, in effect that there should be a mixture of various sizes of farms and not the extremes of the very large and very small that character-ises the Highlands. The case is based on the idea that the population of a country should be 'distributed wisely between the country and the town' and 'in managing this distribution by the State wisdom lies in recognising that the peasantry of a country . . . form in normal circumstances the most healthy, sound, and sturdy class of society; and though they do not live under such strong intellectual and moral stimulants as the inhabitants of the towns, they are for this very reason better fitted to act as a seminary from which all classes of society may be most effectively recruited and repaired' (1880:20).

Blackie goes on to describe the responsibility of the State and of the 'lords of the soil' to nurture rather than extirpate this noble peasantry, the Highland crofters, because from 'their ranks have sprung the best soldiers and the most illustrious commanders that have made the British name re-spected, and the British power feared from the rising to the setting sun'. So not only is their extirpation an act of callous ingratitude, it is also one of the most thoughtless as regards the future. The Napier Commission, generally remarkable for the rigour and objectivity of its observations, subscribed to similar but rather more rarefied and poetic sentiments when it said of country people that they are an 'ever flowing fountain of renovating life' (Napier Commission 1883, quoted by Paterson 1897:278). The Duke of Argyll commented, rather peevishly, that Lord Napier, 'whose own estate is situated among long cleared sheep pastures of the Southern Highlands and in a locality which is specially described by Sir Walter Scott in Marmion as a perfect picture of solitude and depopulation', did not attempt to resettle his depopulated lands (Argyll 1187:442).

The notion of country people as a source of life is not confined to critics of the depopulation of the Highlands. J W Paterson, a demographer, in an article on rural depopulation in the Transactions of the Highland and Agricultural Society (1897) noted that the subject was 'one of the most generally popular topics of the day' but reassured his readers that 'it can never be a source of loss to a country to drive away subjects who have made a living by evading its judiciously enacted laws' (1897:236, 246). Nevertheless rural depopulation does have 'evil consequences' which he identifies as 'the devastating effect which town life has upon the health and energy of the inhabitants'. The health and energy of country people is simply due to 'fresh air, untainted food, abundant exercise, and early hours' . . . 'If a typical rural population is better fitted than a corresponding urban population for actual warfare, for the same reason it must be better for the war of industry' and so a nation cannot be indifferent to securing the continual replenishment of its sickly urban population with vigorous country people (1897:276–8).

This idea that the country is a source of life but the town a consumer of life exists quite independently of the material history of either rural depopulation or the drift to the towns. J-J Rousseau held that 'towns were the abyss of the human race. At the end of several generations races will be degenerating or perishing and will have to be renewed. And it will always be from the country that the renewal will come'. The reason for this, according to Rousseau, is simply that humans are by their nature the least gregarious of animals and we 'poison' each other physically and morally when pressed together. This representation of the relationship between town and country can be traced back into classical literature and is, as it were, available to be deployed as an understanding of the significance of the demographic events and experiences of the nineteenth century.

Rural people are evaluated in these views both in a material and moral or spiritual sense. Not only are they healthy in body so also are they healthy in mind, indeed the distinction is hardly made and it is difficult to detect even the play of metaphor in the use of words such as 'sturdy'. As long as this integrity is maintained then it follows that the rural population needs to be conserved. If, however, the material body is merely a shabby tenement for the eternal spirit then quite a different course of action follows. Depopulation and degradation of the Highland population is only 'the apparition of a passing race [and] no more than the fulfilment of a glorious resurrection before our very eyes . . . the Celt fades but his spirit rises' (1919:246). The resurrection process consists of William Sharp ('Fiona Macleod') and other Celtic twilighters tapping into the uncontaminated perspicacity, vision, and wisdom of the Celts, of people such as "Seumas Macleod, the old isleman who had never been to the mainland . . . Ignorant of the foreign tongue of the mainland, ignorant of books yet he saw so deep into the human heart and into the mystery of the soul' (1910:165). This kind of spiritual life is curiously still and motionless stuff, 'save for the encroaching shadow of death there was nothing to mark the time for the dwellers in Ithona' (1910:163), but in a sense it has to be if the uncontaminated purity of the aboriginals is to be maintained to the present. Songs are 'older than the oldest things, save the summits of the mountains, the granite isles and the brooding pain of the sea' (1910:38). This very spiritual fountain of life is contrasted with the 'feverish', hence agitated and sickly, life of towns.[4]

At the other extreme the concerns of eugenists with racial degeneration had by now engaged, though somewhat tangentially, with the ideas and feelings clustering around rural depopulation. Especially worrying and much publicised was the physical state of the nation as was supposedly revealed by the high proportion of volunteers from the towns presenting themselves for enlistment during the Boer War who were rejected as physically unfit, a war in which it was pointedly noted that an irregular army of farmers was embarrassing the British Army. Eugenists themselves could not accept the basically environmentalist or Lamarckian hypothesis of urban degeneration which entailed a 'Back to the Land' policy rather than selective breeding. And in any case the wilder theories of urban degeneration, for example that some urban dwellers were now so debilitated as to be incapable of even reproducing themselves, were quite contrary to eugenists' belief that the threat to the race came from the relatively high fertility of the urban poor (Searle 1976:20–33). Nevertheless some of the eugenists vocabulary about race degeneration now appears in writing about rural depopulation.

The most notable of these writers was Rider Haggard, better known now for his adventure novels set in Africa and his imperial career, who was a tireless contributor to the public debate and to the advocacy of practical schemes to halt rural depopulation. Accordingly he was consulted by Government on several occasions. In 1906 he published a two volume study called *Rural England* based on observations and interviews with farmers and land owners in a large number of English counties. Later in 1911 he published a study of land settlement laws and practice in Denmark. No one of comparable stature was addressing the issue from a Scottish perspective but Rider Haggard's views were widely reported and debated in the Scottish press.[5] The chapters of his study of rural England are arranged by county and the presentation is a simple direct reportage. However, in the final chapter he sets out some general themes, recommendations, and conclusions.

According to Rider Haggard the situation arising from rural depopulation, or what he calls 'the ominous migration of the blood and sinew of the race' (1906:254), is now 'perilous' and not simply for agriculture in terms of labour supply, because agriculture will get by, but for the nation at large. This peril is the direct consequence of the sate of the reservoir of rural people which has so far continually replenished and restored the urban population thereby countering the effects of urban degeneration. However this state of affairs cannot be sustained. 'As has been shown again and again, it is now common for only the dullards, the vicious, or the wastrels to stay upon the land . . . and it is this indifferent remnant who will be the parents of the next generation of rural Englishmen' (1906:539). 'The desertion of the countryside, if unchecked, will' writes Rider Haggard, confining himself to what he calls 'a moderate statement' lead to nothing less than 'the progressive deterioration of the race', even 'the ruin of the race' (1906:541).

Conserving a rural population

Governments could hardly avoid warnings from several establishment quarters of impending 'race ruin'. However politicians were more comfortable with the familiar implications of those advocating land settlement, the agrarian matters of buying and selling land, of tenancies and leaseholds and freeholds, of reorganising estates, than they were with the application of eugenics. Moreover the public contempt which eugenists showed for politicians and parliamentary democracy was hardly likely to become anything other than mutual. On the other hand, there is a distinct ambivalence in the attitude to land settlement because of its association with radical and Chartist aspirations and projects. The Royal Commission into agriculture in the United Kingdom 1879 -92 considered the feasibility of establishing a system of peasant proprietary but concluded that such a reform would be 'ill adapted to the habits of the people or the condition of agriculture in this country' and it drew attention to the failure of the Chartist National Land Company's project in the late 1840s to give the land back to the people. This project grew out of the dream, articulated especially by Feargus O'Connor, of restoring the village community of 'old England'. But as long as what was intended by 'old England' was not examined too closely then different interests could agree that it was worth defending, and so the Small Holdings Act (1892) results from the Royal Commission's recommendations. Rider Haggard is sent on a Government Commission to investigate Salvation Army land settlement schemes in the UK and the US. The Board of Agriculture and Fisheries looked into the decline of the agricultural population of Great Britain in 1906 and again in 1913. Representatives of the Scottish Chamber of Agriculture, which had resolved unanimously at their annual conferences in 1903 and 1904 'that with a view to promoting the general interests of the country and assisting to stem the tide of rural depopulation His Majesty's Government should take into favourable consideration the expediency for increasing the number of small farms throughout the country' (1906b:355), were invited to give evidence. The land settlement act of 1892 had already empowered county councils in the UK to establish small holdings. In Scotland the Small Land Holders (Scotland) Act 1911 extended much of the Crofters Holdings (Scotland) Act 1886 beyond the crofting counties to the whole of Scotland and in effect gave powers to the Government to intervene and reorganise the pattern of land holding on any estate in Scotland. What is now known as the Scottish Land Owners Federation was formed in 1906 by Scottish land owners to defend their rights to manage their estates in their own interests. In this respect there was a major difference between the land settlement schemes of England and Scotland where in England county councils bought farms which were then subdivided into small holdings and eventually sold to the small holders. However, in general, the aim of these and subsequent land settlement schemes was to increase, or at least ensure the retention of, the rural population on the land and arrest what was usually referred to as 'the drift to the towns'.

The Board of Agriculture and Fisheries in their 1906 report on the decline in the agricultural population of great Britain was, however, rather cautious about the effectiveness of the land settlement policy through small holdings and its hoped for consequence of retaining a rural population. The

Board observed that the land settlement schemes involving setting up small holdings had to be considered within a context where in England 67% and in Scotland 66% of all farms were already 50 acres or less in size. Adding a few more small holdings would have little effect seemed to be the implication of their remarks. In the same year a departmental committee of the Board of Agriculture addressed itself to the specific question of the workings of the Small Holdings (1892) Act and the curious fact that the Act was not a success in terms of fulfilling what had been expected of it. After ten years only five counties in England and one in Scotland, Ross-shire, had purchased land for small holdings amounting to 652 acres of which only 248 acres or 0.0008% of the farmland of the UK had actually been set up as small holdings. On the grounds that 'retention of the population on the soil is a benefit to the entire country' the Report argued that the state should take over from county councils, which bodies the committee reckoned to have been less than vigorous in the implementation of land settlement schemes. A reservation was entered by one member to the effect that 'the evidence of before us shows that rural depopulation is so serious an evil as to demand frank recognition and bold treatment' and demanded Government action on an appropriate scale.

Despite the ineffectiveness of these land settlement schemes, ten years later in the middle of the first world war a Board of Agriculture and Fisheries Departmental Committee on Land Settlement for Soldiers and Sailors was of the view that 'a scheme for attracting a large population to the land is urgently required in view not only of the obligation of the State to ex-service men but of the highest interests of the nation as a whole . . . The stability and physical strength of a nation depends largely on those classes who have either been born and brought up in the country or have had the advantages of country life. It is certain that the physique of those portions of our nation who live in crowded streets rapidly deteriorates, and would deteriorate still further if they were not to some extent reinforced by men from country districts' (1916:5). The Committee were critical of the piece-meal working of the Small Holdings Act 1892 and advocated a state agency to implement what it called 'colonies of land settlers' in the countryside. They reckoned that 4–5,00 families could be settled each year at a cost of £2,000,000 per annum, or roughly £60,000,000, at today's prices. By any measure a considerable sum of money. There is a dissenting minority report which expressed again the view that the measures were inadequate and that the main report did not convey an appropriate sense of urgency.

These huge schemes, some of them very regimented, for colonies of settlers in the Scottish and English countryside, like the homes fit for heroes, came to nothing and so two years on another committee of the Board of Agriculture was still arguing that 'it is an urgent problem of national welfare to increase the rural population' a theme endorsed and taken up in 1920 by the Board of Agriculture for Scotland's Committee on Women in Agriculture. The Committee's views that 'country-bred women are generally superior in vigour and health to town bred women', and that 'agricultural work is a good preparation for motherhood' nicely bring together both the value of women to agriculture and of agriculture to women as regards the breeding of future generations of citizens (1920:2,9).

Given the healthy vitality and honest virtues which country life induces in country people it is rather a mystery why people should 'drift to the towns'. A range of causes are variously invoked, among the most common being 'the restless spirit of the age', the pernicious influence of formal education, and communications, 'the swift travelling contagion of locomotive machinery' in Blackie's fine phrase (1880:4). The 1906 report on the decline in the Agricultural Population of Great Britain 1891–1906, which had been less than enthusiastic about small holdings as a practical solution, cited the state of rural housing as the cause of discontent. And the evidence of Mr T Mackley, representing the Agricultural Labourers and Rural Workers Union, to the Department Committee on Land Settlement for Sailors and Soldiers in 1916 would seem to confirm that view. Asked about his own experience he said, "I was driven into town because we had only one bedroom and I was helping my mother and younger sister. I wanted to get married, and I wanted to go somewhere else where I could get a house. Therefore I drifted into town. The most serious problem is the housing problem, for any decency and morality" (1916:312). The extent to which images of rural depopulation had become naturalised in the popular imagination is nicely caught in Mr Mackley's oxymoronic deliberate 'drift into town'. Mr Mackley, incidentally, must have disappointed the committee with his negative opinion of smallholdings: "the small holder cannot compete with the large farmer, just as the large industrial business can always beat the small one in industry". The 1920 Report on Women in Agriculture for the Scottish Board of Agriculture also regarded the state of housing as contributing to rural depopulation. They discovered that 'water supply in the houses is regarded as a luxury, baths are unknown, sanitary conveniences primitive and inconveniently sited, sometimes non-existent'. Cooking and diet were described by one Medical Officer for Health as 'atrocious'. All of which makes one wonder about the health and vigour of the people.

The Scottish Board's Committee on Women was also convinced that the organisation of employment was associated with rural depopulation. Until the Second World War, when a so-called 'stand-still order' was imposed by the government, farm labourers would sign up to work a farm for a season in much the same way that seamen signed up with a skipper to crew a ship for the duration of a voyage. Labourers could sign up for another season with the same farm and stay where they were or they would sign up to work another farm and move taking their belongings in a *kist* (chest, rather like a seaman's chest). Enough men and women engaged with new farms rather than re-engage with the same farm each year to impress the Committee with the 'extra-ordinary contrast between the migratory life of ploughmen's families and the settled permanence of small holders' and, incidentally, shepherds (1920:12). The 'drift to the towns' was, it seemed to them, only an element in a generally high level of geographical mobility.

Rural depopulation: images and representations

As regards the interventions, the general conclusion was that all the talk of 'rural re-colonisation' and 'land settlement' was in the end only talk, though in Hugh MacDiarmid's view more than that, actually a 'smoke screen', and the schemes were deliberately 'dead lettered' (1934:38). However, it may not now have mattered because by the 1930s it was recognised that the population in rural Scotland was no longer declining. The Scottish Economic Committee's 1938 review, in an appendix on population, was optimistic that the 'Highland people will renew their supply of recruits to Scotland and the Empire without endangering their ability to maintain their numbers in the future' (1938:158). Others were pessimistic. It now appeared that not only had those who moved to towns suffered from the degeneracy endemic to urban life but Rider Haggard's expectation that the rural population itself would shortly exhibit moral and mental decay as a result of depopulation had also, it seemed, been realised. Neil Gunn writing in 1937 about Highland life expresses concern about the state of the rural population in the Highlands and he quotes the Scottish Committee of the British Medical Association to the effect that the rural areas have been 'drained . . . of much good stock . . . Nothing has been done by way of a really serious attempt to preserve the fine type of people, mentally and physically, which the Highlands and Islands have hitherto possessed and produced ' As evidence of the mental degeneration Gunn refers to the statistics for insanity in the Highlands. 'Not only is the pauper lunacy rate for the area far higher than for any part of Scotland, but it is more than twice as high as that for the congested industrial towns of Lanark where conditions amongst the vast mass of the poor have been and are surely dreadful enough' (1992:57–8). This hopeless prospect where faith in the country as a source of life is no longer tenable was elaborated in his novel *The Lost Glen* (1932). The rural landscape of the Highlands is in terminal decline, the houses 'huddled together for warmth' (whereas by contrast in a vital landscape houses always 'nestle'), the people were 'mean and wretched, thin blooded and miserable'. The urban scene is hardly different except for the 'myriad' of people. The imagined solution is a great deluvian cleansing of the land, another cosmogonic flood. Prosaically, in the end Gunn has his three key figures finishing as corpses in the sea.

At the turn of the century the contrast between country as a source of life and the town as a consumer of life, the one positive and the other negative, is presented as self evident but in *The Lost Glen* both are now viewed negatively. After the Second World War Gunn was more optimistic, though the perspectives are complicated by gender, and an enlargement of the scope, and a redefinition of the scale, of the dichotomy between the metropolis and its remote regions. The structure of feeling, in Raymond William's phrase, revolving around town and country is now ambivalent. There is a complementary but asymmetrical relationship between town and country. The law offices, which deal in the abstract administration of things, the affairs of estates, the tenants and so on, are in the town while the creative work of growing things and animal husbandry is in the countryside. Similarly, the artist, in *The Other Landscape* (1954), finds in the countryside a source of creative inspiration but the city is where the music is performed, the books bought, the contracts signed, and ultimately recognition accorded. The town is still associated with death and the consumption of life, so that someone returns to the country from the town 'with the ghost of herself in her face' (1949:254). It is a place where people move 'furtively' and one has to guard against thieves, pickpockets and ' sudden assaults', while all around are the 'unemployed, stagnant yards, derelict areas, slums'. Yet at the same time natural features of the countryside are called upon as figures for aspects of city life. Life in the city 'swarmed and the tenement walls were cliffs' (p. 37). That the metaphorical image of a teeming insect life is at best ambivalent as an evaluation of the town is underlined by the description of the work of the maggot fly on sheep and this image is used of men in the country, 'the maggot men', whose gossip is more 'deadly' than that of women.[6] However, now instead of the nihilistic contemplation of a flood, Gunn finds a new and uncontaminated source of life which transcends town and country. The glen need no longer be lost because of the arrival of a redeemer in the flesh of a new land owner from across the seas:

'This may be the beginning of new life in the glens. He's not the old kind of land lord. He's a colonial!' The vital best could, and did, 'go to Canada, take land, blast the trees off it and make it fertile, build dams and factories, pioneer and create' (1987:159). Now they would return invigorated and more powerful than before and do the same to the Highlands and the nation. The source of life is no longer the remote glens but the remoter Dominions.

Rather than elaborate on this dynamic modern future of building, blasting, felling, and damming Gunn is actually more concerned in his novels to explore contemporary complications. Gender perspectives on depopulation are developed immediately in *The Drinking Well* (1946). The book is divided into three parts where the first and last are set in the glen and are opposed to the second set in the city (Edinburgh). But in the first part a very deliberate contrast is drawn between men and women. As yet unnamed but specified by the definite article 'The woman' is introduced with adjectives such as 'gaunt' and 'weary'. Her eyes are 'sunken' and she moves with 'automatic indifference'. 'The man' on the other hand is 'round chested and strong', his face is 'weathered'. He is 'compact' and moves 'carefully' and with 'dignity'. The woman as a mother takes pride in the fact that three of her four children have been to university, have succeeded, have 'got on' and therefore got away from the glen and are in professional careers in London or North America. Now she says of the fourth child 'I have slaved to save the others and I'll save him too'. But the man, the father is perplexed; they have gone, but are they saved or are they lost? The man 'leisurely surveyed the countryside' and the remaining son sees his father 'directing that living world'. The woman looks up and out and thinks, 'it's so long since I've been anywhere.' However it is the middle class estate factor, a retired army officer, who articulates the problem of depopulation; 'when I see the best mothers driving their sons, their own flesh and blood, away I sometimes wonder. It's a problem. It's perhaps the world's greatest problem' (1946: 1–21).

Gunn is keenly aware of the irony of a situation where young people, especially young men, who are supported by their families in their education and in further education eventually to secure professional careers, are being propelled into that class of men, 'lawyers in big houses in the great cities', from among whom are drawn those politicians who make much of the need to repopulate the rural areas. Furthermore, if a young man does return to the land after a period working in the city in white collar employment, then he wins no respect from his family or the neighbours for his contribution to reversing rural depopulation and saving the nation, even if his motives are wholly positive. In *The Man Who Came Back* (1928) Gunn exposes the bitterness of a son who admires his crofter father and what he does, but finds that he is silently despised even by his father for giving up his city career to return to try and emulate him.

In a study of rural depopulation in Scotland, a demographic process which it was claimed 'must be regarded as a dangerous trend', though these dangers were not specified, the author was 'surprised' by the fact the people in the countryside whom he interviewed did not share his anxieties about depopulation (Hutchinson 1949:3). Many of his respondents felt that depopulation was not an important problem 'while others thought that the population was being increased by newcomers rather than decreased through migration' (1949:3–4). This despite the fact that many of them have clear evidence of emigration from the loss of members of their own households. Moreover in Wigtonshire 14% of his sample actually expressed a wish to leave the countryside for the town, and yet they were 'reluctant to admit the gravity of the rural depopulation problem' (1949:4).

Hutchinson did not pause to reflect on why he, a middle class urban academic, takes it for granted that rural depopulation is a danger while the people in the diminishing population do not, even if they are aware that the local population is declining. Clearly, moving from the countryside to the town from their perspective is a solution not a problem. Hutchinson's survey revealed what one would expect at that time: that the most common motive given for moving to the town was to take a better job. Correspondingly agricultural workers and retired people living in the country were least likely to see advantages in moving to the town.

Hutchinson's surprise that a belief in the dangers of rural depopulation, which seemed so natural to him, was not shared by the rural population illustrates how naturalised such a belief had become and at the same time indicates that it was beginning to be uprooted. A Department of Health for Scotland Report (1951:36) observed that for several centuries land owners had in the course of pursuing their political legal and economic affairs taken themselves off to the towns where indeed, as in Edinburgh's Old Town, many of them maintained residences. Later the legal and commercial interests of farmers took them to the lawyers' offices, to the corn exchanges and auction rings of the market towns while their social interests, especially matrimonial matters, meant attending the assembly rooms and participating in the society of their social equals. The town is the arena of strategy and risk, of problems and conflicts, of deals and the unpredictability of the market, of competition and contract among equals. To return to the country and the farm is to return to an order of seasonal predictability, of social relationships of status, of command, and of deference. Such traffic by landowners and farmers and their experiences of town and country was never represented as threatening the breakdown of the rural community far less the degeneration of the nation as a whole. It was not until the development of a public transport of roads and railways which allowed the rural proletariat to go to towns to share each other's company and extend their social horizons that these movements are cited as a danger to the rural community.

After the 1938 Hileary Report little more is heard of the idea that the rural population as a reservoir of vigorous people to supply the industrial towns and defend the Empire. The Report of the Scottish Land Settlement Committee (1944) which reviewed the previous fifty years of interventions to promote land settlement since the Crofters Holdings (Scotland) Act of 1886 concluded that, despite the creation of over four and half thousand small holdings, half of them in the Lowlands, this had had no discernible effect on the trends of rural depopulation. The Report did think that small holdings were successful in their qualitative and moral effects of engendering independence, self-reliance, frugality and industry but they '*were* essential in an age of mass production to the continuance of a healthy race in both town and country' (1944:18, emphasis added). The use of the past tense is curious and perhaps significant of a scepticism about the whole 'healthy race' argument. The old view, that land settlement would and did reduce rural depopulation and that there is still a continuing need for the yeoman qualities of crofters and small holders, is represented in a dissenting note. 'Such men have in the past proved and still prove a great strength to the Empire, and we must not forget that from their class have been recruited, to a large extent, our gallant Scottish regiments' (1944:72). Naturally enough the note deplores the lack of political will to implement the various settlement Acts. The main report had, however, noted that at the time of writing there seemed to be a constant demand for small holdings in the Lowlands; the only unlet holdings were in the Highlands. In the Lowlands the Committee observed, however, that many small holders had sublet the land to a farmer, used the house as a dwelling, and commuted to work in the towns.

The complete abandonment of a land settlement policy was vividly manifest in the events on Knoydart estate in 1947–8 when several ex-servicemen, a category for whom some of the settlement schemes were specifically aimed, petitioned for small holdings and submitted a plan for 40 holdings to the Department of Agriculture and Fisheries in 1947 in accordance with the various relevant Acts. The proposal pointed out that, among other things, it would halt and reverse the serious decline in the local population and, as part of their case for the viability of the proposed settlement, drew attention to the far higher numbers of people that had lived off the land of Knoydart in the past. The land owner objected, the cumbersome official process was initiated but the Scottish Office procrastinated and so the men of Knoydart, after the manner of the nineteenth century, staged a land raid for the benefit of the press and with the intention of embarrassing the Secretary of State into action. The government responded by staging in turn a public enquiry which resulted in, at five pages, probably the shortest official Report on a Public Enquiry of all time. The report recommended rejection of the settlement scheme.

At the same time another resettlement scheme was undertaken on the Scoraig peninsula in Wester Ross. An association called the Clann Albaiin Society, which had been formed in March 1948 to promote the repopulation of Highland and other rural areas of Scotland, had identified the abandoned crofts of the peninsula as suitable for what the secretary of the society described as 'recolonisation'. The main function of the society appears to have been supplying interest free loans for, in their words, 'the settlers' who were also to engage in a revival of indigenous arts and crafts. Neil Gunn and Hugh MacDiarmid are listed as vice-presidents of the society. In this case the land owner, Sir Michael Peto was actively cooperating with the scheme and the Department of Agriculture had assisted by reseeding 25 acres of pasture. The majority of the prospective settlers were men in their twenties from Edinburgh and Glasgow. In November 1948 there were six of them on Scoraig. The scheme failed. According to the landowner, who was also a Ross-shire County Councillor, this was due to the failure of the Government to provide sufficient funds for the construction of a road into the peninsula, a road which would, of course, greatly enhance the value of his land. Sir Michael was evidently eager to keep the settlers and two years later expressed concern that now they 'would like to get away' (back to the city, presumably). Without people there would be no question of the County Council constructing a road going nowhere.

The whole depopulation issue was officially brought to an end in 1951 with a Department of Health for Scotland review which announced that the problem of rural depopulation is 'a sentimental myth' (1951:69). Echoes of the old cries could be heard in the Taylor Commission of Enquiry into Crofting in 1954, and its opinion that crofting is a way of life with its own intrinsic quality which ought to be maintained in a predominantly urban civilisation. By 1976 a Treasury report on rural depopulation from an interdepartmental group can blandly state that 'we have not started from an assumption that rural depopulation must be prevented' (1976:5). From 1960 until 1985 local authorities in Scotland adhered strictly to a national policy which did not permit new houses in the open countryside unless, and on condition that, such new houses would be occupied by agricultural or forestry employees. Even the addition of new houses in a countryside landscape which already featured dispersed settlement would not normally be permitted.[7] In 1985 this policy was reviewed and constraints upon new housing in the countryside were relaxed from 'not normally being permitted' to 'should be discouraged'.[8] Moreover, during this quarter of a century, while new houses were not being permitted, many already existing houses were allowed to fall out of use as dwellings. In the south west of Scotland, for example, many farm houses and cottages are becoming ruins in the middle of dense forest plantations.

The demand for rural dwellings which is being suppressed by recent policies is indicated by the increase in the number of planning applications for housing in the countryside since the slight relaxation in constraints. For instance, Dumfries and Galloway Region received in 1985, an average year before the review of policy, 40 applications, of which 22 were approved. In 1988, after the policy review, the Region received 165 applications, of which 111 were approved.[9]

Nevertheless, in certain rural localities depopulation is still, for the remaining inhabitants, a reality, but their efforts to hold locals and attract incomers have to made in the face of planning constraints which still 'discourage' new housing and the settlement of the countryside, not to mention the current popular image of the 'problem' of migrants from the cities moving into the countryside. For example, Carsphairn Parish in Dumfries and Galloway has seen its population decline from 250 in 1951 to 183 in 1990, and a number of houses outside the village were lost when the farms were bought by the Forestry Commission and planted with trees 'to the very doors of these dwellings.'[10] The Community Council in 1988 did, however, mount a campaign, which attracted the attention of national television, to reverse the decline, and the Council succeeded in persuading the Region to introduce a 'Small Holdings Policy' as part of the district Local Plan. Whether this local project will be more effective than its national predecessors remains to be seen.

This chapter, then, has shown how the widespread concern and anxiety about the consequences of rural depopulation which prompted Acts of Parliament giving national and local government great powers to conserve a sturdy rural population by means of agrarian changes, had almost no detectable impact on the trend of rural depopulation. Depopulation of rural areas proceeded regardless. National attempts under the auspices of voluntary organisations, such as the Clann Albaiin Society, were no less ineffective. The decline in a local population is now only a matter of concern for the dwindling number remaining in that locality who feel the loss of a closed primary school, shop, or post office.

And yet when anxiety about rural depopulation has ebbed away and is no longer so general and pervasive as it was, only then does there appear demographic indications of a reverse in the apparently inexorable population decline and evidence of the repopulation of the depopulated areas. But these individuals who have moved into the countryside were not recognised as the longed for resurrection of sturdy shepherds, crofters, and fishermen reviving an imagined traditional and virtuous rural way of life. And so, at this level, that of representation, the images are reversed and the 'incomers' are characterised sometimes as uninvited fugitives, 'escapees' from the law, from failure, from reality, or at other times as expropriators, 'white setttlers' grabbing houses, land, and diverting government grants and assistance intended for the 'local' population to themselves, or as both. The appearance of these strangers induces a sense of anxiety, even danger, as generalised and as vague as did the antecedent departure of the local population. This is the subject of the next chapter.

Notes

[1] The table is drawn from J. W. Paterson, 1897. Rural depopulation in Scotland, being an analysis of its causes and consequences. *Transactions of the Highland and Agricultural Society of Scotland* 9:236–278.

[2] In this respect it is worth noting the striking contrast between Hunter's (1976) history of crofters in the north west and Carter's (1979) comparable study of farm life in the north east. The former is dominated by cases of, and responses to, evictions and emigration while these are virtually absent from the latter account. Clearly the impact of demographic change is mediated by social structure. In this instance the different pattern of land holding is very relevant. In the north east there was, and still is to some extent, a well dispersed range of holdings both in size and tenure, from squatters, through small holders, small farmers, large farmers to lairds, all in marked contrast to the lack of intermediate classes in the north west where crofter's stood starkly distinct from and opposed to sheep farmers and landowners.

[3] That 'the Highlander' has a special sense of history is a typical observation, and seems to be based largely on the way residents talk to outsiders about the Clearances as if they happened yesterday, leaving the impression that one might actually bump into Mr Patrick Sellar as he comes out of a lawyer's office in Portree. But is this perhaps no more than the amplifying effect already noted as indicative of remote areas? It may be that 'the Highlander' has, in fact, no more or less oral history than any other comparable individuals. For instance,

here is the experience of a researcher into recent changes in agrarian law and regulations, a subject close to the heart of 'the Highlander'. 'Knowing the importance of oral history in Highland culture, I had expected to find many people with vivid memories of the post-World War I period. This did not turn out to be the case. I had to abandon more than one interview when someone old enough to have lived through that period could talk only of the Clearances (a time when they had not been alive)' (Leneman 1989:192).

[4] Actually Rothesay, of all places! (1910:34).

[5] *The Glasgow Herald,* for example, devoted a leading article to Rider Haggard's views (*The Glasgow Herald*, January 17, 1907). In this and other articles *The Glasgow Herald* took the view that while depopulation of the countryside was undesirable, the land reforms of the Liberal Government were even less desirable. It was sceptical of the view that there was a great demand for small holdings, a demand which the Prime Minister, Sir Henry Campbell-Bannerman, believed existed (*The Glasgow Herald,* April 27, 1907).

[6] For the maggot image and urban degeneration see Searle (1976:25) and *Eugenics Review* 1;275–80, 1909–10.

[7] Department of Health for Scotland (DHS) Circular 40/1960.

[8] Scottish Development Department (SDD) Circular 24/1985.

[9] Figures kindly supplied by the Department of Physical Planning, Dumfries and Galloway Regional Council.

[10] Carsphairn Community Council, (nd). *Carsphairn Facing the Crisis: an Objection to the Proposed Stewartry Plan.* Submitted to the Director of Physical Planning, Dumfries and Galloway Regional Council.

Chapter 3

Changing Places

The great problem of the depopulation of rural Scotland was for long considered to have a straightforward solution: rural repopulation. Indeed, stemming depopulation was adopted as a key policy objective by the Highlands and Islands Development Board (reorganised in 1991 and now known as Highlands and Islands Enterprise) from its establishment in 1965. Yet, now that it is happening, rural repopulation has provoked an ambiguous response, as the popular phrase 'white settlers' indicates, and feelings about the repopulation of remote rural areas are nowadays expressed in rather alarming terms. As was illustrated in the previous chapter, it is remarkable that the depopulation which characterised the previous one hundred years was greeted with virtually the same response. It is important to recognise that some of these concerns address rather general matters such as 'Scottish culture' while others articulate the experiences of particular people. Sometimes they may be congruent but as we have seen with respect to depopulation as a 'problem' they may not. While chapter four returns in more detail to the language and sociological configurations introduced in the first chapter regarding the 'problem' of repopulation, the purpose of this chapter is to describe, at a less general level, the local experience of recent population changes.

In order to do this, firstly, the commentary on the 'Englishing' of Scotland is considered and, secondly, a comparison is made between the south west and north west of Scotland. What emerges as significant from this comparison is not so much the similarities, which was to be expected, but the differences. As will be described, change in the south west is experienced as a change in social organisation and in the quality of social interaction, while in the north west Highlands people, generally, are rather more aware of cultural change than social change. This is not to suggest that social change in the north west has not occurred on the same scale as in the south west, but that people in the north west understand, interpret and articulate their experience of it in cultural terms. This chapter argues that the experience of cultural change has the effect of sensitising people more to population fluctuations and the appearance of incomers than does the experience of social change.

The 'Problem' of Rural Repopulation: The 'Englishing' of Scotland

As a demographic process counterstream migration affects rural populations in various ways, sometimes actually accentuating the experience among residents of a sense of population loss. This feeling of loss, though, is often quantifiable in demographic terms. Rural repopulation does not necessarily mean a net *increase* in population. True, for many areas blighted by out-migration new settlement has seemingly halted population decline, and new migrants have even settled in areas which had become completely depopulated. But some geographers have argued that counterstream migration contributes to rural depopulation, rather than halting it. Most notably, it does so through two processes which geographers have labelled *geriatrification* (i.e. the increasing numbers of retired, elderly people) and *gentrification*, or the gradual dominance of rural areas by the middle-classes (e.g. Robinson 1990). Although some areas may be considered attractive places to retire to, increasing numbers of elderly in-migrants may mask the continuing out-migration of younger people, while one aspect of the process of gentrification is reduction in family size, as middle-class professional couples who move to rural areas may have fewer children than local families did in the past.

In Scotland it has been the emphasis on the negative cultural impacts of counterstream migration that has become central to reports and comments about the changing quality of Scottish rural life, particularly in the national media, which play on the theme of the 'Englishing' of the Highlands. The accompanying vocabulary describing incomers from Scotland's 'rapacious neighbour' south of the border 'swamping' rural communities uses unreconstructed colonial metaphors ('white settlers') or terms originating in critiques of colonialism, such as 'cultural domination', and incomers are generally described as threats to Scottish cultural identity, with the ironic consequence that Scots are as aware now of their national identity as they have ever been.

However, while there is agreement that there are people who can be described as 'locals' and 'incomers' in all rural communities, it is also evident that agreement about who they are is less easily achieved. In reality, the categories 'local' and 'incomer', while often used unambiguously as terms of reference, gloss over a complexity of social relationships. As categories their attributes are static and absolute, and by accepting them merely as such they are analytically restrictive starting points for any attempt to assess the cultural impact of counterstream migration. Considered dynamically in the flow of social life, the words 'local' and 'incomer' are elusive, contested, and their appropriateness negotiated in different social situations.[1]

Perhaps it is precisely because cultural change sensitises people to the presence of strangers that much of the commentary surrounding counterstream migration in Scotland is focused primarily on the Highlands. By comparison, Dumfries and Galloway and Borders Regions receive scant coverage. Media images, particularly those constructed by the Scottish press, continue to depict the Highlands as being 'swamped' by English incomers. Such people are variously described as 'hippies' and 'drop outs', 'the '87 Crash refugees', 'burnt-out yuppies', and 'entrepreneurs'. All are considered to be escaping from urban life in search of an idealised Scotland, with most, having sold their expensive London townhouses, now settled in an idyllic country house. They are regarded as a new breed of invader. 'Venture into almost any part of the Highlands of Scotland these days', raged *The Sunday Post* , a Scottish popular newspaper with a huge circulation in Scotland, on 5th November 1989, 'and you find yourself in alien territory'. The article, a 'Special Investigation', went on to bemoan how

> Soft, lilting accents are drowned out by tongues nurtured in deepest Sussex and Surrey, with a smattering of Yorkshire, Geordie, Lancastrian and Cockney thrown in! What we're witnessing is the invasion of the White Settlers desperate to escape the rat race. They're snapping up bungalows, villas, croft cottages, fishermen's cottages, farms, shops, boarding houses and hotels.

Such reports about what is commonly described as the 'Englishing' of the Highlands are not easy to miss in the Scottish press. Newspapers regularly, and with enthusiasm, recycle predictable stereotypes about incomers being predominantly English, responsible for disturbing the tranquillity of rural life, taking the best jobs, and assuming leadership roles on local councils. The 'ancient' Highland culture is reported to be under so much pressure from English incomers that places such as Mull are described as being 'Surrey-In-The-Sea' (*The Scotsaman* 2 February 1991), while parts of the Highlands and Islands generally are depicted as outposts of England. In *The Scotsman* on 24th April 1991, John Macleod wrote how 'white settlers en masse look ominously like a collective takeover bid' and went on further to describe how

> Plockton in Wester Ross is a *New Sussex*. Ullapool has changed beyond recognition from its days as a backwater port in the early Seventies: you are served from shop-counters in the accents of Lancashire and the tiny Gaelic community has retreated into Fortress Wee Free. The home-made newspapers now proliferating on the western seaboard — in places like Gairloch — are splattered with alien names leading alien activities. *Les bourgeois nouveaux sont arrives*, and in many communities they have taken over.

Surprisingly little press coverage is given over to positive responses to incomers. When it is, a balanced view is sought in an attempt to get at the 'truth' about the relationship between locals and incomers, such as in an article in *The Scotsman* on 18th February 1994. Here, while some local feeling towards white settlers in Kilchoan on the Ardnamurchan peninsula was expressed in terms of 'the new Clearances', on the whole incomers were seen as revitalising the area in some way. And local people were reported as 'astute' enough not to blame house prices on incomers, but on government housing policy.

In all this, it is strikingly apparent that concern over English incomers is directed at their appearance in rural areas and their impact upon them. Incomers to urban areas are scarcely noticed or considered interesting enough subject matter for the press. One of the few articles on incomers settling in Scotland's cities appeared in *The Scotsman* on 18th February 1992 and dealt with the English in Edinbugh. Although members of the English middle class have long been prominent in Scotland's universities and other institutions in Edinbugh, Glasgow, Dundee, Aberdeen and St. Andrews (often to the ire of Scottish intellectuals), the focus on the 'Englishing' of rural Scotland possibly has something to do with the visibility of English incomers. This will be returned to in a later chapter.

Complementing the media, the attitudes of local people towards incomers are often reported to be negative and not altogether welcoming. The results of interviews conducted with residents in several rural localities as part of this research can be used to support this view. For example, one woman from South Erradale in the parish of Gairloch complained that only three local families were left in the neighbouring village of Badachro and that most houses owned by incomers remained empty for several months of the year, generating expressions of discontent among those local people living in caravans. Talking about a smart white cottage in Badachro the same woman said:

> an Englishman bought it. Once he moved in, he started to complain that the three caravans in the field opposite spoiled his view. You know where we live, in our caravan, well I wouldn't like it if someone complained like that. We can't afford a house, especially since N. (her husband) has no regular job. That Englishman knew the caravans were there when he bought the house. He's never here, just comes in summer and flies south with the birds for winter. Look at all the empty houses in the area, while there's plenty of local folk around that need a place to live.

This is a typical expression of a widespread feeling that locals are excluded from the property market because incomers bid up house prices. What is notable in the Scottish context, however, is any talk or evidence of violence towards property owned by outsiders. This contrasts with the situation in Wales, the other obvious case of counterstream migration in the United Kingdom. Over the last twenty years or so, there has been a steady rise in English people either moving into the Welsh-speaking heartlands of rural Wales, or buying houses and cottages (often in a state of chronic disrepair) for use as weekend and holiday retreats (e.g. see Symonds 1990). In response to this, the militant nationalist group calling themselves Meibion Glyndwr (The Sons of Glendower) have, in recent years, pursued a spectacular incendiary campaign focused on second homes and the estate agents in English towns like Chester and Shrewsbury who sell them. Although such violence is not indicative of widespread opinion, ' . . . there can be no doubt that the issue of second homes is one about which many people hold strong views and they may thus be ambiguous about the Meibion Glyndwr campaign' (Jenkins 1991:34).

As yet there have been no reports about arson attacks on second homes owned by outsiders in Scotland. However the activities of two groups, Settler Watch and Scottish Watch, have precipitated debate about the impact of incomers on the Scottish economy, the nature of Scottish identity, and have invited comparison with the actions of the Welsh militants. Yet there are differences between the two situations, especially the distribution of second homes in Wales which appear to be heavily concentrated in the heartlands of Welsh speaking Wales (Day 1989), a distribution which is not paralleled in Scotland. Jenkins argues that anti-English feeling in Wales must be understood with reference to 'the centrality of culture and language in the politics of nationalism' (ibid. 35). Concerned with the protection and promotion of Welsh culture, nationalist politicians in Wales keep the Welsh language high on their agendas. Yet, as must be stressed, both Plaid Cymru, the Welsh nationalist political party, and the Welsh Language Society (Cymdeithas yr Iaith Gymraeg) deplore violence for any nationalist reasons. In Scotland culture and language are not linked to the same extent as in Wales, except perhaps in Gaelic speaking areas. (Although as of 1994, the Scottish National Party, which controls local councils in Grampian and Tayside, has settled on a policy of making Gaelic lessons compulsory in Scottish primary schools. It is significant that such a decision has met with scepticism in Scotland, as Gaelic is not and never has been the national language of Scotland) It is perhaps significant that Settler Watch and Scottish Watch do not originate from, nor are they active in, Gaelic speaking areas of Scotland.

During the early summer of 1993 posters with strange Pictish symbols and the words 'Settler Watch' appeared in various locations in north east Scotland and anti-English graffiti daubed on hoardings and shop fronts in Aberdeen. Police also investigated the sending of letter bombs to the Scottish Office in Edinbugh and Dounreay nuclear power station in Caithness, and two fake bombs which were left outside the Aberdeen headquarters of the Shell and BP oil companies[2]. Two women were prosecuted for the sticking of the Pictish symbol posters. One of the women, a German named Sonja Vathjunker and resident in Scotland since the late 1980s, was a member of the Scottish National Party (SNP) and vice-convenor for the SNP's constituency of Aberdeen South. After being prosecuted and fined she was swiftly expelled fro the SNP. Vathjunker, a fluent Gaelic speaker and former student from Aberdeen University, was described in one press report as someone who 'showed the classic fanaticism of the convert'[3].

Yet, Settler Watch has continued its anti-white settlers campaign by sending anti-English literature through the mail to people the organisation has identified as English. Individuals have also received hate mail and threatening telephone calls[4]. While claiming that English infiltration into the remotest corners of Scotland and white settler domination of small villages and townships does harm 'traditional' culture, many of those 'community activists' and politicians in the public eye were quick to distance themselves from the aims and activities of Settler Watch despite, perhaps, there being an unspoken understanding (although no implicit condoning) for why an organisation like Settler Watch has been provoked to initiate its campaigns. For example Michael Foxley, a prominent Highland regional councillor, was quoted in one newspaper as saying that, while he thought Settler Watch was 'almost amusing',

> Highlanders are very tolerant and courteous, and that is probably their undoing. People move up from England with considerable amounts of capital, expecting a status which they don't warrant in terms of their moral worth or mental ability, and strut around pretending to be lord of the manor. [5]

It is precisely this perceived situation that Scottish Watch, another nationalist group, has set out to rectify. While Settler Watch has its centre of operations in the north east, Scottish Watch is based in Dumfries and Galloway in the south west. Although it has condemned the tactics employed by Settler Watch, Scottish Watch has taken an explicit anti-incomer stance and aims to fight what it sees as 'English imperialism' and 'colonisation by a greedy Thatcherite generation'. Thus, Scottish Watch argues that many problems faced in rural areas, such as unavailabilty of housing and jobs for local people, are attributable to an influx of incomers. Scottish Watch has set itself the task of monitoring the extent of English settlement in Scotland by using informants to draw up 'ethnic maps' of the country [6], which will, among other things, provide information about the numbers of English people in senior managerial and local and regional government positions, and about the influence of incomers on the housing market.

Iain Sutherland, national treasurer of Scottish Watch, likened the members of the organisation as 'freedom fighters' who were filling 'a gap in the political process' in Scotland, and were addressing the situation of English influx and influence that the main political parties in Scotland were reluctant to admit existed [7]. Rather than intimidating English incomers directly, Scottish Watch advocates a policy of positive discrimination to be applied in Scotland and makes it clear that it would take non-violent action against employers and cultural organisations and institutions that did not replace any English employees with Scots. In response to political and public disapproval and condemnation of Scottish Watch, its anti-incomer campaign leader, Robert Dunlop, was prompted to deny accusations of racism, pointing instead to cultural differences between the English and Scots which were at the heart of problems in rural areas [8].

The emergence of Scottish Watch and Settler Watch perhaps says something about perceived threats to Scottish identity and the frustrated political hopes of some individuals for Scottish independence. White settlers are metaphors for change and continued colonialism. As such they are easy and obvious targets for the militant expression of anger and racism dressed up as concern for cultural fragmentation and out-migration spurred by lack of opportunity. While much of the commentary on Scottish Watch and Settler Watch focuses on attempts to understand what these organisations are saying about national identity and nationalism under threat from an 'Englishing' of Scotland, little has been written about what kinds of experiences the notion of 'Englishing' and the reaction to 'white settlers' articulate in small localities.

Stability and Change

Despite the absence of any reports of a resort to physical violence, and although there is no evidence to indicate growing support for either Settler Watch or Scottish Watch, a general feeling remains that incomers and outsiders can and do intrude upon existing social structures in rural Scotland. Although there are no more than 400,000 English-born people in the 1991 Census living in Scotland, it can be argued that 'Englishing' has nothing directly to do with the presence of English people, but with their prominence and visibility. Elias and Scotson (1965) also remarked that newcomers to the Leicestershire suburban housing estate they studied were labelled by established residents as 'Londoners', even though many of them came from northern England, Wales and Ireland. But the majority of 'Londoners' in fact originated from London's East End and were perhaps the most visible and therefore more easily identifiable group ('the cockney colony'). Locals reproduce stereotypical images of incomers, but do so in order to make sense of the group (and, of course, this reproduction of stereotypical images works both ways).

The notion of 'Englishing' also articulates a general experience of the rural-urban convergence and cultural and social change. English presence is felt where incomers tend to settle in larger numbers, so that certain places in Scotland quickly acquire reputations as 'English colonies' and the blame for extraordinary events is levelled at them. The remarkable affair of the allegations of 'Satanic and ritual child abuse' on Orkney in 1991 (see Black 1992) is a case in point: whatever else people might recall about these extraordinary events on Orkney, everyone remarks that either the families, or the social workers, or both, were 'incomers'.

Counterstream migration not only amplifies the experience of depopulation, it is commonly held that it erodes a special quality of social life associated with a small community. This has led local people to respond in various ways, for instance by deliberately expressing the distinctiveness of their specific way of life vis a vis that of incomers and strangers. Above all, most people seem to agree that they are witness to a 'changing way of life'. For people who regard themselves as locals, incomers are either agents of change, or are associated with external causes that bring about change, while incomers themselves often perceive the areas they move into as having already experienced change and decline, and that this is something to lament rather than something which they themselves have contributed to bringing about.

To assess the impact of counterstream migration, we need to recognise that people are articulating their experiences of it from a perspective that expresses notions of a community with specific traditions and a distinctive way of life that can only be shared by members of that community. A sense of belonging is expressed by such cultural markers as kinship, local history, dialect, modes of occupation and so on, which can all be used to distinguish locals from incomers, a community from a neighbouring community, rural life from urban life. Faced with a group of incomers, locals may employ various strategies to exclude them from full membership of their community. As Elias and Scotson's (1965) study of tensions between old and new residents on an English housing estate highlights, the newcomers were perceived by the established residents to pose a threat to ' . . . the standards, the norms, the way of life that had evolved among them. They (the established residents) were all closely associated with their self-respect and with the respect they felt was due to them from others' (Elias and Scotson *ibid.* 148). The established residents felt that direct contact with the newcomers would ' . . . lower their own standing, that it would drag them down to a lower status level in their own estimation as well as in that of the world at large, that it would impair the prestige of their neighbourhood with all the chances of pride and satisfaction that went with it' (*ibid.* 149). In this case, the established residents, who considered themselves superior in manners and morals ('symbols of their own respectability' p. 149), were fearful of contamination, of pollution, of contact, with a lower status group - the newcomers.

Elias and Scotson's study points out the importance placed by established residents on the 'age of families' and 'length of residence' as legitimating their own superiority over the newcomers and thereby underlining the social distinction between the two groups of residents. The established residents, being well aware of the threats posed to them, aimed to ensure that the newcomers remained outsiders by asserting their sense of superiority and authority. While categories of 'local' and 'incomer' express and emphasise perceived distinctions and cultural differences between people, such distinctions and differences are used, as we have seen in chapter one, to construct a simple dualistic stereotype of 'locals' and 'incomers' as exclusive and natural categories. It would be easy to fall into a discussion of patterns of social life that does not move beyond this dualistic stereotype, but this study points to a situation which is rather more complex.

As a demographic and sociocultural trend, counterstream migration can be regarded as one aspect of the progressive extension of individualism and modern society, superseding the original and traditional little community. Much of the literature on Scottish rural life has painted a picture of the community as a well-ordered collection of individuals who have lived in the same place all their lives, with each member able to claim several generations of ancestors lying buried in the churchyard. In his short story 'The Cinquefoil', George Mackay Brown writes that

> A community maintains itself, ensures a continuance and an identity, through such things as the shop, the kirk, the stories told in smithy and tailor shop, the ploughing match, agricultural show, harvest home, the graveyard where all its dead are buried. (It is the same with all communities - city or island - but the working out of the ethos of a community is best seen in microcosm, as in the island of Selskay.) Most of all the community ensures its continuance by the coming together of man and woman. There will be a new generation to plough and fish, with the same names, the same legends, the same faces (though subtly shifted, and touched with the almost forgotten, the hardly realised), the same kirkyard (1983:121-22).

The drama of community life, the rejoicing and quarrelling, fighting and loving, together with its inherent sense of continuity, is played out against a backdrop of sea, mountains, moorland, lochs and rivers. So much so that

> The little Highland community in which Kenn lived was typical of what might be found anywhere round the northern and western shores of Scotland: the river coming down out of the wooded glen or strath in the little harbour; the sloping croft lands, with their small cultivated fields; the croft houses here and there, with an odd one on a small ridge against the sky; the school, the post office, and the old church, where the houses herded loosely into a township; and inland the moors lifting to the blue mountains (Gunn 1937:17).

In such descriptions, while rural life is not always idealised, there is a characteristic and vivid sense of stability, of knowing one's place as a part of a locally circumscribed structure of social relationships. As we shall see in chapter six, underpinning both the realities and images of this sense of community and cultural continuity in the Highlands and Islands is the croft, which ' . . . condenses the past through the landscape itself, and through its associations with the natural calendar; with an earlier mode of subsistence and the ideal of self-sufficiency' (Cohen 1987:109). This image continues to appeal to the tourist and visitor in search of peace and tranquillity and an experience of another, radically different way of life, and is common in the vocabulary of motives offered by residential incomers for their moving from urban areas (e.g. see Forsythe 1974, 1980).

The image of the little community is well represented in the popular genre of writing known as 'Kailyard'. In Tom Nairn's (1977) analysis of Scottish nationalism and culture the success of Kailyard is attributed to exiled Scots who were the most ardent consumers of such books, and who, presumably, liked to think that *Auld Licht Idylls* and the rest represented the kind of society they had left behind. All of which is, moreover, dressed up in what George Rosie calls 'Highland kitsch'. The claim that much of Highland tradition is invented (Trevor Roper 1984) is well known, but there are those who would argue that the misuse of Celtic paraphernalia, such as the kilt and bagpipes by Lowland Scots, has become an essential part of Scottish cultural identity. For instance, Highland dress is what George Rosie, writing in *The Scotsman*, considers as

> one more manifestation of that pervasive syndrome I've come to think of as "Highlandism". I'm not talking here about Gaelic literature, poetry, music and song all of which are showing signs of a real and vigorous revival. I'm talking about that debased, silly, music hall version of Gaeldom that has seeped into every corner of Scottish culture. And which, I would argue, enervates and muddles Scottish culture (Rosie 1991).

In such a setting the idea of the 'incomer', 'the white settler', is a metonym for changing economic systems and cultural circumstances that are seen to be replacing kinship, locality, and other defining components that go to make up a community and underpin a unique way of life. It is not simply that the host population is confronted with a problem of assimilating a new-comer into an existing social milieu and complexity of social relationships. The incomer as a symbol of change captures the feeling of transition and adjustment to a situation where specialised roles, individuality, and con-tractual relationships as opposed to social relations supported by morality, intimacy, and sentiments of belonging, become increasingly dominant and in fact corrode a state of being that appears to be receding into the past. In order to explore these themes, in the rest of this chapter the experiences of both those who define themselves and are defined by others as incomers and locals, will be considered.

What follows is distilled from fieldwork and interviews in Nithsdale and Wester Ross. In Nithsdale, in the south west, the appearance and disappearance of people is not, on the whole, talked about to the same extent as in Wester Ross, in the Highlands. Although in Nithsdale 'white settlers' are topics of conversation from time to time, many locals do not recognise any persisting and immediate interaction with incomers, who, despite the efforts of Scottish Watch in Dumfries, remain somehow as 'shadowy' figures on the social horizon. In the north west Highlands, on the other hand, the sense of the presence of incomers is immediate and is perceived as a direct threat to a special sense of Highland identity and distinction. With entire glens and townships depopulated by the Clearances, and with current social and economic problems contributing to make out-migration a continuing and persistent trait, the disappearance of people from the Highlands is amplified by the appearance of residential incomers.

A View from the South West:

'There's no sense of community, nowadays . . .'

In this section we focus on accounts from people in two parishes, Keir and Penpont in Dumfries and Galloway Region. The response of people who were born and have lived most of their lives in these parishes towards in-migrants is considered, together with the experiences and commentary of some of the in-migrants themselves. This will be contrasted later with the situation in Wester Ross. While there are some obvious and expected similarities between the accounts from these two areas there are also some significant differences between Nithsdale and Wester Ross. As will be argued, people in mid-Nithsdale talk generally about change in terms of what might be called social organisation. What people in Keir and Penpont call a 'close-knit community' is a local society that is socially differentiated and with a marked division of labour such that there is a keen sense of mutual interdependence. With the transition to a local society now internally divided by class cultures into residential groups of an otherwise rather similar nature, and with an almost negligible division of labour, the loss of a sense of community is mourned. People now simply dwell in proximity to each other and may, or may not, associate simply as neighbours.[9] This has considerable implications for the way incomers are perceived, and how sensitive people are to their presence.

The recent history of mid-Nithsdale has followed a pattern familiar to that of rural parishes in many parts of the British Isles. Over the one hundred year period between the 1850s and 1950s, for example, the demographic trend in mid-Nithsdale, and elsewhere in the Dumfries and Galloway Region, had been a gradual depopulation of rural areas. This was partly attributable to a declining agricultural labour force, and to the growth of the town of Dumfries owing to the increasing centralisation of trade and commerce, service industries, and local government. In the period leading up to World War II there was very little manufacturing industry, and the population was predominantly rural. The two main occupations in Dumfriesshire were agriculture and textiles, but between 1851 and 1951 there was a decline in the percentage of people in the area employed in these occupations from 55% to 24%. There were also considerable changes in the numbers of women employed in agriculture. On the other hand there was a significant rise in the percentage of people who were associated with commerce and the professions, from around 5% to 39%. This is representative of an overall economic transition from primary industries to tertiary industries. There was also quite significant growth around Annan in the 1960s, as a consequence of the opening of the Chapelcross nuclear power station in 1959.

While the population of Dumfries and Galloway declined from 150,268 in 1891 to 143,187 in 1971, by 1991 there had been an increase to 147,732. For the region as a whole, the 1991 Census recorded 82.6% of the population as having been born in Scotland. The breakdown by districts is as follows:

	Total population	% Born in Scotland
Annandale & Eskdale	37,087	76.8%
Nithsdale	57,012	87.1%
Stewartry	23,629	78.4%
Wigtown	30,087	84.5%

(Source: 1991 Census Monitor for Dumfries and Galloway Region)

Although the population of these districts is predominantly of Scottish origin, incomers tend to be labelled as 'English white settlers', and this even applies to those of Scottish origin who have moved into the area from elsewhere.

Much of the material that follows comes from older people born in the parishes of Keir and Penpont. During interviews most informants would refer to recent history, looking back over their lifetimes to talk of a distinctive sense of community they regard as having once existed but has now disappeared. In many cases, this knowledge of local history is a way of demarcating the boundary between locals and incomers. Locals, people in Keir and Penpont say, are easily distinguished from incomers by their knowledge of past events and by being able to trace their origins in the area back through several generations.

When asked about how the area had changed in recent years, people would often talk about the decline of essential services and sources of employment, and about the disappearance of artisans, merchants, and shopkeepers. One woman in her late seventies from Penpont commented

> In the early part of this century there were a lot of tradesmen — masons, joiners, blacksmiths — and there were jobs in the woollen mill. This has all changed, now. I remember there being plenty of dry-stane dykers and there were quite a few shops in the village, including a bakery. You have to go into Thornhill for shopping now, or even to Dumfries, but without a decent bus service it's not that easy.

By the 1950s there were few tradesmen in Penpont; the tailors, drapers, bakers, butchers, grocers, and shoemakers were almost consigned to history. The last baker in Penpont, for example, closed in 1953. The main sources of employment for people in Penpont and Keir were now several miles away, mainly in a bacon factory in Thornhill, in the grain mills in Closeburn, and in Dumfries. Nowadays, Thornhill is the nearest centre for essential services apart from Dumfries. In Thornhill are the secondary school, a small supermarket, a baker, bank, chemist and some small shops. However, Dumfries is the main centre for employment opportunities, especially for the young adults.

The community that old people feel they once belonged to, but which they feel has now almost disappeared, was one characterised by a complex division of labour and high degree of specialisation. This was a socially differentiated local society of farmers, agricultural workers, carpenters, blacksmiths, masons, weavers, tailors, bakers and merchants. It was a society with a noticeable degree of mutual dependence, and a kind of social solidarity that reinforced co-operation. For example, in Keir and Penpont local needs were virtually satisfied by local people, and this is illustrated by the importance of the mill. The mill at Keir, which dates back to 1780, was supplied with corn by local farmers, who, incidentally, would also depend on local mills to get their corn ground into stockfeed. Keir Mill produced bruised corn, mash and oatmeal, the latter primarily for local bakers to make oatcakes and bannock, and for local butchers who needed it as an essential ingredient in puddings, sausages, and haggis.

Underpinning this rural society was the estate as a unit of social organisation, and indeed, a central topic of conversation among informants concerning recent changes in the area was the virtual disappearance of a social structure of landlords and tenants. In the recent past, a large number of people depended on the estates in Keir and Penpont parishes for employment and rural society was stratified into landlords and tenants and their employees, various artisans, servants and labourers and some clerks in the former case, and the farm workers of the latter. With declining incomes from rents and increasing costs together with inheritance taxes, landowners have sold portions of their estates, or have even broken up the estate in its entirety. Generally, in Keir and Penpont the number of tenants has decreased, attributable mainly to changes in tenure patterns, and to the fact that fewer people are now dependent on the land to earn a living. However, there are still some smaller, estates in the area, notably Barjarg in Keir and Capenoch near Penpont. While it has become common to sell off the houses of estate workers, in some cases even the landowner's mansion house has been sold. In Keir parish, Barjarg Tower, the Barjarg estate's 'big house', is now a hotel, catering mainly for business executives. The landowner lives a few hundred yards away in a place called Newhall, where he farms. The Barjarg estate itself now comprises just two tenant farms, 'Netherkeir' (dairy cattle and sheep) and 'Glenlough' (hill cattle and sheep). The other large estate in Keir parish was Waterside, owned by the Dalrymple family from its foundation until the mid- nineteenth century, when it was bought by a member of the Hoggins family. The estate was broken up and sold in 1954. Waterside House has, since the mid-1980s, been owned by a retired couple of Anglo- Scots origin, while the gardener's cottage is owned by a retired English couple.

The general situation at present is that estate houses and cottages have been sold or are rented to individuals who are not employees of the estate Many of these residents may be either retired people, urban-rural migrants, or commuters who work in Dumfries, Kilmarnock, Ayr, and even Glasgow, and they tend to retain an urban-focused lifestyle, social network and image of the countryside. Furthermore, because of the proximity of Dumfries, and even the declining mining areas of Sanquhar, Kirkonnel and Cumnock, the Dumfries and Galloway countryside has become an extension of suburbia for people who depend on urban areas for employment and pleasure. That the urban and the rural have converged upon a common structure, with the distinction between them blurred, is an accepted sociological perspective, although from the perspective of people living in rural areas, the urban is considered to have intruded upon rural values and a well-defined social structure. In response to this, one of the most common complaints from elderly people in Keir and Penpont is that, while there are shops, a post office, and bus services in Penpont, there is 'little sense of community, nowadays'. A seventy four year old woman said of Penpont,

> Apart from the retired people in the village, it seems that most folk that live here are incomers. There seem to be an awful lot of commuters here, going off to work in Dumfries. There's no work to be had locally, not like how it used to be. I can't really keep up with the new folk who move here and wouldn't say I know who many of them are. We used to be more or less self-sufficient here. Folk would help one another, and rely on one another.

Many of the elderly people interviewed were born in the area and had been involved in agriculture and estate work. One seventy nine year old woman, who was born in the back lodge on the Barjarg estate, where her father had been head gardener, said she could remember when most people in the Barjarg area had been involved in the estate in some way:

> There was a limestone quarry at Barjarg, and there was work to be had for seven or eight months of the year. But I think it closed in the early years of the century, maybe in 1905 or 1906. I can remember the remnants of the quarry and the pulley bridge that the workers would take to get across the Nith, on their way to and from Closeburn.

Through memory and reminiscence, people and events are located in the landscape and reference is made to a sense of place and community. But this connection with people, whether kin or non-kin, and with events and places is regarded as absent from not only the experience of incomers, but from the experience of 'local' children. One man, in his mid-sixties, recalled how

> School was a two mile walk from Barjarg to Barndennoch, and that always seemed a long way then. Nowadays, the children go to school in Thornhill and learn about the world. But they don't seem to know much about the area they live in. With all the old people dying and newcomers moving in, no-one gets to know one another. My grandchildren wouldn't know who lives in most of those houses in the valley.

Change in the area, then, is characterised by a transition from a socially differentiated yet mutually dependent local society, to a society where people are less dependent on one another, and indeed are hardly known to each other. Social relationships are fragmented rather than differentiated. Such change, however, is not attributed to wholesale depopulation. Indeed, people in Keir and Penpont seem to be less aware of depopulation than do people in the Highlands. Rather, change is the result of external influences that act to extinguish people's 'traditional' roles and occupations. Nowadays, rather than there being a 'community' to which people feel they belong, people simply reside together in the same locality, and whatever relationships arise do so on the basis of sharing this residential area, instead of being founded upon, and deriving meaning from, social differentiation and a division of labour.

Social fragmentation is likely to persist because, on the whole, incomers to Keir and Penpont retain their links with their previous places of residence, with relatives and friends. Together with their work, it is the previous, or already existing network of relationships that informs their feelings of social involvement. One couple, in their late forties, who had moved in from Dumfries complained that

> Local people tend to be parochial, unsophisticated and not too worldly-wise. We don't feel that we're accepted here, probably because we're not farmers or interested in entering home baking competitions at the village show. But we do have our own friends scattered around the country, so we tend to just keep in touch with them.

The couple who bought Waterside House said that they felt they had not been totally accepted and were still considered incomers. They regarded the local area as 'still structured' in terms of established social relations, and illustrated this by recounting how, on first moving to Keir and attending their first church service there, they were told by several people that they were expected to sit in the Waterside pew. Because of this and other experiences, they described local people as 'forelock tugging', adding that despite several years residence they were still addressed formally by other residents. It is interesting to note that many incomers in other areas, such as Gairloch, also felt that being addressed by their fore name was an indication of acceptance.

One reason for this feeling of non-acceptance may be that the reality of rural life is blurred by the image incomers often have of it and which they bring with them. What is taken for ignorance, or indifference, are likely to be instances of reserve, and of respect for people's independence, self-sufficiency and privacy. The idea of self-sufficiency is used here to refer to the attitude that people living in rural areas have been forced to adopt because of their changing circumstances. Too often, bus services are reduced, post offices are closed, and employment opportunities restricted. There is a lack of some foodstuffs, and even in agriculturally productive areas this can extend to bread, basic groceries, and fresh vegetables. There is also a lack of amenities and paucity of advice from local authorities. Shops can be distant, and it may be a two-mile walk to a telephone box. In Nithsdale, while the loss of a sense of community is regretted there is a persisting respect, at least outwardly for individual privacy and an attitude that people's affairs are their own. This is an interesting point, however, as gossip about other people's business and activities forms the bulk of much conversation. Quite often, though, the details of interest are farming matters.

Some of the incomers to Keir and Penpont admitted that they thought they were entering a close-knit, self-contained little community where everyone helps one another. When they found they were not participating in social relationships of mutual aid, they believed the community out there was closing ranks to exclude them. It is then that locals are described by incomers as 'yokels', and 'parochial to the extent of ignorance'. Most locals recognise incomers as belonging to different and already existing social networks. They are regarded as 'sophisticated', 'educated', people from the big city 'with letters after their name'. Both incomers and locals belong to different social worlds, yet reside in the same geographical locality. Individuals from each of these networks can of course deliberately exclude the other, but it is more likely that each has preconceived ideas about the other that precludes the building of intimate relationships. In his study of agricultural workers in East Anglia, Newby (1977) pointed out that newcomers do not necessarily have to struggle to be accepted by the community receiving them. Rather, they can afford to ignore the values and social conventions of the village by establishing contacts 'among fellow-newcomers or even outside the village altogether' (1977:330).

But, as elsewhere, incomers do not share the historical background and cultural experiences that give, or have given, locals in Keir and Penpont a sense of continuity and community. There are no 'memoryscapes' for incomers and no acceptable way they can explain their present attachment to the area in terms of 'roots', unless they are able to trace genealogical links to antecedents who have resided in the area, but even these appeals may be met with scepticism. Unlike many locals, incomers have no knowledge of the landscape and of the specific characters who inhabit it, both in the past and in the present, that can provide the basis for feelings of locality and belonging. Much local historical knowledge is not of 'significant' events in global terms, but stories, reminiscences of childhood, or of different ways of life, farming methods, significant features of village life, the estates, old cooking methods, crops and vegetables that were once grown, and of people. Such information differs from the kind of historical knowledge that incomers seek. Like the initial research of the anthropologist or local historian, incomers derive much of their knowledge from books on the area, from the Old Statistical Account and so on. For example, the owners of Waterside House are interested in the history of the estate, its families and its boundaries. Since buying the house and moving in, they have spent a lot of time and energy researching the Hoggins family history and collecting old maps of Keir (mainly by scouring antique shops and old book and map shops in Edinburgh and Glasgow). They have also restored the stables and outbuildings, dug out the well and have tried to build up a picture of what the house and grounds looked like during the 'golden age' of the estate. Despite this, there is a sense in which such knowledge of the area though sometimes of considerable historical depth has nevertheless a shallow quality since it has no foundation in a practical knowledge of the area acquired over many years. For incomers interested in local history, many of the area's social characters appear only in black and white photographs. People's knowledge of the area is bound to differ, however. A large number of local people, especially those involved in farming, said they would not have the time to indulge in archival research in the Ewan Library in Dumfries, whereas retired incomers are able to do so. By focusing on specific themes, the image of a rural idyll is allowed to persist, and those incomers who are aware of changes in the area can nonetheless construct images of a not too distant past that looks similar to the one that is preserved in pictorial displays in museums and heritage books.

As will be discussed below, it is a characteristic trait of incomers that they tend to join local historical societies, while locals do not. In Nithsdale many local people admitted they had no interest in the kind of historical material that incomers were eager to discover. For example, Bob and Margaret H., who farm in Keir have no particular in-depth 'historical' knowledge of their farm in the same way that the couple who own Waterside House have of the old estate, rather than a rough idea of the age of the farmhouse. This is illustrated by a letter Margaret received in 1987 from a woman in New Zealand who was a descendant of people who were tenants on the farm in the eighteenth century. She explained that she wanted to trace her ancestry and requested information about people and dates, and some general historical information about the farm. By 1991 the letter remained unanswered, because Margaret said she would not know where to begin to find out what the letter writer wanted. Again, this points to a different kind of historical knowledge. It does not suggest that Margaret has no interest in local history, just that there are different kinds of local history. Indeed, rather than taking an interest in specific dates and the kinds of events that may interest incomers, Bob's knowledge of his farm is personalised. As a third generation tenant, he is attentive to the kinds of details outsiders would perhaps not find too significant, such as changes in patterns of field drainage, and in the layout of fields and dry stone walls over the years. A family friend once when visiting the farm asked about the 'Preaching Stone', a large rock to be found on the farm's rough pasture on the Keir Hills, and something he had identified through study of an Ordnance Survey map, only to receive Bob's astonished reply that, while he knew of the rock, he had never known its name.

Yet it is not only incomers who are excluded from local knowledge. Because so many young people work in Dumfries or elsewhere, their social networks extend over a wider area, beyond the farming interests of the locality. While it is true that farmers throughout Nithsdale know one another, meeting at market, shows, union meetings and so on, many young people are not involved in farming, even though they may be of farming stock. The immediate area is no longer the main focus of people's lives, and work and leisure activities focus mainly on Dumfries. In this way, specific places, names, personalities, stories and events, do not figure prominently in the social worlds of even some locals. Friends and personal networks extend and cover a wide social landscape.

Again, this indicates how misleading is the assumption of the objective reality of a well-established rural host community, that can trace genealogical connection, 'rooted' in the landscape, with those who have lived in it over several generations under threat from a flow of incomers from urban areas. Like other Scottish rural areas, the rural landscape of Nithsdale is in flux, and in-migration is part of this process. But commentary on the demographic trend of in- migration in Nithsdale's rural areas remains subdued. A sense of threatening in- migration is not as immediately apparent in Nithsdale as it is in other Scottish rural areas, such as Wester Ross to be considered in the next section of this chapter. Nithsdale is in relative close proximity to urban areas, so there are people, both locals and incomers, who commute to work and depend on those urban areas for their livelihood. For many locals in Keir and Penpont, incomers do not figure prominently and immediately in their social worlds. Their presence is suspected in the rising house prices in the area, but this impact is not one of appropriating aspects of culture, or of taking the jobs that would otherwise be available to locals, largely because there are no jobs, or at least relatively few jobs, to be had in the area. Many incomers, excepting those who are retired, already have jobs and move to the countryside because it is in reasonable commuting distance to Dumfries. That incomers tend to be rather shadowy figures is partly attributable to this fact. This is far from the case elsewhere in rural Scotland and, as the next section illustrates, in areas where people are more sensitised to depopulation and the appearance of incomers the response is hardly muted.

A View from the North West:

'There are no real crofters in this part of the world'

In this section we turn to the Highlands and focus on the Gairloch seaboard in Wester Ross, an area where incomers are perceived to be a direct threat to a 'traditional way of life' by many people who would consider themselves 'locals'. As a region, Wester Ross has experienced a population growth of 39% since 1971, which is one of the biggest increases for any comparable area in the Highlands and Islands. The increase has taken place mainly in Gairloch and Ullapool. Such an increase is attributable partly to in-migration for reasons of retirement and employment in the tourist industry, and partly to fewer people leaving because of enhanced employment opportunities, for example in fish farming and fish processing. A population growth of 25% between 1971 and 1981 in the Kishorn, Lochcarron and Strathcarron area was mainly due to the Kishorn oil platform construction yard (Highland Regional Council 1985). While the population in these places is expected to grow, this depends to some extent on how the area will continue to recover from the loss of the Kishorn yard (Highland Regional Council 1989).

Despite the growth in population and the increasing numbers of in-migrants to Wester Ross, it is far from easy to construct in objective terms a realistic version of the dualistic stereotype of 'locals' and 'incomers' and then assess the impact of counterstream migration. Although there is a widespread impression that incomers are thick on the ground they defy definition, and descriptions and attributes are matters of personal perspective. While there are English incomers, including many who would correspond to popular images, there are also incomers from urban parts of Scotland and from other rural areas of the Highlands and Islands, such as Skye and Lewis. The latter, however, are not usually regarded as incomers in the usual sense, as the English and urban Scots are. Whatever the differences, it is the purpose of this section to illustrate how the image of the 'incomers' comprises among other attributes a threat in terms of being representatives of other values, and ultimately represent agents of cultural change.

The Gairloch seaboard area, including Gairloch itself and several small townships, which are based mainly on crofting, has a population of about 1000. The exploitation of natural resources underpins the economy of the area and, as well as crofting, people depend mainly on shell fishing, fish farming, fish processing, and quarrying. As Gairloch is a service centre for much of Wester Ross, there are also casual and seasonal employment and income generating activities to be found, especially in tourism, which is increasing in importance for the local economy. The history and institution of crofting is discussed at length in chapters five and six, but it is worth pointing out here that crofting differs from part-time farming in that it is constituted legally as regards tenure in a unique way. It is also restricted to the so-called crofting counties in the Highlands and Islands, of Ross and Cromarty, Inverness, Argyll, Caithness, Orkney, Sutherland and Shetland. Most crofters are tenants on the estates of Highland landlords, but they have rights over permanent tenancy, the right to a fair rent (which is fixed by the Scottish Land Court) and the right to assign the tenancy of the croft to someone else (although the assignation of a croft to a non-relative is subject to approval by the Crofters Commission). Crofting also differs from small-scale farming because of its communal nature and its historical development has nurtured a unique sense of community and identity.

In addition, crofting by itself has never been a viable agricultural proposition and crofters have always had to find other forms of employment to supplement their work on the croft. Yet, because of the demands of the croft, people have never been freed from its responsibilities to take permanent employment. In the past, this situation bound the crofter both to the land and to the landlord. The crofter, says David Kerr Cameron (1980:14) '. . . ran in the double harness that was the curse of the old crofting existence: working away by day and coming home to his croft by night, often enough by the light of the wintry stars'. To this day, crofting can only be sustained by diversification and pluriactivity. In Gairloch, for example, most crofters and their wives find employment with the regional council, or in fish farming, or are self-employed as builders, carpenters, painters and fishermen, or obtain seasonal work in the fishing industry. Others travel to distant parts of Britain to find short term and casual work, including offshore jobs in the oil and gas industry.

Gairloch is recalled as, until recently, a predominantly Gaelic speaking area, and local people talk of there being a continuity in the Gaelic culture and the crofting way of life before incomers started to arrive in ever increasing numbers. Incomers are identified not only as agents of cultural change, but as part of a gradual process contributing to the disappearance of a way of life. A crofter from Port Henderson recalled how

> I grew up speaking Gaelic and only started to learn English when I went to school. Children had their knuckles smacked if the teacher found them speaking Gaelic in the classroom or in the playground. Many children lost the Gaelic and I live in an area where there are few Gaelic speakers. Parents didn't think it was important for their children to speak Gaelic anymore, because, I suppose, they had to get by in English. What was the use of Gaelic?

Today it is primarily elderly people who speak Gaelic as a first language, and accompanying this loss of language is a strong sense of the loss of a distinct culture. This sense of cultural change is experienced as something that marginalises people. For example, crofting is described as 'a struggle' or as 'a hard life'. Another crofter from Port Henderson, who inherited his croft from his father, expressed his feelings towards modern crofting as follows:

> I feel very negative about diversification schemes, ever since I was encouraged to go into egg production. I got a grant, but invested a lot of money of my own in the thing. I also invested a lot of time and energy, only to be hit by the salmonella in eggs scare. Now I have an empty shed and my wife and I are thinking of going into cheese making. I'll have to approach the local enterprise company for a lot of money, but I'm doubtful if it's worth bothering about. There's no money in crofting, and lamb prices are low. It's hardly worth taking them to market. Crofting is dying.

It certainly does seem to be the case that crofting is dying in some parts of Gairloch, especially at Big Sand. Here, on the north shore of Gairloch, there is considerable croft land that is poorly used and managed and there is a particularly acute problem of absenteeism. Croft houses lie in ruins and much croft land is under pressure from incompatible property development projects, such as tourist facilities and holiday homes. The situation at Big Sand is illustrative of what can happen to a crofting community when too many decrofting applications are granted and croft land is lost, and when occupancy is no longer permanent on some crofts, to the general detriment of the crofting community. (When croft land is decrofted, it is taken out of the statutory regulations of the Crofters Act. Quite often, once this is done, croft land is lost and development can take place). When permanent occupancy and the working of a croft is interrupted when a crofter dies and the croft is inherited by a person who, owing to whatever circumstances, is unable or unwilling to live and work on the croft there is an appreciable weakening of the crofting township as a whole. Because crofting, unlike the working of other small holdings, is necessarily also a communal activity because of obligations in connection with common grazings, absenteeism and decrofting threatens the viability of a crofting township as an active crofting settlement which may, as a consequence, be reduced to a mere aggregate of people doing no more than inhabiting dwelling houses.

The fragmentation and loss of croft land is also cited as a problem elsewhere in the Gairloch area. At the same time people are also hostile to the idea of incomers acquiring crofts, partly because young local people are denied what is described as 'the right to enter crofting', but also because of a fear that once incomers have acquired a croft, then a successful decrofting application to the Crofters Commission would result in yet more land being, as it is put, 'lost'. One woman who works a croft with her husband in South Erradale explained that

> We see the land in a different way. Incomers see it as having an economic value, but crofting land means something else to the crofting community. Ken (her husband) inherited this croft from his father and the thought of it being lost eventually is something we can't bear.

However, being a 'local' croft tenant or owner does not necessarily guarantee that crofts will remain within the legislation of the Crofters Act. As the same woman's sister complained:

> Local people are as much to blame as incomers for the loss of croft land. They've sold out and taken advantage of the demand for crofts from strangers.

Here, then, is a feeling that some locals have 'sold out' to the values of incomers and the wider society. Of particular concern for the crofting communities of Port Henderson and South Erradale, on the south shore in Gairloch, was a case in 1991 where a local woman applied, in her son's name, to the Crofters Commission for the tenancy of a croft in Port Henderson. While putting forward her son's case (at the time he was sixteen years old) to the Crofters Commission that it was his intention to go into crofting as soon as he finished school, people in the area had grave worries as to her long- term plans. The woman already owned several properties in the area, which she let out as holiday accommodation, and did not come from a crofting background. It was feared that, if she was successful in acquiring the croft, she would submit a decrofting application to the

Crofters Commission and, once the land was decrofted, she would build holiday homes on it. A cousin of the woman commented that "She's thinking of the future, about the value of the land, not about going into crofting". The woman's application was unsuccessful, and the Crofters Commission allowed the assignation of the tenancy of the croft to a local man from a crofting background, having been satisfied that he would work it and fulfil his obligations to the crofting township. It remains, however, that the future of crofting is felt to be is precarious because of the demand for land from other interests.

It is not only crofters, however, who say they are struggling to maintain a way of life. A Gairloch man in his early twenties, who was experiencing difficulties making a living as a shrimp fisherman, said he was doubtful whether he would be able to stay in the area, because ". . . hard working fishermen are being forced out of business by spiralling costs, EC measures and competition from east coast vessels". This comment comes despite the optimism of Highland Regional Council that Gairloch can benefit from public and private investment in the development of the west coast fishery. A recent extension to the pier has been accompanied by an initial expansion in fish processing facilities, but this has done little to make local people feel secure about the future of the fishing industry in Gairloch. The same man thought that ". . . while there may be jobs for folk on shore, there's no way fishermen can compete with other ports along the coast. And we can't expect to survive with these new tie-up rules".

The marginalising felt by crofters and fishermen is accentuated by the growth of other industries in Gairloch that are gradually replacing their traditional occupations. Most significant is the tourist industry. Certainly, the casual visitor to Gairloch must be impressed by the numbers of hotels and guest houses, and by the numbers of holiday homes in the area. Tourism is of increasing importance for the local economy, and is one way that crofters are able to diversify and generate additional income. But it is the development of tourism in the Gairloch seaboard area which, perhaps more than anything, sensitises people to the presence of incomers and to their impact on local culture. An example of this can be found in the village of Badachro.

Badachro is situated on the south shore of Gairloch, and in the past was the centre of the Gairloch cod fishery. Today, fishing has declined, but many buildings which were used as fish curing stations still stand, testifying to the previous importance of fishing for the local economy. In recent years, Badachro has become a popular place for retirement and holiday homes. During the tourist season it is also a centre for recreational activity.

This is focused mainly on the harbour, which in summer is a somewhat congested anchorage for yachts. Compared to the nearby crofting townships of Port Henderson, South Erradale and Opinan, the population of Badachro is almost entirely made up of seasonal and permanently settled incomers. Badachro is considered a good example of the encroachment of incomers that begins in Gairloch, but reaches into more 'traditional' crofting areas. As elsewhere in the Gairloch area, some incomers in Badachro have moved in and taken over old businesses. The storekeeper in the village, a doctor who took early retirement, is originally from Arbroath on the East coast of Scotland. Similarly, the Badachro Inn is owned and run by a couple who retired from Edinburgh. Other incomers originate from Cheshire, Orkney, and Yorkshire, while some are conspicuous by their absence, returning to the village only during the summer months and leaving their houses empty for the rest of the year.

The presence of incomers and the exploitation of Badachro by strangers causes occasional friction and discontent. For example, those who patronise the Inn complain that during the winter it is only open for three nights a week, but is open every day during Easter and throughout the summer to cater for tourists. "They wouldn't open at all in the winter for the people who live here, if they didn't need the money", was one comment. Quite often, however, it is the established incomers as well as some of the local people who are resisting further change, development and in-migration. For example, the Old Post Office, a disused wooden building in the centre of the village, was bought by two men from Yorkshire in 1989. There was considerable opposition from Badachro residents, both incomers and locals alike, towards their plans to convert it into a holiday home. Residents argued that as it had been a community building in the past, when it functioned as a post office, it should have been put to community use. However, it transpired that the owner, a local woman, sold the building to outsiders. The new owners, aware of the opposition to their plans, decided, as they explained, "to leave it for two years, until the dust settled". In 1991 they completely renovated the building and began to let it to holidaymakers. Shortly before their work was completed a large stone was thrown through one of the windows. During this time, discussion among residents centred on exaggerated guesses about how much tourists would have to pay to stay in the building, and on how it did not benefit the local economy, but "lined the pockets of two sharks down south".

Throughout the Gairloch seaboard area, incomers are again usually cited as the cause of rising house prices and thereby denying young people the opportunity of acquiring their own house in their home communities. Many young adults live in caravans while they are on a waiting list for a council house, and others are forced to leave. Incomers cannot be blamed entirely for high house prices and a lack of suitable accommodation for young people, however. As has been noted, some local people themselves are selling out to incomers, or are owners of holiday homes which they let out to tourists in the summer. There are numerous examples where locals own several houses. For instance, in Badachro, one local woman owns four houses which she lets out as holiday homes, while one of her sons lives in a caravan with his wife, unable to find rented accommodation at an affordable price.

In Badachro and neighbouring townships, the consensus is that incomers who fit in are generally accepted, but that many of them tend to create too much fuss and are ignorant of local ways. During spring 1991, one Englishman found himself the butt of many jokes throughout the Gairloch area. At a meeting of the moorings committee which, among other things, discussed the speed of water skiers in the loch, he startled many people by suggested that the words 'SPEED LIMIT' be painted in six foot high letters on a rock face overlooking the harbour at Badachro. This spurred comment that incomers are active on too many committees that make decisions that affect the area. A fisherman living at Big Sand, who originated from Lewis, said "I really start to worry when English people get all the top council jobs. There's an arrogance about them". The Badachro Residents' Association, which has retired incomers among its number, has also caused friction because of its opposition to locally-based development. For example, one local man's application to Ross and Cromarty Divisional Planning Committee to build a storage shed for his business received objections from the Residents' Association and several other individuals. The man, a builder and joiner, wanted to build the shed on ground next to houses which were used as holiday homes. The proposal was accepted by the Committee,[10] which rejected the claim that the building would spoil the view from the houses. It is notable that one of the objectors was also granted permission to build a property to let as a self-catering holiday home, and received no objections from any Badachro resident.[11]

It is not only local people who talk about the loss and decline of culture, the decline of crofting and of the Gaelic life. Incomers themselves are aware that they have moved to an area that is experiencing change. Sometimes, however, assumptions about cultural change are founded upon scant knowledge of the realities of a way of life such as crofting. The owner of a teashop, who hails originally from Kent, commented that

There are no real crofters in this part of the world anymore. I know people who claim to be crofters, but they do other jobs, like driving lorries for the council. I also know a guy in Port Henderson who's gone and bought himself a computer . . . for his sheep, he says! No, I think the real crofting areas are in places like Skye and Lewis.

Such misconceptions are guided by ideas of 'tradition' and images of what the area was like in the past. It can be assumed that most people feel they can only get an idea of what 'real' crofting is from the exhibits in the Gairloch Heritage Museum. Crofters who drive lorries for a living, have other jobs and use computers are therefore not considered 'real' or 'genuine', those who are seen to use 'traditional' methods and live in a state of grinding poverty presumably are. This points to the disappointment that some people feel when they move to an area which they had expected to be full of bucolic folk. One man, a retired dentist from Edinburgh, felt

the area lacked colour because there aren't any characters, like I suppose you found in the old days. I would imagine you only find them in Wales, as that seems to be more of a traditional place.

Individual incomers do not identify themselves as agents of change but, like locals, may see other incomers as bringing about undesirable change. Unable, perhaps, to assess their own impact on the areas they move to, they are, from their own understanding of the situation, witnesses to a changing way of life. This may account for their participation in local historical societies. Possibly because they have no sense of historical continuity with the area, with its people and landscape, incomers appropriate aspects of cultural heritage and also set out to preserve local traditions.

While the opinions of local people towards incomers reproduce increasingly predictable stereotypes, the views of return migrants offer an important and slightly different perspective. Return migrants, those local people who have returned to settle after living elsewhere, are especially perceptive and sensitive to change, perhaps because they have lived away for some considerable time. Return migrants have often moved away for specific reasons, to find work elsewhere, to go to university, to join the armed forces or, in the past, the merchant navy. During their time away, however, they often retain kinship and friendship links with their home community, thus maintaining their social presence despite their physical absence. Attachment to place in the Highlands is commonly expressed through a nicknaming system and out-migrants, or 'exiles' also have nicknames that define them as social persons and locate them in the community (Mewett 1982).[12]

One area left wide open for further research is the role played by return migrants in rural development and tourist-related activities. Throughout Scottish history agents of change have been unambiguously defined as 'outsiders' (which is often synonymous with 'the English'). The exile is a victim of circumstance, of eviction and colonialism and remains a powerful symbol in the cultural repertoire many Scots use to construct and define their own identity. The idea of them returning and disrupting the very area they were forced to leave is an uneasy one.

In the Northwest of Scotland it does not seem that the return migrant represents a particularly problematic category of person. Elsewhere in Europe, for example in the Greek Cyclades, return migrants do create difficulties for both locals and the researcher when working out a definition of 'islander' (Kenna 1983:90). Return migrants have often lived in urban areas, notably Athens (and may have been members of Migrants' Associations), and back in the Cyclades many of them are involved in tourist enterprises, sometimes leaving themselves open to accusations of contributing to a changing island life (and thereby making the sociological discussion of tourist development as one of conflict between locals and outsiders far too simple). Return migrants are differentiated from those who consider themselves as 'real islanders' and sometimes labelled 'urban interlopers', although as Kenna points out, one definition of a 'real islander' as someone who spends the winter on the island is problematic in so far as many elderly long-term residents and their children now spend the winter in Athens. Kenna goes on to say that 'The definition is further complicated by the role of some migrants themselves as holidaymakers, included, when it suits a particular argument, in the category "tourist" by both locals and migrants running tourist-related businesses' (ibid.).

In the Gairloch area, some return migrants maintained they always intended to come back, whether at an earlier stage in their lives or to retire. Others return to help aged parents. One forty year old man returned to Badachro when he was twenty seven, "to settle my parents in their retirement home. I thought I'd go back to Edinburgh, but if you come back here for three weeks, you'll stay". There are also those return migrants who come back because they inherit crofts, or they return to help out on crofts run by their siblings.

Kenny U., for example, is about 60 years of age. A bachelor, he lives on a croft shared with his younger brother in a township a few miles from Gairloch proper. In his twenties he left the area and worked for many years as a hotel caterer, in several different cities in both England and Scotland. The longest period spent in one place other than that of his birth, was thirteen years in Edinburgh. He returned to the Gairloch area in 1981 to look after his aged mother following the death of his crofter father. His mother died in the mid-1980s. The running of the croft is the responsibility of his brother, also a bachelor, who works as a labourer for the roads division of Highland Regional Council. While Kenny helps out on the croft, he is responsible mainly for letting the old croft cottage next door as a holiday home (the house in which they live was built only recently). Although Kenny enjoyed his time in Edinburgh and other cities, he says he would not now leave the croft to go back "to the kind of life there", and talks about his sister, who lives in Perth, as someone who would be unable to live anywhere more remote than Dingwall. Dimensions of remoteness are a constant topic of conversation for Kenny, and it is this aspect of Wester Ross that he believes most attracts incomers. It is also something he emphasises when taking bookings from holidaymakers, observing that "The view from the house, after all, is what people come up here for".

Kenny is not against incomers moving to the area, but his idea about what the Gairloch area should be like is informed by his own memories of the place before he left as a young man. Much of his conversation revolves around discussion of the old people he visits in the area, and of a time "when people mostly spoke Gaelic". While he recognises that incomers "mostly mind their own business", he laments the fact that "they like to bring a Little England with them", and that this "is bad for the area". Above all, Kenny talks about the disappearance of people he knew and the replacement of the characters who populated his childhood landscapes with strangers "who organise themselves in a circle that tends to include only incomers".

Wester Ross is an area valued by incomers and tourists for its scenic beauty and its 'empty' landscapes. But while the landscape may seem empty to the casual visitor and the sojourner, it has its own austerity, another sense of emptiness for those people who can be considered locals. In many places along the Gairloch seaboard, there are croft houses and buildings, the reminders of past lives, that stand in dereliction. It is a landscape that bears the scars of cultural change and widespread evictions. It has been a landscape without figures, but one which has now the setting of a tremendous growth in population that, far from rejuvenating a way of life, has contributed further to its overall decline, or rather to a heightened awareness of it as something that has its existence in the past rather than the present. The significance of the changing meanings of the landscape has already been referred to in the first chapter and it is one which will be returned to in chapter five, but before that the sociological implications of the terms 'local' and 'incomer' as representations which shape social and cultural realities are analysed in the next chapter.

Notes

[1] This point is well made by Phillips in a study of a Yorkshire Dales parish (1986). Philips also notes that the distinction between locals and incomers can be either rigid or blurred depending upon the particular setting and the persons involved. In other words if someone is not to be defined as an 'incomer' then others in the situation must renounce being 'locals'.

[2] *Scotland on Sunday* 1st August 1993.

[3] *The Guardian* 5th November 1993.

[4] *Scotland on Sunday* 1st August 1993. The newspaper reported how an Englishman living in Gairloch since 1969 had been targeted, and also that an English woman who had written a letter to the Aberdeen Press and Journal expressing her opinion 'that the use of the Saltire was akin to the use of the Eire flag by the IRA' had been advised to leave Scotland by Settler Watch (it is probable that many Scots who would not have much sympathy for Settler Watch, would nonetheless consider such an opinion provocative).

[5] *The Guardian* 5th November 1993. Dr. Foxley is also quoted as saying "Highlanders are an endangered species – this is no joke. The playing field is stacked against them . . ."

[6] See Scottish Watch (1993a) *Constitution of Scottish Watch* and Scottish Watch (1993b) *The Struggle for Scotland* .

[7] The inaugural conference of Scottish Watch, which was held in Perth, received coverage in the English press. See *The Independent on Sunday* 17th October 1993. It is worth noting that the Scottish National Party also distanced itself from Scottish Watch. In the same newspaper article, Margaret Ewing, the SNP MP for Moray, was reported as saying the members of Scottish Watch '. . . are doing the general cause of Scottish nationalism no favours whatsoever', while the Labour MP Bryan Wilson called Scottish Watch 'unpleasant nonsense'.

[8] *The Scotsman* 25th October 1993.

[9] It is curious that this subjective experience of social change is, despite the use of terms such as 'community', in many respects the reverse of Durkheim's idea that human social history can by summarised as a movement from primitive society where social solidarity arises from similarity, so that people are drawn together because they have so much in common, to modern society where social cohesion is a consequence of social differentiation based in a division of labour and mutual dependency (Durkheim 1964). Ferdinand Tonnies described something similar in terms of a historical movement from society where sentiments of community (*Gemeinschaft*) predominated to modern industrial society characterised by individuality and recurring but transient association (*Gesellschaft*) (Tonnies 1955). Informants in the southwest project back onto the socially differentiated setting of their early lives the sense of community which Durkheim and Tonnies believe characterises an undifferentiated society.

[10] Highland Regional Council's Local Plan for Applecross, Gairloch and Lochcarron laid out a strategy for the development of local businesses and service industries.

[11] *West Highland Free Press* 21st January 1994.

[12] Mewett's study has drawn attention to another aspect of remote areas. If remote areas are indicated by a sense of the immediate presence of strangers, then, as a kind of corollary, there is also a heightened awareness of the absence of particular individuals, 'locals' who have migrated and are now described as 'exiles' (Mewett 1982:240-1).

Chapter 4

Incomers and Locals

Tourism: A Threat to Tradition?

That tourists, by their very activities, bring about the destruction of precisely what they seek to enjoy is nowadays a commonplace remark. Tourists themselves seem to believe it, and are therefore sometimes embarrassed by each other's presence. To describe a scene as unspoilt is to say that there is no discernible impact on the people or landscape from the intrusive activities of the tourist, or other industries of exotic origin. In areas of low population densities the seasonal appearance of tourists may involve a high proportion of the people in servicing directly, and indirectly, the demands of tourists rather than indigenously generated community needs. Moreover, tourists typically are not supposed to share the values and way of life of the residents, since the difference is part of the reason for travelling. In the Western Isles there is considerable pressure from tourists for facilities to be made available on a Sunday and now shops, public houses, petrol stations are opening on Sundays. 'The whole blame could not be placed on incomers for the erosion of the Sabbath' according to a Free Church of Scotland Minister. Tourism not only erodes traditions and ways of life but also that special reality of community which is so valued both by those who enjoy it and those, such as tourists, who seek it out.[1]

Yet this sense of imminent and rapid change should alert us. After all, tourists have been travelling in Scotland for more than 150 years. Indeed, it is possible to say that there is a tradition of tourism in Scotland that predates strict Sabbatarianism, and is older and more traditional than some of the items and events, such as Highland Games, which tourists come to gaze upon and which have, in some cases, come into existence in order to deliver what the tourist has travelled to find. In the Victorian era there were regular fast steamship services from Glasgow to the Hebrides, and Macbraynes advertised summer cruises. The Highland Railway in 1876 offered ten tours of the Highlands and Islands from Inverness and their handbook for 1894 describes how 'year after year thousands visit the island of Skye'. The popular tradition of railway travel is today maintained on the Fort William to Mallaig line by trains hauled by preserved steam locomotives during the summer. 'Steam through the beautiful Highland scenery that flanks the West Highland line to Mallaig and you'll feel yourself transported back into history' promises the brochure. For considerably greater sums of money you can also experience the traditional train travel of the Edwardian rich in immaculately restored dining carriages, observation salons, and sleeping cars. The rich also cruised in luxurious yachts and crewing these boats during the summer season was, according to the Secretary of the Congested Districts Board in 1906, a regular form of casual employment in the Northwest Highlands. 'In Skye many of the people are yachtsmen (i.e. crew). They go away in the beginning of the yachting season, and they remain away until the season closes'[2]. Tourists and touring in Scotland has now a history and traditions of its own which can be exploited to develop and sustain contemporary tourist projects so that tourists may, if they wish, experience the tradition of touring in Scotland.

Some holiday makers are looking for entertainment facilities (watersports, chairlifts, fast food outlets, serviced campsites with play equipment for children, amusements, discos, bingo etc.,). The facilities may be dressed in a half hearted way with some tartan bunting and identify themselves by appealing to some easily recognised icon (The Rob Roy Tea Room, The Lord of the Isles Lounge Bar) but they are otherwise essentially similar to the thousands of other tea rooms, bars, fast food outlets, or what ever, all over the UK. Whether such enterprises represent more of a threat to local traditions and ways of life than the Chinese restaurant in Portree, is a fruitless debate. While such facilities are inspired by the latest from elsewhere and from other holiday centres, there is, on the other hand, a considerable cultural production for tourism of a quite different order which finds its inspiration and resources not outside the region but in the particularities of local history. In this process both the tourists and those critical of tourism conspire together, often unwittingly, since both are in pursuit of authenticity, of the real Highlander, the genuine tradition.

The excellent current guide to Castle Tioram in Moidart accounts for itself as an 'answer to the forlorn cries from visitors to the area for information on Castle Tioram' and is the work of three residents, two from Ardgour and one from Acharacle. The text was written by the Secretary of The 1745 Association. The reader is assured that it is the result of the 'daunting task of sifting through the truths and half truths which lie behind today's ruins' (Aikman nd). It would seem that the task might not have been undertaken but for the demands of visitors. West Highland Publications of Oban produced in the 1980s The West Highland Series which has been 'specially designed to help visitors learn something of the history, traditions, and topography of this richly varied area'. The author of another recent and local publication about the traditions of Skye remarks that because of the 'swelling of our incomer population and the influence of television much of our fine social tradition has been abandoned.' According to the author, only fifty years ago (probably the 1930s) 'almost every Skye man could give the colloquial name of any local spot and could often recall a legend or saying pertaining to it' (MacDonald nd). Again, had it not been for the demands of the visitors, it would seem that the abandonment of the heritage would have consigned it to oblivion.

The local production of histories written by locals for visitors is as old as tourism itself. In 1840 the publisher W. R. McPhun of Glasgow produced *The Scottish Tourist's Steam Boat Pocket Guide* to 'our western Highlands'. *Dumfries-shire Illustrated* is published in Dumfries in 1894 and the author, Peter Gray, hopes that it will 'commend itself to both residents and visitors'. From the offices of The Badenoch Record appears *A Guide Book Compiled for the Benefit of Visitors to the District with an appendix of traditionary tales'*. Of particular interest is the provenance of these tales. The guide explains that they have been 'handed down from generation to generation through the medium of the *ceilidh*. But these have been culled from the columns of The Badenoch Record to which most of them have been contributed by a worthy old native, the late Mr Malcolm Macpherson, Kingussie, who in his younger days made a hobby of collecting them.'

In 1981 Ardnamurchan Kirk Session published *Ardnamurchan – Annals of the Parish* to commemorate the 150th anniversary of the opening of Ardnamurchan Church but the foreword makes it clear that the booklet is also intended for people 'beyond these parts'. The first edition has apparently provoked not only complementary but also critical comment, and a working group of residents was set up in 1988 to produce a new edition and the group has appealed for suggestions, information, and new material. Critical commentary can take other, more public and complex, forms. Especially striking are the 'folk museums' which have been quite deliberately put together by residents who have reacted to the representations of local traditions, material culture, and ways of life expressed by other 'visitor attractions'. A notable example is provided by the museums established in Skye by 'local man Peter MacAskill'. The first was at Colbost in 1969 and was provoked by the very different house and museum of 'local man' MacLeod of MacLeod of Dunvegan Castle on the other side of Loch Dunvegan. The mud floored and thatched roof house of the Colbost Folk Museum leaves an overwhelming impression of the tools, equipment and simple furniture of a practical and hard working people who could turn their hands to the skilled production of a variety of useful goods. On the opposite shore, the vast pile that is Dunvegan Castle is like the towering superstructure of a great battleship, and is all about consumption and superstition: sumptuous dining rooms, The Dunvegan Drinking Horn ('a great clan treasure'), a magical 'fairy' flag, and sundry other fetish objects, such as Flora MacDonald's corsets, and a lock of Bonnie Prince Charlie's hair. Authenticity and the truth lies not with one or the other, or even somewhere in between, but in the dialogical relationship between them. And this dialogue is self consciously conducted before the gaze of tourists who, all are agreed, must not be allowed to leave with the wrong impression. McPhun was anxious to point out that his *Steam Boat Guide* included only what was 'worthy of the stranger's notice'.

Thus representation is met with counter representation, which may vary from the gentle comment that the Gaelic spelling on a craft shop sign is wrong to George Rosie taking up two pages of *The Observer* to berate his fellow Scots for going along with a bogus Highlandism and kitsch customs, such as Burns Suppers.[3] There can be few now who have not learned to be wary when in the presence of anything which announces itself as a 'tradition'. This sort of dialogue can and does have real consequences. One can imagine that the Gaelic spelling on the sign will be corrected. On a larger scale the appearance of 'clan centres' during the last twenty years, of which the Clan Donald Centre in Skye is perhaps the best known, constitute a move away from simply opening up the castle to the public and displaying some dusted down antiquities from the attic each accompanied by a fable. The Clan Donald Centre is owned by a trust, The Clan Donald Lands Trust, and declares itself to be undertaking an ambitious programme of restoration based on thorough and sensitive historical research, and the Centre includes a library, study centre, and archive of historical records. Anybody with the appropriate surname is eligible to be associated if they wish and, by emphasising the clan rather than a privileged hereditary clan chief and his possessions, appeals to clan loyalty rather than deference to an individual. By describing itself as a 'Centre' of, by implication, schol-

arly historical research, scientific conservation and preservation, it skil-
fully distracts the visitor from cynically viewing it as a trading enterprise in
the heritage and tourist business. There is an unmistakable impression that
all this work would be going on even if no visitors turned up at all, and this
is something the visitor is happy to collude in since it is for them indicative
of the authentic, as opposed to a show for visitors which is the mark of the
inauthentic. The Centre cannot easily be dismissed as, objectively, yet another 'theme park'.

The tourist is provoking representations and counter representations in a
dialectic which ransacks, trawls, and cultivates an ever renewable and expanding history. Arguably never was Scotland, and the Highlands in particular, so rich with traditions. Yet such a creative nurturing of tradition is
perceived as a destruction of tradition. The appearance of the stranger as
tourist provokes, for the first time, the search to identify what is objectively
worthy of attention and this distinction thereby lifts whatever is identified
outside the relativising stream of personal events to become deserving of
respect as timelessly traditional. While all can agree that there are things
worthy of the stranger's attention, and others that they ought not to see,
what these might be is contested. The tourist induces tradition but in circumstances such that it seems to those involved as if tradition is being
eroded.

Threatened Communities?

But is tourism not loosening the bonds of community? Are locals joining
with the atheist incomers to worship at the Golden Calf of tourism instead
of attending church in Christian fellowship on a Sunday? Given that the
tourists have been around for five or six generations, it is perhaps a conceit
to imagine that only now, in our adult lifetimes, will the historical and
irreversible consequences of this be witnessed. It is also worth recalling
that not only has remote Scotland been regularly invaded each summer
for the last a hundred years and more, but there was also a vast seasonal
movement of the locally resident population out of the north west to the
fishing ports of the east coast of Scotland and England, when the men, at
least those who were not crewing yachts, worked the herring drifters, and
later the women, in increasing numbers, worked on shore as gutters and
packers. This seasonal labour migration grew rapidly after 1850 and by
the 1870s in some districts, of the adult male population, only a few old
men and boys were left behind. Not only did the 'outside world' thoroughly

penetrate the remotest glen, the inhabitants annually experienced for themselves life in other parts of the UK. In those robust and dynamic times, isolated but tightly knit communities were to be a thing of the future rather than the past.

As with culture and tradition, so then with communities. Isolated and fragile communities clinging to precious fragments of their ancient language and culture are being tracked down by tourists in the grip of nostalgia and by researchers after authenticity. Thriving communities around every turn of the road, next to every pier and jetty, in every suburb and housing scheme could hardly be the object of a quest. The more isolated, lost and precarious they are, the more compelling and attractive are their attributes. Yet, as before, it has to be asked whether this is a trick of perspective.

Where the traveller stops, and becomes a sojourner in some settlement, which the traveller somehow knows is where they should stop, there they will find the community. Here, far from their own familiar network of personal relationships and patterns of interaction where the spatial dimension of the relationships is usually insignificant, being the outcome of contingencies such as work relationships, housing moves, and a history of personal encounters, the sojourner finds that there is nothing but shared residence in the same locality as the basis upon which to build personal relationships. From the sojourner's perspective, this can only have the effect of promoting in any interactions a marked sense of the spatial dimension in social relationships. The people of the settlement are all just that, the inhabitants, the locals. For those already resident and working in the locality, as it was for the sojourner before leaving to travel in search of community, the spatial dimension is unmarked, or at least taken for granted. The pattern of networks of interaction follow the contingencies of work and the inter-sections of personal histories, and as such will spread far beyond the named settlement. Yet interaction with the sojourner can only be on the basis that the sojourner is now residing, though temporarily, in the locality. For a resident this spatial dimension only emerges as salient in interactions with the sojourner. So, for both the sojourner and the resident then, interaction unavoidably and unintentionally brings into the foreground an awareness of themselves as homemakers in a settlement of other homemakers, in other words, of what is usually called a community.

A number of other factors are also at work in ways which amplify the sense of community which is unavoidable in such interactions. First of all, there is the simple rhythm of the seasonal appearance and then disappearance of the sojourners, who leave behind their shuttered houses to remind the residents that they, the residents, are, by contrast, still here. Thus the annual rhythm of the sojourners contributes to a feeling among those who are permanently resident that they share, as against the sojourners, their permanent residence in the settlement. This is an aspect of community awareness among the residents which will cut across networks of personal links to individuals within and beyond the settlement.

Secondly, the jealously guarded boundary between the private and the public domains of life is brought into play in such a way as to reinforce a sense of a boundary between a local community and the outside world. Those who come to stay for a summer holiday are typically families who rent, or own, a house which they use as a holiday home, and the work of the holiday is a kind of elaborated second order domesticity, of 'the family getting together and doing things'. Children paint, make natural collections, keep diaries, log the weather and tides, chores are turned into team games, elaborate duty rosters are drawn up, picnics and hill climbing parties are organised, and in this way a great deal of work is put into a highly condensed burst of self consciously elaborate homemaking which 'nestles' the house into the landscape. If the community is a localised group of homemakers, more or less aware of themselves in this function, then the spirit of community flows especially powerfully in the sojourning household and this will affect all those who come into contact with them.

Yet domesticity, unlike relationships arising out of work and employment or recreational pursuits in clubs and associations, can only be a limited basis for the elaboration of relationships between sojourners and residents because the domestic domain is, above all, private. It may be shared only with family members and the most intimate friends, and information which goes beyond these relationships becomes gossip. Alasdair Maclean, though writing about the etiquette of visiting and mealtimes in Ardnamurchan, draws attention to this boundary; 'when you arrived too early you were then, by crude means, placing yourself in a position to note — and retail -how well they did themselves at table. It was perfectly acceptable to acquire such information by stealth, usually by rooting among the order boxes while the grocery van driver's back was turned, but it was generally acknowledged to be bad form to obtain it openly' (Maclean 1986: 73). This respect for each other's privacy among neighbours can be taken to remarkable extremes. One of the authors recalls that in a rural parish in Aberdeenshire, a woman invited her neighbour, two fields away and of thirty years standing, into her house to meet her mother only after the old lady was dead in her bed. So, unable to take an overt interest in each other's contemporary domestic affairs, the attention of sojourner and resident is then displaced onto the most public and literal of common grounds, the physical landscape of the settlement and its history, which is nothing less than the expression of the boundaries of the community in space and time.

As against the analysis being presented here, that talk about, and an awareness of, community is a product of a particular perspective, it might be argued that a sense of community is a feeling and value engendered by local loyalties and sentiments, which are developed and sustained through rivalries between settlements. So we, the residents of Glen Bogle, are distinguished from others elsewhere as the tenants of the most noble (or venial) landlord in Scotland, sharing the freshest water, finest views, cleanest air, mildest winters, richest folklore etc. . . It is, however, recognised that these claims can only be held against exactly similar claims being made by the residents of the next glen, and must therefore be continually contested. Such an agonistic theory of community has a long history in anthropology because of the discipline's concern to explain the social order evident in societies without any obvious unifying hierarchical and governmental institutions. It was theorised that community A and community B define themselves and come into being through mutual opposition, but then come together as the wider community X in opposition to community Y, and so on through higher orders until eventually the whole population is embraced as a single community of the highest order. It is familiar enough in such notions as Argylls and Seaforths being deadly rivals but standing shoulder to shoulder as Highlanders against Lowlanders, and Highlanders and Lowlanders uniting against the English. However, though there is plenty of competition, and not infrequent expressions of hostility, even violence, little, if any, of these contests and fights can be taken as evidence for an agonistic community structure.

It is true that in various sports, teams may be identified through their names as the representatives of particular localities, and the success of the team is, to some extent, enjoyed by more than those who play or are members of the club. Rivalry between localities may appear to extend to fighting and brawling in and around public houses between men from different settlements, and this is usually reported as if it were a fight between the two localities. But again such reports are an illusion of perspective, the perspective of the outsider. The individual players in the football team, the club, their relatives, wives and girl friends, husbands and boyfriends, see it as their success, and one which has nothing to do with 'the community'.

Fights in public involving several people usually break out as the consequences of someone aggravating a previous slight or injury of one sort or another, and in origin are of a quite personal and private nature. They may even be an expression of long standing feuds between individuals, supported by their respective relatives and friends and who may not all be residents of the same settlement. It is not altogether accidental, however, that the parties to the fighting are often from different settlements, though this has less to do with any sense of community than with personal relationships. Fighting between individuals from different settlements is almost always started by the visitors since it is not in the interest of a local to be banned from his nearest public house, perhaps the only one for several miles. Fighting at dances in the village hall is not constrained, however, by such considerations.

Such outbreaks of physical violence have a certain symmetry, in the sense that blows and abuse are exchanged, and this may contribute to their misinterpretation as the expression of mutual rivalry or balanced conflict between similar communities. There are, however, from time to time, incidents where the expressions of hostility are evidently asymmetrical. Reports that Highland landowners and their guests, attending the annual Skye Ball in Portree in September, are sometimes pelted with tomatoes by some of those excluded, who happen to be the inhabitants, rather than the owners, of Skye, may or may not be true, but all agree that the ladies and gentlemen do not throw tomatoes back. There is, unlike the Saturday night fights, nothing personal about this but, on the other hand, it can hardly be read as something equivalent to a fight between the Glen Bogle lads and the boys from Hourn Bridge. It is, of course, a traditional, if rather attenuated, expression of class conflict. Nevertheless, these real hostilities, contribute to the imagined hostilities between local communities.

The active front is not so much in the environs of the venue for an exclusive night of Scottish country dancing, which is a mere local skirmish, but along the banks of salmon rivers. This is a vast and fascinating topic but it is only the implications for the notion of community that are relevant here. In matters concerning angling, public attention is more often directed to the importance of the money which is spent by anglers visiting Scotland for an abstraction called 'the Scottish economy ', rather than to the owners of fishing rights and their interest in the asset value and income from the rents of their salmon fishing rights.[4] These values are peculiarly difficult to form a judgment about and depend on the audited records of salmon caught and receipts from letting the rights. Illegally taken fish cannot, of course, be included in the record and sporting tenants, who have paid considerable sums of money to be allowed to fish, are likely to be upset by evidence of others taking fish for nothing. This creates a situation in which the owners of the rights and those who infringe them both have an interest in operating covertly; the latter for obvious reasons, and the former because they wish both to prevent infringement of their rights and to deny that their water is heavily poached. Organisations of proprietors, each based on a river, hire watchmen ('water bailiffs', who do not come to this kind of work after a career in the 'caring' professions) to deter illegal fishing. Proprietors who join such organisations and contribute to the cost of these watchmen are, under recent legislation (Local Government Finance Act 1987), exempt from local government taxation of their very lucrative fishing properties. Occasionally the low intensity warfare between poachers and bailiffs breaks into the newspapers. A typical incident was reported in *The Glasgow Herald* as follows;

> Bailiffs, who took part in a cross-region car chase over Soutra Hill with fleeing poachers, eventually cornered them on Haddington golf course where fighting broke out . . . The men, from the Dalkeith area, made a get away, but were caught during a later raid.'[5]

While a few deliberately hire 'outsiders' from Glasgow or Edinburgh as bailiffs because they recognise that the poachers are really the people living outside around the castle walls, on the whole proprietors like to believe that the people living around their properties, the 'locals', respect them and their rights, and that poaching must therefore be the work of outsiders. If locals do take the odd fish, this is nothing as compared to what is done by the 'organised gangs from the towns and the South'.[6] It seems that owners may also come to arrangements ('easements') with local residents which allow the latter discreet access to the fishing in return for which they are supposed to deter outsiders from poaching.[7] Obviously, such easements divide the population into those who enjoy them, and those who do not and if this division does not distinguish between locals and outsiders, it will certainly help to identify the 'real locals' from among the other residents. Payments of 'compensation' to 'local communities' by disruptive industrial developments, such as the proposed super quarry on Harris, are similar in their consequences in so far as a defined local community is induced into existence as the beneficiary of the compensation. By working with the notion of locals and outsiders, and by attempting to invest the former with real interests a powerful material basis is introduced to sustain the distinction between a community of locals and a collection of outsiders. However, the net effect is one of ambivalence, or contradiction, because the local community is never quite achieved even in these instances. At best some statutory body, such as the District Council, is vested with an amenity, a sports and leisure facility, or heritage centre, but which anyone from anywhere can enjoy as a beneficiary. And so one encounters a curious and paradoxical structure of feeling about the community in which it continually comes into existence so that it can continually decline.

Matters of Perspective

If tourism can 'undermine local values, make a living museum of a vital if quiet countryside, and encourage activities which can be alien to local cultures'[8] then how much more threatening must be those tourists, and sojourners, in rural Scotland who decide to stay and settle. And yet such subversion cannot be the intention of people who come to live permanently in remote parts of the country. On the contrary, individuals who actively work to promote and defend the traditional way of life are often, paradoxically, identified as 'incomers'. For example, the views just quoted are those of a North American who settled in a croft in Skye in 1971. Why is it that incomers are perceived as a threat to the ways of life of the localities in which they choose to settle, a view which, it seems, is shared by the incomers themselves despite the fact that no one comes to remote rural areas with the intention of changing what they find? In order to answer this question it is necessary to consider some of the other qualities which are attributed to 'incomers'.

'Incomer' is a relative term and its counterpart is 'local', and the two words identify not so much kinds of people as clusters of contrasting and complementary values and images. What is particularly striking about these elaborations on the attributes of these two categories is that they do not summarise the collective experience of individuals designated local and incomer in their interactions with each other, but rather represent inverted images of the speaker's self image. This is especially marked in descriptions of the attributes of incomers. 'The stereotype of the incomer — as used by the Orcadians — is of someone running away from trouble/problems but bringing it with them, having unrealistic views of what it means to live on an Orkney island, being on the dole, giving nothing to the island, wanting to change things, bringing in outside agencies (police, social workers etc. . .) to sort things out, and "not like us"' (Stead 1990:22). By simply inverting these characteristics it is possible to compose someone who faces up to difficulties, is realistic, hardworking, generous, independent and resourceful, and who values local traditions, or in other words, the local Orcadian view of themselves. Since a degree of modesty is also a local virtue, it is tempting to suppose that claims to such noble attributes can

might use in conversation with another man when he asks, 'And how's the family Angus?' where 'family' means Angus's wife and children, and Angus, as the father, is the 'root'. Sometimes family just means children, descendants, as when a woman might ask of another woman, 'do you have any family?' It has the same meaning in a phrase such as 'family croft', or 'old family' but is not the same as the word family in the phrase 'family car', where 'family' means a distinct and separate domestic group of husband, wife and their offspring. 'Locals', on the whole, dwell in a world of families in the first sense, 'incomers' families are the relatively impoverished, genealogically speaking, separate and bounded domestic groups. 'Locals' are residents who are related to each other in ways which are often known only to themselves. Others may be warned when speaking about someone not present in the company that there are 'friends' (*fri:nds*), in the old sense of kinsmen, of theirs present. Outsiders are often led to speculate about 'tight-knit communities', and even to fantasise about 'in-breeding'.

Confronted with a vocabulary and an elaborated figure which articulates and represents the presence and destiny of 'locals' in such a way as to pre-empt any other way of belonging, the incomer is apparently at a disadvantage from the outset when called to account for his or her presence in the same landscape. However, this is not the case and one is frequently offered an appeal to an equally powerful figure which appears at first far removed from that of 'roots' and a 'family tree'. In-migrants often say of their chosen place of residence that they 'fell in love' with the locality.[9] This expression is dense with meaning and is intended to convey a feeling of attachment to a locality amounting to a transformation and commitment of one's self and one's life. The vocabulary displaces attention from the personality and attributes of the incomer as, for example, a rational agent exercising a calculating utilitarian attitude to the area (cheap housing, healthy environment, business enterprise grants, good schools, cheap labour etc.,) and instead appeals to a notion of destiny and of the incomer moved by a passion. Rather than acting as an agent in the rational pursuit of personal benefits, the incomer is inviting his conduct to be understood in terms of the locality itself, such circumstances as the captivating charm of the vernacular dwellings, the enchanting landscape, the magnanimous inhabitants who respect wisdom and are not driven by material values etc. . . The 'love' is a kind of courtly love where the lover is compelled to submit to the demands, however whimsical, of the object of his love. It is, however, a privilege to be in this relationship to the land because the relationship is a source of virtue and nobility, perhaps even more virtuous than that which flows from having 'roots' in the land. The latter does not exclude a love of one's country, but it is, by contrast, a pietistic devotion, the love of offspring for parents. While individuals mature into adults the landscape of childhood persists, to evoke in adulthood those first and vivid emotions of childhood. So though in the appeal to the complex of feelings expressed in the phrase 'falling in love' the 'incomer' acknowledges that they are incomers and that therefore others are 'locals', they counter the claim to 'roots' and the virtue of descent with an appeal to a different but equally noble devotion and commitment to the locality. Both deny contingency and make claims to an unfolding fate in their relationships to the landscape.

To what extent this vocabulary of 'falling in love' which is offered by the incomer is recognised by others as a valid account is difficult to judge. It may be that those who feel themselves to belong to the land and express this in terms of 'roots' cannot recognise some other attachment and suspect that claims of being 'captivated' conceal a falsity, and a concern with the picturesque quality of the landscape. The latter attitude may show itself as an excessive preoccupation with preserving and even improving the appearance of the landscape.[10] However, when the incomer claims not to have chosen Glen Bogle but to have fallen in love with it, or fallen under its spell, this accurately expresses a kind of constraint which the incomer experiences. In the days spent confronting the choice to be made, of where to settle, the prospective incomer experiences an unnerving sense of detachment but as soon as the choice is exercised, it now compels the incomer, and all sense of being an active agent is lost to the object of choice which now determines the incomers conduct. The movement from utter freedom to live anywhere to 'not being able to contemplate living anywhere but here!', is absolute. The devotion to the preservation and care of the landscape flows from this compulsion. The difference in the structures of feeling between those 'in love' and those 'with roots' is evident in numerous daily incidents. For instance, one of the authors while waiting for a small Highland ferry, watched a sea trout easily circling in sun dappled shallows, recovering perhaps from being hunted by otters. Two residents also notice what we all agree is a beautiful creature. But then, while one telephones, from the nearby call box, the local hotel to negotiate a price, the other has, with skills learned in childhood, gaffed the fish, and it's out of the water and into a plastic bag, all inside two minutes. One might say that the land looks after its own as a father provides for his children.

The idea of 'roots' also evokes an impression of enduring presence. Locals comprise the 'old families'.[11] 'Old' here refers neither to the biological age of individuals nor to the length of their pedigrees, since everyone's pedigree is, at any one time, the same age. An 'old family' is one that can, in the first place, 'trace its roots' in the locality. Others have lost their roots, and therefore the limbs and branches of a network of *fri:nds*. Because the distinction 'old' necessarily involves 'roots' and 'branches', there must always be a plurality of locals, of their families, and of 'old families', though they are usually specifically identified as 'the Robertsons', 'the Macleans' or whatever. Married daughters from these 'old families', though they nowadays take their husbands surname, a relatively recent popular convention in Scotland (Clive 1992), retain their membership of an old family and it is always part of their identity ('Of course, she's a Robertson, ye ken!'). Incomers, even those with large households, do not qualify for the distinction of a plural patronymic.

A plurality of 'old families' is also necessary for their persistence because only through their mutual recognition can they sustain the distinction of being 'old'. The Macleans know about themselves but they also know the affairs of the Robertsons, as do the Robertsons know about themselves and the Macleans. Being known extends beyond the living representatives of the 'old families' to include dead parents, grand parents, even great grand parents. Incomers are by increments introduced to this knowledge which at first may be little more than genealogical ("Angus, who started the drainage, was, you realise, his grandfather, so Donald and Mary are cousins") but then may be more detailed and hint at scandal ("Fiona and Mairi are nae full sisters, ye ken!" . . . "No, there's actually four brothers nae three, but granny cannae blaw aboot James, the eldest.") The incomer may feel privileged to be allowed to share such information, but he or she needs to reflect that no one is taking much interest in their grandparents and genealogical tree. They are unknown except to the incomer.

The enduring presence of 'old families', their 'rootedness', tends to displace change and amplify a timeless continuity. Death may physically remove an individual but even when alive and as a 'character' his or her deeds had always lived in their telling and representation, and in their evocation by the marks they left in the landscape rather than in the transient reality of the memorable events themselves. Representation has a fascination and interest for those involved which the real thing lacks. Moreover, representation does not share the mortality of who and what is represented. Among 'old' families personal histories and family lore and the morality which is embedded in them are not transmitted from generation to generation any more than the air people breathe is passed on from parents to their children. Change and the passage of time and a sense of handing on a tradition from generation to generation is the outcome of moving between the subjective and the objective, between the perspectives of local and incomer.

To stand with the incomer and share that perspective is to adopt, however fleetingly, an objective perspective. What was taken for granted, like the air we breathe, becomes, with an accompanying sense of anxiety, a subject of reflection which is now seen as something vulnerable and fragile which needs to be recalled from the edge of oblivion. Attributes which were previously 'second nature' come to be recognised as properties possessed by individuals which have to be deliberately repaired, secured, placed in a museum or put between the covers of a book or else, just as deliberately, destroyed.[12] For this, the stranger, the incomer, is held responsible. The ambivalent feelings aroused in relation to the past, to something that is now the past but what was, it seems only yesterday, the unchanging and enduring present, are projected onto the outsider, amplifying and resonating with his or her inherent ambivalence as the outsider who is also here among us.

Incomers are also a threat in so far as they are unaware of, and are excluded from, the processes of social ranking of the locals. They are excluded partly because they are ignorant of the history of the families which is the basis for ranking them as collectivities and their members individually. The code that personal history is private and not in the public domain is observed by all, but locals actually know more about each other than they ought to, and the only way incomers can acquire this information which locals share is by illicit means, namely through gossip. Incomers appear to respect the privacy of others but only because they cannot do otherwise. They know little or nothing about the locals or each other. As the length of residence of an incomer increases so also does the shared history with other residents, including locals, accumulate, but there will always be a deficit, a lack of 'roots'.

But incomers are also excluded because they exclude themselves as a consequence of their disposition to see the settlement and its residents as 'a community'. As outsiders they can do little to avoid an objective view, and in fact they find it natural, even virtuous, to 'treat everyone equally'. This is an attribute which residents find very useful in matters affecting those interests which they do hold in common (water, roads, bus stops, sewage etc. . .) and incomers will soon find themselves on Community Councils, School Boards, District Councils and the like representing the community especially if sojourners of long duration, such as the minister, the doctor, or teacher, are unavailable.[13] Incomers may find this flattering and presume that it is indicative of their integration into the 'community', or, less generously may talk about the 'apathetic locals', when actually their worth lies in their ambivalent position in so far as they are residents in the settlement but yet are also not part of 'the community', and so 'objective' in their concerns. So-called 'community leaders' necessarily speak of 'the community' as a naturally harmonious, united, and bounded totality, otherwise they could not claim to speak as representatives. Community leaders are people to whom formal and official visitors are referred, and through whom governmental and non-governmental organisations, deal with the residents of the settlement. The community is a phenomenon which is constituted by the gaze and activities of outsiders. In Ralph Glasser's book *Scenes from a Highland Life*, the Chairman of the Community Council is a 'local' and would seem to controvert the analysis. However, he is also the owner of the only shop in the locality, and everyone has to use it. His success as a trader depends on him dealing with everyone equally and 'objectively', and therefore he comes to acquire some of the valuable attributes of the 'outsider'. So he locates himself in a position from which the residents, his customers, come to appear to him naturally as members of a community.[14]

Since ranking exists only through its acknowledgement in the mundane activities of daily life, it is therefore exposed as vulnerable in interaction with those who are incapable of acknowledging the rank order. Incomers, because of their disposition to 'treat everyone equally', undermine judgments about the worth of individuals, and therefore the values from which these judgments flow. For the incomer, the outstanding characteristics of the 'locals' are what they share and hold in common, and so social diversity is muted. Yet the indigenous view reveals diversity rather than homogeneity. However, this diversity is complicated by gender. In rural Scotland class differences are objectively more evident among men than among women: men employ other men, men pay rent to other men (even where the land owner is a woman her agent is usually a man) and there are obvious differences among men in terms of class culture such as, for example, with the regard to speech and table manners. Class relations among rural women are consequently mediated and their domestic work is much the same, all of which contributes to an apparent attenuation of class distinctions, again for example, as regards speech and table manners. Yet it is women who are generally more sensitive to issues of class divisions, of someone's background and family, than are men. Men seem to be more concerned with personal integrity and the esteem which can be won from the outstanding performance of a role, as shepherd, cattleman, ploughman, fisherman, craftsman etc., and there are medals and silver trophies to be awarded in formal recognition of such achievements.[15] When an old farmer, third generation on the same land died, his body, as was usual, was laid out in the 'front room'. Another local farmer, his neighbour, remarked to an incomer that "Bob had looked fine, really fine wi' a' his medals laid oot beside him." "These must have been first world war medals, then". "Naw, man", with some exasperation, "his plooin' medals!" In unmarked contrast it is unimaginable that a dead woman would be laid out with her winner's certificates from years of devoted support of SWRI baking competitions. For women achievement is a matter of social mobility, of changing classes upwards, rather than winning public recognition or esteem. Alasdair Maclean, recalling his upbringing in a crofting family noted that 'I had been the brainy one, the one whose emergence into adulthood, clad in a neat blue suit with a collar and tie and a solid professional career stretching ahead, Mother had most looked forward to' (Maclean 1986: 109).

The Scottish author Christine Marion Fraser, who lives in Argyll and whose five volume Rhanna romance is set in the period between the twenties and the sixties, constructs a landscape of social structure for her characters. In the opening pages of the first book, *Rhanna* , tenant farmers and their farm servants, crofters, professionals (veterinary surgeon, doctor, teacher, minister), shopkeepers, and landowners are all introduced as are the subtleties of social ranking: the crofter addresses the tenant farmer as 'Mr' Mackenzie but Mr Mackenzie calls him 'Dodie', as does the author herself. The land owner's wife considers the doctor an acceptable dinner table guest but wonders whether the tenant farmer is equally acceptable. All this and more is described incidentally while in the foreground the hero's wife dies giving birth to their daughter (Fraser 1978: 1–20).

It is notable that by contrast Neil Gunn's novels tend to minimise social structure and he prefers instead to focus on landscape, culture, and personality. While the diverging experiences of men and women are often explored, the relationships of class as they might structure the feelings of people are muted if not absent. The inhabitants of 'the glen' are, apart from their personal identities, uniformly pastoralists and the tenants of a landowner whom they deal with through a rather peripheral estate office. At the end of *The Drinking Well* the crofter hero is sitting down with the landlord to plan together how the estate will be managed in the future! In his last novel, *The Other Landscape* , the possibility of such unlikely scenes is dealt with simply by quickly getting rid of estates, land lords, and farmers. On the morning after his arrival in Balrunie, the hero is told by a local woman that "The whole estate was broken up and sold many years ago. There's none of the old laird's family left." "So they were 'cleared ' too! And the sheep farmer — what happened to him?" "When the estate was broken up, many changes took place. There hasn't been a sheep farmer in the white house for many's the year' (Gunn 1988: 35).

It is tempting to suggest that these differences of emphasis, on the one hand a concern with social structure and social differentiation and, on the other, with culture and men engaged in heroic and classless metaphysical struggles for 'cultural renewal', are not accidentally associated with female and male authors respectively. However, it is obviously not impossible for men to write about rural class structure. Colin Macdonald, a crofter's son and contemporary of Gunn, who became an extension officer in the Department of Agriculture and Fisheries, and in which capacity he returned to the Highlands, also wrote articles between the wars for the *Highland News* and the *Ross-shire Journal*, and published several books about his experiences of rural life in Highland Scotland.[16] His version of the social structure of the Highlands is virtually identical to that of Christine Marion Fraser.

According to Macdonald (1943: 18–19), there is first of all the 'farm servant class', a 'prolific breed with large families. Only God and their mothers knew how they were clothed and fed'. They are a 'tough and hardy race' but 'below average in scholastic attainments' and given to frequent flittings and changes of employer. Secondly, there were the crofters, 'up on the braes', described as a 'community' rather than a class. They shared a certain hardiness and that quality that comes from agricultural and pastoral work with the farm servant class but otherwise were very different and sought to present an image of permanence and solidity, taking pride in inhabiting the same land holding for generations, a holding which they had been 'permitted by our landlord to settle'. Their children are the 'schools best scholars'. Clearly feeling superior to the shifting rural proletariat they focused their contempt on what are called 'villager's families' comprising local merchants or shopkeepers, and estate clerks and office workers. According to Macdonald they are 'comparatively well-to-do' and 'esteemed themselves superior to crofters' (1943: 18–19). Shopkeepers and estate clerks are people with whom crofters are necessarily involved and who could exercise an irksome control over credit and agrarian matters. They would, perhaps, come to know too much about their private circumstances for comfort in each others' presence, all of which would compromise the crofters' valued sturdy independence. Macdonald also identifies the tenant farmers' families, the employers of the farm servants as a class but does not elaborate on their distinctions nor on their relationships to the other classes. It may be noted in passing, however, that the social and cultural differences between Highlands and Lowlands is a consequence of the relative proportions of crofters on the one hand and of farmers and their employees, the farm servants , on the other. The Board of Agriculture's

Committee on Women in Agriculture reported being impressed by the High-landers' 'love of the land' but they were also astute enough to notice that evidence of such sentiment only came from crofters. 'With reference to Highland farms the same state of matters obtains as in the Lowlands', namely, an instrumental orientation to the land uncomplicated by senti-ments described as 'love' (1920:24). Yet this 'love' of the land and pride in permanent settlement of the same land for generations is combined with an ambition if not for themselves at least for their children ('the schools best scholars') which must in the ways and with the consequences described by Gunn drive them from the land. No aimless 'drift to the towns' here.

'Permitted to settle' is a telling phrase and captures an aspect of the com-plex of feelings involved. Others, Macdonald seems to imply, have not been so favoured by the land lord. A croft , 'the favour', is heritable but cannot be sold. If there are no heirs or heirs decline the inheritance, then the croft must be assigned to some other candidate in a complicated legal process involving the land lord, the Crofter's Commission, Land Courts and Grazing Committees.[17] Does the croft belong to the crofter, or the crofter to the croft? Does an heir inherit the croft or does the croft inherit him? It is notable that though shame, disappointment and bitterness may accompany 'the man who comes back' this is not the case with someone who returns as an heir and the next generation to continue working the croft. It is hardly surprising that this 'favour' which at once confers distinction and hardship should evoke such complicated, even ambivalent feelings, as to deserve to be described as 'love'. It may also be fertile ground, as it were, for the sustenance of doctrines of an elect of God and practices of exclusion which are a characteristic of the strict Calvinist churches which have survived with congregations largely drawn from the crofters, or as one minister be-gan his sermon, sensitive to the presence of visitors in the congregation, 'we who have been born and bred here.'[18]

Ideas such as 'community', 'locals' and 'incomers', obliterate not only the perception of the divisions of the class structure but also the fine dis-tinctions and gradations of ranking of the families and the individuals in these social classes. It is to be expected that 'incomers' would reject the suggestion that they are a threat to traditional values and social structures, and individuals who consider themselves to be 'incomers' certainly do not regard themselves in this way. But it is also true that incomers, paradoxi-cally, accept the views held by locals about themselves as incomers. Incomers and locals come together in agreeing that if there are individuals posing a threat to the community then these individuals are incomers. A freelance journalist, Roger Hutchinson, who has settled in Skye, took up three pages of *The Weekend Scotsman* to describe, under the titles 'Paradise disturbed: the Englishing of Mull' and 'Shadows of a Lost Culture', how 'the traditionally classless tenant peoples of the Hebrides have been all but overwhelmed by settlers from elsewhere . . . who have trodden all over the fragile Hebridean way of life'. The curious phrase, 'classless tenant peoples', simultaneously manages to obliterate class distinctions, which are replaced by the notion of a community 'existing for its own sake' while acknowledging in the word 'tenant' the existence of class structures and the feelings they will induce. It is the perspective of the outsider condemned to seek endlessly for the community 'out there' and it is strikingly expressed in Hutchinson's opening sentence. 'Early last year, I journeyed to a remote part of the Italian Alps in search of the descendants of a rumoured Scottish Gaelic community, supposedly lost, isolated, and clinging to fragments of their language amid an alien culture.'[19]

The View from Within

The argument of this chapter has been that an awareness of tradition and community and therefore talk about community and tradition is a product of a particular perspective, one which has the qualities of objectivity and these are typically embodied in the ambivalent figure of the stranger. Not the stranger who comes today and goes tomorrow but the stranger who comes and stays. Someone who is therefore both near because resident among us, and distant because not one of us. Community, like tradition, seems to be one of those fugitive states of being which, when they become the objects of reflection, and explicit concern, fade and seem therefore to have their existence only as memories, or recollections, of the recent past or some other place. Just as there is no means by which someone enclosed in the hold of a ship can ever come to know whether the ship is underway or not, except that they come out of the hold and adopt a standpoint outside, so the community can only be known from the outside. Local-outsider is not a classification of people but a configuration of perspectives and an associated structure of feelings which not only provoke tradition, community, and their historiography, but also enter into the productions as an inherent attribute of them. In other words, if the local-outsider configuration has the properties that are being attributed to it here, it might be expected that it would be possible to trace its presence in its consequences. This is best done by a detailed reading of a substantial text and for this purpose a recently published history of the people of the Scottish Highlands is eminently appropriate (Hunter 1992).

The book is described as one where the author, a Scottish Highlander, searches out 'my people's origins' and attempts to identify 'what it was that made us what we are'. The author, James Hunter, though an accomplished historian, explicitly denies that what he has written is a history, and this can, perhaps, be taken to mean that he sees and feels himself to be a part of what he is writing about in a way which is not usual among professional historians. Social anthropologists would recognise what he has written as a kind of ethnography, but written from within, by an insider not an outsider. The author not only identifies himself in general terms as one of the people he is writing about but also includes in the text details arising from his enquiries into his own genealogy. He writes, for example, that;

> The story of the Aoineadh Mor evictions, as recorded by Norman Macleod, was published in English in the early 1860's. And no mention was made . . . of the identity of the man then occupying the shepherd's cottage which figured so prominently in the printed account of Aoineadh Mor's destruction. That man was called James Dempster. He was my great grandfather (p. 46).

And here the author proclaims his identity with the people he is writing about;

> It is my hope . . . that there will not be broken, for a long time yet, the link forged, over the greater part now of two thousand years, between this place of ours and us, its people (p. 188).

It is possible to say that the book contributes, and is probably intended to do so, to fashioning what it is writing about. The feelings expressed are the feelings of a Scottish Highlander. A Scottish Highlander is someone who can write a book like this. Therefore a careful reading of this book should be a test of the analysis of the discourse of tradition and community which has been presented here.

In a general and formal sense the project is a search for a solution to the paradox of continuity in change, of identity in diversity. This is achieved in three ways. There are two relatively objective and explicit factors, place and language, which contribute to a sense of continuity. So Morvern the place is the setting for Columba to establish another church; for Somerled to battle with pagan Vikings; for the Lord of the Isles to assemble an army to invade the Lowlands. It is where the campaign against the Covenanters began and where the infamous Patrick Sellar owned an estate and cleared out the population and where, as a consequence, the author's great grandfather worked as a shepherd. Historical figures known to Highlanders generally are, through attending to place, linked to individual personal history. Place also structures the book itself. The chapters are numbered but untitled yet they could each be named after particular localities.[20] The places are also places in Hunter's life and that of his family. For other Highlanders we may suppose that, though the places in their own histories might be different and the events different in detail, nevertheless, the same structures of experiences and feeling would present themselves. These places are not represented merely as names for the abstract conjunctions of latitudes and longitudes. Though the landscape that one may gaze upon is a record of events, it is also unchanging: 'You can be fairly confident that the trees you will see around you . . . have been following on their predecessors, generation after generation, since the wood itself first began to take shape in the aftermath of the last Ice Age' (p. 61).

The 'ancient' Gaelic language is the second point of reference. Language is no empty container of meanings but comes loaded with significance and so, 'it is still possible on the Scottish side of the North Channel and especially in the Hebrides, to come across surviving remnants of those endlessly retold legends concerning the doings of the likes of Deirdre and her doomed compatriots' (p. 18). The integrity of language, ideas, and place through time explains how the Celtic church accommodated pre-Christian beliefs, traces of which survive to the present in the Gaelic language. Thus on Iona, up to the early nineteenth century, there was performed a sacrifice to the gods of the sea. 'This ceremony, local tradition has it, took place in the vicinity of the little hill known as Dun Mhannannian. That hill shares its name with one of the Celtic gods of the Sea. Nor are such survivals limited to Iona' (p. 35). Speaking Gaelic is a necessary condition for thinking and acting as a Gael (p. 77).

Place, however, fluctuates in extent. At first it is virtually confined to Iona from where Columba set about extending the Christian religion to indigenous Picts and to the Gaels who had settled this part of the western highlands and islands which came to be known as Dalriada. By the eleventh century Malcolm Canmore was the Gaelic monarch of a Gaelic speaking land that extended over most of what is now defined as Scotland with the exception of the Hebrides and the northern isles which were, by that time, controlled by Norsemen. Since then there has been a contraction into the north west highlands and islands so that now, in the Hebrides, Gaelic speaking people dwell in a landscape of Norse names, while in the lowlands English speakers are surrounded by Gaelic place names. There is a suggestion that this retreat into the heartland includes Ireland as the Irish and Scottish Highlanders in the late nineteenth and twentieth centuries rediscovered their common origins.

These fluctuations correspond to the social changes which are the history of the Scottish Highlands but through which persists that special quality which distinguishes the Scottish Highlander. This, the third factor, is implicit but nevertheless basic to Hunter's enquiry. It is the contrast between a timeless community on the one hand and the ebb and flow of events which constitute the trajectory of history and society on the other. It is the contrast between what the German philosopher Tonnies called *Gemeinschaft* and *Gesellschaft*, between community and society. The latter is the field of change, while the former is 'the lasting and genuine form of living together. In contrast to *Gemeinschaft*, *Gesellschaft* is transitory and superficial' (Tonnies 1955:39). According to Tonnies these terms describe existentially different kinds of human social relationships but they also correspond to the configuration of perspectives associated with the duality of local-outsider.

The special qualities of community are embodied in St Columba, 'the earliest and greatest Scottish Highlander' (p. 38). Though no doubt regarded as an incomer by the Picts, he is for Hunter and by implication, other Scottish Highlanders the original 'local' and this is evident in the importance attached to his family tree and roots. First of all, according to Hunter 'immense store (is) set by birth and lineage' (p. 101). Followers were bound to followers and to their leaders 'in principle at all times and usually, too, in practice (through) ties of blood relationship' (p. 100). In the case of Columba his descent is unquestionably noble. He is descended from aristocrats on his father's side and from royalty through his mother. Though he was 'proud and imperious . . . he had no use for riches or the common trappings of great wealth. He sought no high office. He lived all his life in turf and stone cells of the kind which were inhabited by the lowliest of monks. He took his turn at manual labour. And he toiled all his days in the scriptorium, or writing house, where monastic penmen, of whom Iona possessed some of the most skilled in the world, ensured the transmission of all sorts of learning . . . Thus it came about that Europe's oldest vernacular literature consists of the lengthy Gaelic tales which celebrate the deeds of Cu Chulainn, Oisin, Diarmiat, Maeve and Deirdre . . . Men of Colum Cille's stamp did not denigrate folk culture. They recorded it . . . (p. 33–5). Indeed, they may even have contributed to it, as Hunter speculates that Columba may have composed poetry inspired by the Highland landscape (p. 36).

Though there were certain quite important ruptures, such as the synod of Whitby, there is a discernable and uncomplicated continuity from Dalriada to Gaelic Scotland under a Gaelic monarch. It is from this point that a process of differentiation begins and from where Hunter has to track with care the tradition of the Scottish Highlander and that lasting and genuine form of community. The virtue is soon lost to the monarchs. Robert Bruce was, in Highland tradition, 'the last of Scotland's kings to speak good Gaelic'. He was also 'the most outstanding of Scottish monarchs' (p. 78). From this pinnacle there could only be decline and so by the time of the union of the crowns, the Scottish King, James VI 'regarded the Gaels as savages . . . To the men who governed Scotland from this place (Edinburgh), in King James's time and later, the Highland Line was not at all unlike America's Indian frontier; and the Gaels, to them, were no more part of civil society than were the Cheyenne or the Sioux' (p. 73). It was, according to Hunter, the tragic role of the last of the Stewarts, Prince Charles Edward, to bring about unintentionally what his predecessors had been attempting for two hundred years (p. 77).

The agents of this history of decline are unambiguously identified as English incomers. The Stewarts are introduced as the descendants of a rootless self seeking Englishman from Shropshire called Walter. During the reign of David and his immediate successors, 'there was a considerable movement into Scotland from England. One such came North from Shropshire in the 1130s. He was the younger son of a Breton immigrant who had risen high in the service of the English king' and 'was to do still better for himself in Scotland' (p. 75–6). The contrast with the noble Columba, who did not seek high office but took his turn at manual toil, could hardly be more stark. Hunter draws back from joining those who would seek to identify Margaret, Malcolm Canmore's second wife, as the 'villain', and from describing her as a 'simple agent of the kingdom in the South', but he nevertheless concludes that with her English and European background she 'was the means of exposing her husband and her husband's country to external influences of a quite new kind'. For a start 'she spoke no Gaelic' and she gave her children English names. In the Church she completed the process begun at Whitby and 'eliminated much of what remained of the lingering institutional inheritance of the likes of Colum Cille (Columba)' (pp. 74–5). Scottish monarchs were no longer buried in Iona and the monarchy cut itself off from its West Highland origins. It now sought to emulate the south and east.

To recover the *Gemeinschaft* tradition, Hunter turns back to the clans and their chiefs, especially Clan Donald and their leader who styles himself the Lord of the Isles, and whose seat of power is Finlaggan on the island of Islay. This is the true line of the Dalriaddan inheritance. Accord-

ing to Hunter, Finlaggan provided Gaelic speaking Scots 'with an organi-
sational focus of the kind which had been lost as a result of the anglicisation of the Scottish monarchy' (p. 81). From the point of view of a modern
political historian such as Mackie, Black Donald (Lord of the Isles), was
simply another baron engaged in enhancing his power and promoting his
interests, and so in conflict with other barons in an arena over which a
weak Scottish monarch exercised little authority (1964:102). Mitchison
downgrades these struggles to little more than an expression of a political
economy of internecine warfare and the pursuit of booty, to which all parties were too much addicted (1982:58–9). For both, the importance of the
Battle of Harlaw (or the Battle of Garioch, as it is called in the Highland
tradition) between the forces of Black Donald and his cousin, the Earl of
Mar, has been over rated in Scottish historiography and 'misrepresented as
a struggle between Highlander and Lowlander' (Mackie 1955: 102). Yet
this was clearly not the view of the Corporation of the City of Aberdeen
when, in 1911, it chose to erect a great monument at Harlaw to commemorate those burgesses who, five hundred years before, had gone out and died
defending their city, their society, and their property from Black Donald's
Highland followers, to whom he had promised the city as plunder if they
would fight for him. Nor is it the view of Hunter who endorses 'the essential truth' of the old misrepresentation and quotes approvingly Hume
Brown's comment that 'Never since that day has Teutonic Scotland been in
real danger from the Celtic race' (p. 88). For Hunter the misrepresentation
is of the Highlanders as the caterans, bandits and outlaws, and the burgesses of Aberdeen as the representatives of civilisation.[21]

The clan structures of patronage and clientship in an idiom of kinship
which were headed by individuals such as Black Donald were continued
by clan chiefs such as Ruairi Mor of Dunvegan. The clan structure and
ethos was that of the clan chief's household writ large. 'To Dunvegan came
Niall Mor MacMhuirich, a member of the bardic family which had earlier
served the Lords of the Isles but which was now part of the entourage of
those other island chieftains, the ClanRanald MacDonalds. Six nights he
spent within the walls of Ruairi Mor's Dunvegan, Niall MacMhuirich
subsequently recalled; six nights of eating and drinking and music and
merriment before the castle's blazing fire; six nights when the sound of the
harp mingled with the songs and laughter of the younger members of the
household' (p. 99). However, they were, in turn, not immune from what is
called the 'anglicising process' which had split the monarchy from Gaeldom.
So the chiefs unilaterally rewrote the relationship between themselves and
their followers in terms of landlord and tenant, where access to land is

exchanged for rent, while the people persisted, at least for a time and for obvious reasons, in dealing with the chiefs as patrons who are supposed to respond with displays of noble generosity in return for expressions of admiring loyalty.

When chiefs renounced the political economy of warfare and looting and adopted Lowland institutions, their trusty warriors became redundant. Pillaging and blackmail of Lowlanders by Highlanders was morally justified in the eyes of the latter because the Gael once ruled in Lowland Scotland and so that land, in some sense belonged to him, and how can one steal from one's self? Now that the chiefs have declared themselves to be Lowlanders in all but name, so the land they now claim to be theirs can be pillaged as the land of Lowlanders was before. 'It is in this sense that the man who takes a salmon from a land owner's river – as I have done myself – stands, to some small extent at least, in the shoes of those of his ancestors who once came at night to carry off the Lowland farmer's livestock' (p. 115). The sundering of the community of clan and chieftains could not be more complete, only the common clansmen have retained the true tradition.

The clan chiefs of today are no longer real but representations of a past reality, a kind of pageant of 'kilted and bonneted individuals who like to call themselves clan chiefs and relieve you of £3.30 at their castle gates' (p. 101). They have 'rejected their own background' and 'ingratiated themselves with the lowland and English establishment' (p. 119). Instead the nobility that was claimed by the chiefs and acknowledged by their bards is now withheld from them and retained by the latter's successors, the literary men and women of the Scottish Highlands who manifest, and are honoured for, their 'bardic dignity' (p. 102). They are poets such as Sorley Maclean, or folklorists, such as his brother Calum, or artists, such as their nephew Cailean whose photographs illustrate Hunter's text. Now 'the best features of Gaelic civilisation', as carried forward by the essential Scottish Highlander, are to be found among the commonality, among fishermen, crofters, shepherds, roadmen, and tinkers, especially those with a reputation for lore, song and poetry, the inheritors of the bardic tradition. They are 'an aristocracy more prestigious by far than the anglicised and titled landed gentry in their castles and big houses' (p. 123). So Hunter reproduces Calum Maclean's literary portrait of one John the Bard of Lochaber who travelled eight miles through sleet and hail to attend Mass; sturdy, alert, active with piercing eyes; the composer of over two hundred songs, crofter, and road builder, a latter day Columba (p. 120–1).

These parallel aristocracies, one the authentic bearer of the noble virtue, the other a kilted and bonneted sham, are reflected in their monuments. The great pile of Edinburgh Castle, housing the crown of Scotland and still garrisoned, commands attention and receives it, while the small outcrop of rock in Argyll that is Dunadd, distinguished only by the pathetic outline of a boar carved on the rock, a few lines of the mute Ogham script, and the shape of a human foot, is virtually ignored. At Finlaggan are some almost forgotten ruins. Meanwhile, inside Dunvegan castle, where the woman at the gate who sells the tickets 'does not have an island accent' (p. 98) are clan archives, silver and gold artefacts, historical objects, ancient heirlooms and legendary antiquities All stand in stark contrast to the demotic heritage outside the castle. This boulder on a hillside is a Mass stone, a makeshift altar of seventeenth and eighteenth century hillside Catholic services and symbol of the oppression of these times; a great MacDonald warrior is said to have threatened to hang a local bard from that tree; there is a rock upon which two of Montrose's men sharpened their swords. The landscape is a natural and timeless historical text. However, though anyone is free to walk through this landscape of natural antiquities, they are invisible to the stranger, the text is obscure. On the other hand the castle is closed except when it announces that it is open, and inside artefacts such as Somerled's drinking cup, Ruarie Mor's hunting horn, the Fairie Flag and all the rest present themselves fully explained to any stranger who has bought a ticket. And the car park, we are told, is full of coaches from Holland, Germany, England and elsewhere.

This boundary is made all the more vivid and personal by the use of kinship in the text. If, as the author maintains, kinship, in principle and usually in practice, is the foundation of Scottish Highland society, then it is to be expected that genealogies should figure prominently. Ancestors are traced back eight generations and among his contemporary kin, the author notes that the Edinburgh historian, John Bannerman, is his father's mother's mother's mother's sister's son's son's son. 'There is, quite literally, no limit to the network of family linkages that can be constructed in this way' (p. 176). However, no genealogies are presented linking anyone to a clan chief. Kinship links people who are Scottish Highlanders, and clan chiefs are no longer reckoned as such.

Hunter's own genealogy, which can be constructed from details scattered throughout the text, is not without interest. It is at once apparent that Hunter's own links to the Highlands are enormously strengthened through maternal relationships. His father's father is a Lowlander, a gamekeeper, who settled in the western Highlands but his father's mother and his own mother link him to the Inner Hebrides and to Ardnamurchan respectively. His father's mother is clearly a pivotal figure and in life was a formidable woman of considerable accomplishment, and it is striking that the genealogical details provided by Hunter present her as the last of a matriline. While the anglicised landowning aristocracy may insist upon patrilineal descent, it would seem that, to quote Tonnies once more, 'the core of genius, nevertheless, is usually a maternal heritage' (1955:177).

Such a structure of the history of the Scottish Highlander is recapitulated in the biographies of individuals and so the subjective locks onto history and confirms the latter's reality, while historical images are used as figures to express the experiences of personal biography. Anglicisation begins in the disciplined world of the school and maturation is completed by an often traumatic, since it is typically and ironically the mother who is instrumental in arranging for her children to 'get on in life', migration to the lowland world, a move from a rural to an urban setting, from the Gemeinschaft of the domestic family to the Gesellschaft of wider society. This experience is naturally enough a frequent theme of Highland authors.[22] One obvious quality of this movement is a sense of loss, which is amplified by a return to the scenes of childhood. The return, instead of recapturing the lost world, results in a deeper sense of its passing. 'Innes MacColl's family is now the only one in Duror to have roots that stretch back to James Stewart's time . . . We are speaking, as we do in the course of all our occasional encounters, of the extent to which Duror has altered in recent decades; of the fact that there is scarcely a person in the district with whom either of us went to school; of how there is nobody here about from which it is possible to hear Duror tradition of the sort so familiar to Innes's father and to others of his generation (p. 155). To appreciate that this is a wholly subjective perspective one need only consider the views of Highland folklorists since this experience, expressed as witnessing 'the passing of a way of life' is the justification for collecting folklore. If one goes back to the generation of Innes MacColl's father when the traditions were familiar, Calum MacLean reckoned that the 'best lore had gone to the grave with those who had it' thirty years before he began collecting in 1945 (1990:13). At the turn of the century Carmichael reckoned that he had collected all that remained and that the 'tradition bearers' were 'almost all dead now leaving no successors' (1900:xxxvi), and J F Campbell in 1859 thought that the traditions he was collecting were 'about to perish' (1983:iii) (see also Chapman 1978: 114–7, 143).

This chapter has shown how the distinction between 'local' and 'incomer' as different kinds of people is generated by a configuration of perspectives and feelings which also induces a sensitivity to 'tradition', 'ways of life', 'community', and 'belonging'. As we are propelled by events through the temporal landscape it is only in the rear view mirror, so to speak, that we see a diversity of traditions and a plurality of communities continually appearing and then receding, but which appear to be quite absent from the homogenous future ahead. This is nicely illustrated in Diana Forsythe's concluding remarks to her study of urban rural migration to an Orkney island:

> The processes of change set in motion by the widespread migration of city people out into rural areas will reach their culmination when urban people and attitudes have transformed the countryside into an extension of urban industrial culture and society . . . The diversity of people and culture that has characterised the West for thousands of years will have been welded into the mass-produced metropolitan culture and experience of the late 20th century, and the agents of that process will have been the very individuals who sought to escape to the country to an impossible dream (Forsythe 1982:95).

Though purporting to be an objective view of the trajectory of human history, for all the reasons put forward in this book and in this chapter in particular, it is essentially a partial view. The ambiguous figure of the stranger is not only perceived as a generalised threat according to indigenous utterances and texts, but also makes possible the articulation of precisely what is threatened, tradition and community. The relationship between the ideas of local and outsider enters into the very heart of people's feelings about themselves and their historical identity. And for reasons which remain obscure, strangers seem especially prominent in remote rural areas. Consequently it is in remote rural areas that people have an acute sense of being in the presence of fragile communities and elusive traditions. It is hardly surprising that when numerous unknown migrants from the city did appear in the countryside to settle that such events should be endowed with an amplified surplus of significance.

Notes

[1] 'He said that the change in the crofting Acts had led to croft houses changing hands to incomers for high prices. This was leading to the death of the crofting way of life in an area given over to tourism.' Reported in *The Glasgow Herald* 23 May 1991. 'What is to be done

if we are to avoid the absurdity of tourists popping across from Skye to gawk at the quiet of a Harris Sabbath, destroying it in the process? Rev Donald Macleod, *West Highland Free Press* 12 February 1993.

[2] From the evidence of Mr R. R. MacGregor, Secretary of the Congested Districts Board. In The Report of the Departmental Committee of the Board of Agriculture and Fisheries to enquire into and report upon the subject of small holdings in Great Britain. 1906. Cd 3277, p. 352.

[3] The Observer 23 June 1988.

[4] During the eighties the value of salmon fishing rights increased twelve fold (Wigan 1991: 66).

[5] *The Glasgow Herald* 8 March 1989 p. 11.

[6] 'Game Wars' *Channel 4* , 5 May 1991.

[7] 'The river and loch are kept private but an easement is given to the Ullapool Angling Club for two single weeks fishing by members during good periods in the season. This type of arrangement is one of many such local measures of expediency which are made on the initiative of landowners and local residents in various parts of the Highlands.' (Millman 1970:48).

[8] Proceedings of the Skye Forum Tourism Seminar, 13 April 1991, Portree, p. 28.

[9] 'The white house had been advertised for sale for a long time but no one would buy it. They had got to hear about it as a house to rent when they were doing a tour of the Highlands, came and saw it, fell in love with it, could not buy it and actually got it to rent.' Gunn 1988: 37). Note that the house ('no one would buy it') is destined for its eventual occupants.

[10] 'In his [Gilpin's] anxiety for the ideal of picturesque correctness, he seems moved less by piety to nature than by something like Victorian prudery; indeed, as Hussey puts it, he makes a comical figure, "first abasing himself before nature as the source of all beauty and emotion; then getting up and giving her a lesson in deportment"' (Salvesen 1965:66).

[11] The analysis at this point owes much to Elias and Scotston's insightful account of the configuring of social relationships between locals and incomers (Elias and Scotston 1965).

[12] 'The decline in croft production has produced a loss of the old folklore that once surrounded this activity. It is manifested in the reluctance of the older people to pass on the oral history and knowledge of the "old ways" to the younger generation . . . One crofter, for example, explained to me that an uncle had cleared their barn some years before of all the, by then, redundant equipment because "he did not want anything to do with the past."' (Mewett 1982:227).

[13] At the Skye Forum Tourism Seminar already referred to, the only speaker identified as a 'Skye Resident', and presumably representing the interests of residents, came from North America and settled in Skye in 1971. Skye Forum describes itself as 'a community charitable trust'.

[14] 'They moved slowly through a long agenda: sewage disposal, goal posts for the football pitch, street lighting proposals — again turned down, protection of the lifebelts from vandalism by visitors, control of campers, beach pollution, distribution of a Home Office book-

let on nuclear fallout, the mobile library.' (Glasser 1981:163) Note the necessary assumption that deviants, 'vandals', are not members of the community. Only an outsider would draw attention to the rusting cookers, washing machines, broken arm chairs and other detritus dumped around most Scottish rural settlements.

[15] This passage owes much to James Littlejohn's unsurpassed and still relevant analysis of class cultures and gender in a rural Scottish parish in southwest Scotland (Littlejohn 1964).

[16] For a story written, apparently quite unselfconsciously, in the 'tales from the Raj' genre in which many colonial and imperial officials cast their memoirs on retirement (a retirement which often took them to remoter rural Scotland), see the chapter entitled 'Friendly Official — Modest Native' (MacDonald (1943: chapter 11) It is hardly surprising that the 'natives' take up this kind of discourse and give it an ironical twist with phrases such as 'white settlers' to characterise counterstream migrants.

[17] Subject to the usual assignation process (see chapter 6), the new tenant's name is entered against the croft in the Commission's register of crofts. The money which is handed over to the person relinquishing the croft and status of crofter to the new crofter is compensation for the improvements carried out by the crofter. To all intents and purposes it constitutes the purchase price of the croft.

[18] Scottish Television 10th May 1992. The Prince of Wales was in the congregation.

[19] In *The Scotsman* (Weekend Supplement), 2 February 1991, pp. 12–14.

[20] In fact Hunter's book resembles the latest edition (1990) of Calum MacLean's 1947 study of the Highlands in a number of ways. Both are from the same publisher and both are illustrated by Cailean MacLean. The Chapters of MacLean's book are actually given place names as titles.

[21] Nor is the significance of Harlaw lost to today's Aberdonians. In 1974, as a result of local authority reorganisation, a respected high school in the city was renamed Harlaw Academy, and the bar of the Caledonian Hotel, where advocates, businessmen, and councillors may be found taking a drink, is decorated with vivid scenes depicting the battle. When one Aberdonian was asked about the significance the monument at Harlaw, he immediately said, 'It means no Heelanders past this point!'.

[22] For example Gunn (1946).

Chapter 5

Contested Landscapes

The repopulating of rural Scotland by residential incomers contributes to, and is also indicative of, an already changing way of life, which is not only experienced in terms of perceptions of social and cultural change, but also in terms of a threat to individual and collective identity through the subversion of the relationship between persons and places which is a crucial component of these identities. It is the purpose of this chapter to explore how in-migration contributes to the redefinition of known landscapes and the resulting loss of a local sense of place, by considering some of the different and often contested cultural meanings that people draw from and attribute to places in the Scottish Highlands. Firstly, by focusing on the crofting landscape, the significance of a local sense of place will be explored. Secondly, we examine how some incomers perceive the landscapes in which they live. Finally, we consider the appropriation of landscape on a national scale and the conceptual transition from 'landscape' to 'environment'.

For planners and developers, rural areas may be considered to be rejuvenated by in-migration, unless the in-migrants are overwhelmingly of retirement age, in that by their very presence incomers are deemed to add to the kind of 'healthy' demographic profile that provides the basis for local services and facilities, (such as shops, schools, bus services and so on), but incomers often have their own perceptions about those areas which are at variance with local perceptions. This has far reaching consequences because, in so far as a particular place is seen in relation to both person and community, and as one of many significant centres around which people construct their cultural worlds and their identities, then repopulation has the effect of emptying the landscape of people through the erosion of an association between past and present:

The old home was now occupied by strangers. He looked at it over his shoulder, Already he had seen the harbour deserted of fishing craft. How typical he was in himself of countless Highland lads who had come back to the scenes of their boyhood! How many had returned after the Napoleonic wars to find that even the ruins of their homes had been obliterated! (Gunn 1991:220).

Place is an important referent of a society's identity, constructed from experience and a continuous cultural and moral exchange between people and landscape (Tuan 1972, Weeden 1992). It is also vital for a sense of self, so that what threatens the landscape threatens, impinges upon, and diminishes personal identity. Entrikin argues that the significance of place is associated with the fact that '..we recognise that as individual agents we are always "situated" in the world' (1991:3). Yet, the cultural meanings individuals attribute to places are often ignored by the objectivity of the theoretician who adopts a decentred approach in the search for universal qualities of place. Entrikin makes a distinction between attempts to understand the experience of being 'in a place' and being 'at a location'. To understand what it means be in a place is to take a centred view, one that is concerned with the specificity of place and the '. . . significance of the moral particularity associated with the individual's attachment to a place-based community' (Entrikin 1991:3). To adopt a decentred approach, on the other hand, is to transcend what is regarded as provincial and particular in an attempt to discover the 'essence or universal structure of place'. What is lost in scientific theorising, however, is a sense of ourselves acting within and engaging with the world. By failing to take into account experiential aspects of culture, a decentred description of place does not consider how human knowledge of the environment is actually constructed, or that people imaginatively create their environments and attribute meaning to and draw significance from the landscapes in which they live.

Both locals and incomers recognise that they are 'situated' in the world, and both attribute meaning to the places they live in. It would be naive to suggest otherwise. We have argued that 'local' and 'incomer' are contested categories constructed and negotiated in different social situations, but in attempting to understand the relationship between people and place it is perhaps tenable to associate the complex we are calling 'local' with being 'in a place', and the complex called 'incomer' with being 'at a location'. This is not to say that locals have a special relationship with a place while incomers do not. Rather, the orientation to place is qualitatively different. Associated with the complex called 'local' are feelings of belonging, personal and community identity, lineage, and 'roots', while the structure of feeling associated with the complex called 'incomer' is informed by a different orientation to the landscape which, as will be explored, is that blurring of regional and national images of landscape referred to as the 'environment'.

A Local Sense of Place: The Crofting Landscape

All over Scotland the contemporary landscape is a planned system of fields and boundaries that dates from the period of agricultural improvements between 1700–1850. The land surveyors of the Improving Movement were responsible for the geometric patterns now regarded as a traditional feature of much of the Scottish landscape. Roads were integral to the reshaped landscape, important in opening up the Highlands and were a boon to agriculture, providing easy access to markets at a time when agriculture was experiencing commercialisation and an end to the system of payment in kind. Very little evidence of the previous Scottish agricultural land pattern survives.

Before the creation of crofts the pattern of agriculture throughout the Highlands was that of the runrig system, where people lived in clustered settlements known as clachans and held the arable land in common. The runrig system represented a period of continuity which lasted until the Clearances and the creation of sheep farms. Typically, tenant farmers kept herds of small black cattle and a number of small livestock, although the latter would have been of little market value. Each year, at the end of May, in a system of transhumance, the herds and flocks were taken to upland pasture at the shielings (*airidh*) where they remained until the end of August. Access to pasture and cultivable land was a function of kinship and the obligation of clansmen to share access to clan lands among clan members. To a lesser extent unrelated families acquired access to land through marriage or the patronage of a powerful individual clansman. Such arrangements were overseen by the clan chief and his immediate subordinates, the tacksmen, who together extracted tribute from the clachans, displayed generosity to clansmen and hospitality to clan guests, organised the defence of clan lands and herds, and mounted raids on the herds of other clans.

Within an overall historical context of upheaval and cultural devastation in the Highlands, extensive sheep farming developed against the backdrop of the increasing pace of the disintegration of the clan system and the Anglicisation of the lairds following the Jacobite rebellion of 1745. From this time the lairds were drawn increasingly into Lowland society and, because of a need for a regular cash income to sustain an increasingly Lowland and urbane lifestyle, the previous network of allegiances and payments in kind that characterised the clan system was replaced by cash rent. For many of the lairds, the attraction of the rents paid by sheep farmers and the prospects of huge profits to be made from sheep were more compelling than feelings of mutual aid and clan obligations to tacksmen and their sub-tenants. To make available the land for the grazing of Cheviot Blackface sheep, widespread evictions followed. To this day, the Clearances remain a symbol of the appropriation of the Highlands by outside interests, and are regarded as the beginning of a continuing process which manifests itself in various ways, such as afforestation by the Forestry Commission and by private landowners. In the Highland and Islands , the Clearances are often spoken about as if they occurred yesterday.

The first large sheep farms were created in the late eighteenth century. Writing of the creation of sheep farming in the parish of Gairloch, Dixon (1886:137) tells us that

> the commencement of sheep-farming in Gairloch does not seem to have been accompanied by any noticeable friction. If one or two small townships were abolished to make way for the sheep farmer, the inhabitants had other more desirable quarters provided for them. The population of Gairloch steadily increased from the date when sheep farming began.

At first sight, Dixon's comment seems to reflect the prevailing attitude of the early nineteenth century that the establishment of sheep farms was an act of benevolence, with the Clearances seen as a necessary part of the Policy of Improvement. With the larger areas of grazing given over to sheep farming, small individual crofts were created on marginal land and people worked at generating income from fishing and kelping. Together with the creation of sheep farms the development of crofting ended the communal agrarian system of the runrig. However, not all crofting systems were designed to retain labour for kelp production, fishing and other estate work. For example, crofts on the Gairloch estate were created when Sir Kenneth Mackenzie was laird in 1845 and 1846, much later than elsewhere in the Highlands and Islands, and were designed for improvement in agriculture and the social and economic conditions of the estate's tenants. The factor, Dr. John Mackenzie was responsible for the design of the new system. Each tenant was assigned a croft of about four acres where they could grow oats, potatoes, barley and turnips. In addition, each crofter kept an average of four or five cows and between five to ten sheep. Of 364 tenants on the estate at the time, only 94 were moved to crofts on other farms, the rest being able to take crofts on the farms where they were already living (Caird 1987:73).

The development of crofting, then, rearranged the social and physical landscape of the Highlands and Islands. New settlement patterns were established and poor land was reclaimed for agricultural use, often by hard physical labour; owing to the rocky terrain crofters could only bring their land under cultivation with a spade or a foot plough (*cas chrom*). From the middle of the nineteenth century a new system of agriculture and estate structure evolved, and the practice of crofting became part of the new land use system. Crofting, by retaining a common grazing land shared by a group of crofters, provided a basis for communal activity and a sense of continuity with a previous agrarian pattern now recalled as more equitable than that being visited upon the inhabitants of the land (Hunter 1976).

Today, there are over seventeen and a half thousand registered crofts in the seven former counties of Ross and Cromarty, Inverness, Argyll, Caithness, Orkney, Sutherland and Shetland, with croft land occupying about one-fifth of the total land area of the Highlands and Islands. As well as the croft house and garden, the croft consists of the croft land, which is usually next to the croft house, but can in certain circumstances where land is better used for production than as a site for house, the croft house may be separated form the croft land. In addition, each crofter has rights in and obligations to the community land, known as the common grazing, or in local terms 'the hill'. Common grazing is usually high moorland, encompassing several thousand acres in some instances. The arable land is called *gearaidh*, and the moorland is the *monadh*, areas of peat bog in many cases, where the sheep of the crofting township are put to graze for most of the year.

The crofting landscape is a social landscape associated with people and events. This is not only evident in settlement patterns, the organisation of fields and boundaries, and the traces of deserted and ruined crofts and townships, but in cultural meanings and human actions which are beyond what is visible and immediately apparent. Places in the landscape ' . . . take on the meanings of events and objects that occur there, and their descriptions are fused with human goals, values and intentions' (Entrikin 1991:11). This is illustrated by place names, the majority of which are Gaelic or anglicised versions of the original. Gaelic place names are not necessarily restricted to geographical description, although the name of every place will be a picture of what will be there, so that a man will almost know a place on its first seeing by its likeness to the name that will be on it. Say Achadh nam beith to a Gaelic man and he will be seeing in his mind a level place and the birch trees growing here and there, and they white and slender. Say Achadh nan siantan and he will be seeing a little plain between great mountains and the rain driving down on it (MacColla 1932:70).

Place names in the crofting landscape are multi-dimensional, and also contain mythical, factual, historical and personal meanings. They tell of personal experiences and of community events and activities, both in the past and in the present, and have a richness of meaning that goes far beyond the concern with simple reference to spatial location or to a single event. In this way, place names bind the landscape with human imagination and experience and inform us about a multiplicity of close associations which thereby blend the human and natural worlds into one (Nuttall 1992:50–58).

For example, in the Gairloch area Gaelic place names include Lochan nan Breac (lochan of the trout), Loch nan Eun (loch of the birds), Bac na Leth-choin (shelf of the crossbred dog), Beinn Aridh Charr (mountain of the rough shieling), Cnoc a chrochadair (hangman's hill), and Cnoc na mi-chomhairle (hill of evil counsel). The latter name has its origin in the 1840s, when Allan MacLoud was laird of Gairloch. His wife was the daughter of the sixth laird of Kintail and sister of Hector Roy Mackenzie. But Allan's two brothers, the story goes, did not want Mackenzie blood in the veins of the sons of the laird of Gairloch, so they decided to kill their brother and his two sons and inherit Gairloch themselves. They killed Allan and then his two sons and buried them at a place that came to be known as Craig Bhadan an Aisc, 'rock of the place of interment' (Dixon 1886:25–26). Other examples of place names in Gairloch parish include Eilean na h'Iolaire (island of the eagle), Meall Lochan a Chleirich (hill of the loch of the priest), and Blar na Falla (plain of the blood). This last name is one that was given to a place where cattle were taken to be bled.

It would be possible to give numerous other examples of Gaelic place names from all over the Highlands, but for the purposes of this discussion it is enough to note that features and characteristics of the landscape are not only described, but are commemorated by names, and that very few places remain unnamed. Thus, a small rock may have significance because it was once used for a specific purpose in the past and its name will refer to this use, or a place used as the site for a fish-trap (*eileach*) will be recognised as such by its name.

More importantly, place names have contextual and subjective meanings which are elusive and therefore often ignored. This is illustrated by the fact that many place names are not written on Ordnance Survey maps, but are only known in local memory. For local people with knowledge of Gaelic, and especially with knowledge and memories of past events, the landscape is a living landscape and place names are mnemonic devices that trigger recollection of particular activities.

Connecting People and Place

But the local landscapes of the Highlands are also personalised landscapes, in the sense that a footpath through a peat bog may be named after the person who first cut it, e.g. 'Kenneth's Road', or specific places may have particular associations with an individual, such as 'Lochan nan Breac is the place where Niall almost drowned when he was out poaching', or 'Jock's broken leg way' (the name for a footpath where a man named Jock once spent a day and a night with a fractured ankle, waiting for help). As a form of commemorative shorthand such places are given new names, for example Niall's Lochan, which are often not known to many people beyond the locality. Places named for people in this way are not done so in order to establish a claim to possession, or for purposes of power. This is a colonial habit that reduces the landscape to a vast area of impersonal and empty territory. Rather, by naming places after people or by commemorating an event with a name, people are located in the landscape, giving a sense of social continuity.

This linking of persons and local topography is a characteristic feature of agricultural and maritime societies throughout the North Atlantic region. Anthropological works that touch on this include Cohen's (1987) monograph of life on Whalsay in Shetland, Robinson's (1986) study of the Aran Islands in the west of Ireland, Gaffin's (1993) account of landscape and personhood on the Faroe Islands, and Nuttall's (1992) ethnography of a remote hunting community in northern Greenland. Both Gaffin and Nuttall point to the importance of place names for giving meaning to the social, physical and conceptual world of the Faroese and Inuit respectively. What is clear from these accounts is that outsiders are effectively denied access to knowledge about specific aspects of culture, local personalities and particular events encoded in the landscape if they do not know the meaning and significance of place names. For Greenland, Nuttall shows how a local landscape finds expression in the cognitive maps used by individuals to orientate themselves and their sense of community in relation to it. The significance of places for personal, family or community life is often difficult for outsiders, including Danes resident in Greenlandic villages and well as people from other communities, to grasp (ibid.). Illustrating the intensely personal nature of the landscape, Nuttall (1993a:84) recalls that

> 'an elderly hunter from the settlement of Kangersuatsiaq told me how, having been on a hunting trip, he had discovered his footprints at an old campsite of his that he had last visited twenty years previously. To misunderstand the significance of this is to misunderstand that there are many layers of meaning in what, to this man and others like him, is a cherished and known landscape'.

And as Gaffin (ibid. 67) puts it:

> '. . . placenames, in addition to having historical, economic, ecological and social dimensions, are densely symbolic of the culture at large. They are the fora for a community to portray itself and to gain distinctive cultural identity. The identity arises and constantly reaffirms itself in contrast to other island regions and, in being general Faeroese practices and traditions, contrasts with Danish and other continental cultures with which they have had contact. People construe their culture as the knowledge, sentiments and attitudes associated with place'.

In the Scottish Highlands, local landscapes are memoryscapes of events, experiences and associations that tend to become integral elements of the places where they occur, and indeed cannot be separated from them. Every place name is an inscription, the writing of human activity and personal and collective experiences on the landscape, although the place name may not immediately reflect this. Stories and myths unfold against a geographical backdrop, and there are people who pay great attention to detail in the landscape, who are able to read it and to use its named places in everyday conversation and in narrative in order to capture particular moods, moments and episodes in a community's history.

Place names are important for a sense of place, for nurturing a relationship between self and place, and between community and place. However, meanings differ between members of any given community. While many place names are shared collectively, others are highly personalised and are generally not known by a large number of people. Furthermore, some place names serve to demarcate, either symbolically or directly the boundary between communities, so that to enter another locality is to have no knowledge of its places other than as geographical locations. In such a situation, named places produce 'vivid pauses in the imagination' (Gunn 1969:34) for those who have no experience of them.

It is precisely this lack of knowledge and experience of local places on the part of outsiders that makes some official decisions and actions by local and central government controversial. Speaking of a new single track road bridge built by Highland Regional Council to replace an old footbridge over a stream near Lochinver, an elderly crofter said he had disagreed with the council over the bridge, not because of any environmental impact, but because of a change of name. As he put it

> The old bridge that was there was a footbridge and we called it Allt na t-Strathain ('stream of the strath') in the Gaelic. That's the name of the stream, but we always called the bridge by the same name. The council built the new bridge and called it the Ardroe Bridge. It's not good that they do these things, change the meaning. The new name isn't even a Gaelic name. I wrote to the council about it.

The changing of a name is only one way of losing the original name, and thus its meaning, and ultimately the connection between people and place. To name some other, 'we always called the bridge by the same name', not only identifies whatever is named, but also, and more fundamentally, distinguishes and identifies the authors of the name. In the case of a collectivity, of the living and the dead, however imagined, a common unity or community, is brought into being out of a plurality of individuals by the one name, 'the same name'. To obliterate or deny the existence of the name is to subvert the identity, authority, and even existence of the bestower. It is precisely at the point when names disappear that their significance becomes apparent, especially when a new name imposed on a place from outwith the locality contains information about power relationships. Moreover as people die, the local knowledge they possess and the names they give to places may die with them. What is lost is an intensity of association between moments, memories and places. To move across the landscape is to encounter it and become involved with elements of it, or to re- encounter memories from childhood, or a complexity of experiences and emotions from various stages of individual, family and community history. Yet multifarious understandings and the uniqueness of places make theorising and an objective study of place difficult. Places are contexts of human action and events.

Alasdair Maclean, in his elegiac account of his own family's struggle in a dying crofting community on the Ardnamurchan peninsula, writes that the loss of place names is '. . . one of the most vital yet least considered areas of cultural erosion' (Maclean 1984:185). His lament for the passing from memory of an intricacy of place names during his own lifetime is something that many people throughout the Highlands share. As a boy, Maclean wandered the local landscape and recalls how

> Often on these expeditions I was accompanied by my grandfather, who had a name for every least hillock, ever creek and gully. It was by his side that I first became aware, albeit dimly, how such knowledge set one apart. It was not simply that it gave him material advantage over me, although it did, but that it invested him with a form of spiritual privilege (and of course with the concomitant responsibility). He lived in a different landscape from me, seeing it in a different way and - I came to feel - being seen differently by it. He was accepted, or rejected as the case might be, where I was merely and constantly tolerated. He moved through the mansion of his world as a blood relative where I was but a paying guest. (1984:186)

Later, Maclean says he came to know a few of the names his grandfather gave to places, but his grandfather's death '. . . turned most of that huge upland into mere undifferentiated terrain' (1984:187). Maclean suggests that some of the names of places of the Ardnamurchan peninsula, such as around the townships of Sanna and Plocaig "linger in the archives or in the care of the Ordnance Survey. If you had a good enough map, or were a good enough researcher you would find them. But these are flies in amber. Names preserved in that fashion, the few that are preserved, are preserved scientifically, not culturally; they are perpetuated by means of ink, not semen' (1984 186–7).

Place name surveys are being conducted in many Highland localities, often by people who live in those localities. For example, the head teacher at Farr Secondary School near Bettyhill in Sutherland is involved with compiling an extensive place name database. Each place name collected is put into the database, together with its meaning, pronunciation, an associated story, and map reference. In Gairloch, the Gairloch Heritage Museum is carrying out a similar project. The aim is to collect as many place names as possible that do not appear on any map. This is urgent work as there are few surviving native Gaelic speakers in the Gairloch area who know of these names. The decline of Gaelic as an everyday, spoken language means that the transmission of place names to others becomes increasingly unlikely. But most of these places are no longer used or thought about, so for many people there is no need to learn their names or the stories associated with them.

The Gairloch place name survey is conducted by an incomer, an Englishman who speaks fluent Gaelic and who has lived in the area since the late 1960s. Almost single-handedly he has promoted the Gaelic language and precipitated something of a modest revival. He is passionate about Gaelic because he feels a loss of Gaelic entails a loss of identity. For him, knowing Gaelic is essential for knowing one's place because the physical environment cannot be separated from culture, it cannot be seen as a distinct entity. To know Gaelic, to speak it fluently and to be able to think in the language, is also vital for his own sense of place. There are few other incomers who share his sentiments, however. As the rest of this chapter shows, local landscapes are being transformed, re-created and attributed new meanings.

Moving into Places

Recent incomers usually have no previous connection with the landscapes they move into. Their knowledge and experience of it may come from holidays to the area, and, through a lack of the Gaelic language, the meanings of place names are not generally learned. This is also true for some local people, especially because there are no longer specific social and cultural activities associated with certain places and, as has been mentioned, because of the decline of Gaelic as a spoken language in some areas.

Some of those incomers who do make an effort to learn the meanings of place names make the same mistakes as the early map makers who Anglicised the landscape. In Gairloch, a retired Englishman from Kent who had lived in the area for eight years, and who agreed to be interviewed about his feelings towards the landscape, said of the view from his sitting-room window

> If you look out, you can see Skye. On the other side of the bay you can see Badachro. And this small island, here, is called Eilean Glas in Gaelic, which means Glass Island. You can see why it's called Glass Island because of the way it shimmers in the sunlight.

In English Eilean Glas means 'Blue-green Island', but it is easy to understand this man's mistake. And it is not an isolated example. Native Gaelic speakers are aware of this kind of renaming of places and react accordingly. For example, while discussing such changes of place names with a retired crofter from Drumbeg, a man in his late 70s, the response was unequivocal:

Last year some tourists knocked on my door and asked me to give them directions to the Black Loch. I told them I hadn't heard of any place called Black Loch in this area, that I'd lived here all my life and that the Black Loch they were wanting must be somewhere else. They went away, but you know, they were wanting Loch Duibh and I felt a bit angry that they'd asked for it by saying the name for Loch Duibh in English. It has a proper name, a Gaelic name. I know people like those tourists don't have any Gaelic, but it seems that more and more places are becoming known by their English names. People don't use the Gaelic anymore.

Just as with the death of Alasdair Maclean's grandfather the landscape was 'set free' and 'reverted to hostile wilderness' (1984:186), so the loss of place names for other people in Highland communities means the loss of a distinct sense of place. This is not to suggest that the naming system has been stable and unchanging. Yet while it has been dynamic in the past and while one place may have several names, one name is perhaps always considered definitive. It is locals themselves who seem to be reifying 'tradition', by constructing a rhetoric that assumes the system of place naming *has* been stable in the past but is now only changing as a result of the pressures that accompany in-migration.

Incomers move into places with which they are unfamiliar and impose their own meanings on the landscape. The point to be made here is that knowledge of local events that are somehow inscribed in the landscape is perhaps unavailable to the majority of incomers. Seemingly empty, 'set free to revert to wilderness', the landscape is there for the imagination to reshape and recreate. One obvious result is that the original meaning attributed to places is irrevocably lost. But despite this loss of meaning, new meaning is attributed to places. It is just that the '. . . casualty of such change is the sense of attachment that comes from the stability of meanings associated with places and landscapes' (Entrikin 1991:57).

Stewardship and the New Ruralism

When asked about their first impressions of the landscapes they had moved into, a large number of incomers interviewed during the research said, with certain predictability, that they had 'fallen in love with the place'. One couple, in their late forties, moved to the north Sutherland coast from the south of England in 1988 and now own a large hotel. Having travelled around Scotland looking for a place to settle, they chose their present home because they "fell in love, not so much with the hotel, but with the view at the back". They say they are sensitive to the wishes of the people who come and stay at their hotel, "for the same reasons as we felt we needed to get away on holiday in Scotland before we settled here. People come here to get away from the noise of televisions and traffic." The leaflet they produce to promote the hotel describes it as a 'sanctuary from the stress of urban living'.

In-migrants and tourists alike are attracted to an idealised rural Scotland, and many seek out what they believe to be the last remaining areas of wilderness in the British Isles. Much of this image is reinforced by a steady flow of coffee-table books, for which there is a ready market, celebrating the grandeur of nature and the magnificence of Scottish scenery. Furthermore, there is a genre of wilderness writing, such as the works of Mike Tomkies, that points out the fragility of wildlife habitats and the ever present threat that the last wild places in Scotland are in danger of disappearing.[1] These are solitary places, it is argued, essential for the well-being of the human spirit in a complex and alienating age, as well as a refuge for a diminishing variety of indigenous flora and fauna struggling to survive the onslaught of modern industrial society. Characteristics become attributable to certain places, so that they become places of pilgrimage for tourists, or are known to be 'inaccessible' and relatively remote (such as Knoydart, Scoraig and Orkney) and thus attractive to potential incomers.

This image is reproduced in the accounts migrants offer to explain their moving away from urban life to the live Highlands. Certainly, many of the incomers to Orkney in Forsythe's (1974) study saw the ideal of self-sufficiency afforded by crofting and small farming as a way of 'escaping to fulfilment'. Others emphasise the attraction of the promise of beauty and tranquillity to be found in a group of islands far from any metropolitan centre. With fewer people in Britain involved in agriculture directly, or dependent on employment in rural based industries, images of rural life are constructed by an urban population rather than by those actually working in the countryside, and so the rural is a kind of blank screen upon which can be projected images which offer an alternative to the urban setting. As was described in chapter two among urban residents there is a deeply ingrained belief that life on the land is the true and natural heritage of the nations of the British Isles, the source of each nation's life and identity. Glasgow is, as Edwin Muir remarked, merely another industrial city, not a Scottish city. To find that distinctive Scottish quality one must turn to its source, the landscape and its inhabitants. The love of countryside is a national obsession, cultivated by the heritage industry and the proponents of a new ruralism that sees the landscape as '. . . our living link with our history, the visible expression of our British roots, and that if we allow it to change, the link is broken forever' (Sinclair 1990:6).

Incomers describe the Scottish Highlands as offering an alternative to what they believe to be a pervasive materialism that motivates life in urban centres. For some, finding the place they eventually settled in was the final resolution of a journey, an end to searching for somewhere they believed existed for them. Gavin and Kay L., a couple in their early forties and originally from Ayrshire, settled in Skerray on the north Sutherland coast during the late 1970s and, explaining their reasons for choosing Skerray, said that "We knew we had to be here". Neither came from a farming background, although they had grown up in rural Ayrshire. After several years studying art and living in Leeds they made their move. Now, they live in an owner occupied croft with their three children, keep sheep and goats and raise beef cattle. Additional income from the sale of organically-grown vegetables to local hotels is supplemented by part-time casual work, and by lobster fishing. Kay also works whenever she can as a supply teacher in the Tongue primary school.

Both Gavin and Kay readily admit that they are white settlers, but Skerray is an area that has suffered more than its share of depopulation and locals, generally, recognise that its survival depends on people moving in. In north Sutherland as a whole, the population has fallen by 12% since 1971. Settlement is dispersed and the local economy is heavily dependent on crofting, forestry, estate work, and tourism. Dounreay in Caithness is also vital for providing employment. However, population is still declining absolutely and is expected to continue to do so unless there are increased opportunities for income generation. A decline in public services, together with substandard difficult makes living in Skerray less attractive to a wide range of people. While unemployment is not particularly high, a quarter of the population of north Sutherland is above the age of retirement.

Gavin and Kay have involved themselves in efforts to revitalise cultural life in Skerray and the surrounding area. Most notably they organise concerts and other cultural events in the village hall, bringing in theatre groups, folk musicians and artists, and arrange exhibitions. Gavin also derives inspiration from Skerray as a place, as a community, and has embarked on a long-term video project to record the 'essence' of Skerray; in short, what animates the settlement as a community and what makes it, as he believes, "a special place", together with the ways people living there express their sense of belonging. There is a pervading ambivalence in so far as people in Skerray are aware that the area is in a situation of decline, yet there is also a evidence of a vibrant living community.

Gavin's own sense of place, of belonging to Skerray is informed and given meaning by the croft which he works, and by feeling he is part of a crofting community with a distinct history but which is also part of the wider crofting network extending throughout the north west of Scotland. His commitment to crofting is inspired by a belief in its importance for Skerray's future. He shares the opinions held by Skerray's longer-term residents that existing crofting legislation denies young people the chance of entering crofting, and that as crofting in Skerray declines more croft houses will become holiday homes. Above all, however, Gavin represents a new kind of crofter who places emphasis on the ecological importance of crofting, a theme to be elaborated in chapter six.

It is evidently not, if indeed it ever is, simply an escapist wish that motivates incomers to relocate. One challenge of living in remote areas, often with no road access and public services, is about 'doing something' with the land. Rather than being 'refugees from the rat race', there are those incomers who are inspired by an environmental ethic, informed by ideas of stewardship and custodianship. People in Scoraig in Wester Ross, for example, are well aware that there are many, particularly the inhabitants of nearby communities, who label them as 'drop-outs' and 'hippies', but they are quick to point out that it is easier to be a drop-out in an urban environment than it is in Scoraig. "Survival in Scoraig", one man argued, "is only possible through hard work, by earning one's own living, and by being integrated with the wider economy, not isolated from it." The population of Scoraig is around seventy, and the people generate their own electricity through windmill power, they keep sheep and raise cattle, they grow organic crops and vegetables, they build and repair boats, make musical instruments, produce pottery and other crafts, and are engaged in fish farming. There are others who also derive some income from limited and specialised tourism.

Tom Forsyth was one of the first settlers to repopulate Scoraig successfully after the failure of earlier attempts in the late 1940s, and he arrived by way of several other places, including the Iona community. Dissatisfied with materialism, his was almost a spiritual quest for a place in which to explore the possibilities of the self and to lead a meaningful way of life. Tom Forsyth considers himself first and foremost a crofter, but his home is also open as a retreat for others who wish to experience Scoraig and to share the vision he has of Scoraig setting a precedent for a different kind of environmental ethic and land use practice throughout the Highlands. This vision is one of communities integrated with the environment, and of people nurturing a sense of place through a deep intimacy with their surroundings. It was this vision that inspired his involvement with the Isle of Eigg Trust.

The Isle of Eigg Trust was set up in 1990 to raise enough money from individuals and organisations to purchase Eigg after the Court of Session ordered the owner, Keith Schellenberg, to sell it. This state of affairs came about because of a long and drawn out legal battle between Schellenberg and his former wife over the estate. Schellenberg had bought Eigg for a quarter of a million pounds in 1975, thus becoming the latest in a long line of owners dating back to the nineteenth century. The mismanagement of Eigg over a long period had resulted in a situation of decline familiar to other parts of the Highlands which the Trust hoped to reverse if it succeeded in buying the estate. According to Tom Forsythe, rather than see the estate owned by yet another remote individual, the Trust's aim was to see the interests of the inhabitants served in a way that would allow the island to develop. Once bought, the estate would be held in trust for the island's residents, the majority of whom were said to support the Isle of Eigg Trust and its plan for a new type of land ownership. Residents would be involved at all levels of decision-making; decisions affecting their lives would no longer be made within a context of an anachronistic, feudal system of land ownership.

Central to the Trust's plan for Eigg was the importance placed on an increase in population if the island was to prosper. It was hoped that much of this increase would be brought about by in-migration. New land holdings would be created and incomers encouraged to settle on the island. In order to ensure the stability of these new holdings, the Trust would guarantee security of tenure worked out along the same lines as that enjoyed by the existing crofting population. As well as the planned population growth, transport facilities would be improved, including the renovation of the harbour and pier, and EC grants would be secured for this purpose. Other facilities envisaged for the estate included a community hall, and a schooling system based on that developed in Scoraig. In Scoraig, parents had reacted to having to send their children as weekly boarders to Ullapool High School, and seeing them only briefly at weekends, by declaring educational independence and teaching them in their own school. The long journey to Ullapool and a prolonged absence from home was said by parents to place unnecessarily high levels of stress and strain on their children. There is a primary school in Scoraig and older children have been attending the community's high school for the last six years or so. The teachers remain self-employed, and the school's Apple Macintosh computers are powered by their own locally generated electricity.

The Isle of Eigg Trust also planned to build what it called a Life Centre. This would be a centre designed to explore the possibilities of alternative energy and technology that could be used on the island. It would also be a place where urban residents could come and seek new perspectives on life, and so return home having acquired 'a sense of balance' that would allow them to get some satisfaction out the urban experience. The Trust envisaged professional and managerial people coming to the Eigg Life Centre to learn how to build dry-stone dykes, to work on crofts, to help at lambing time, and to shear sheep and so on.

Tourism was also something the Trust wished to see developed on a significant scale. Not only would tourism bring much-needed income to the island, tourists were considered key contributors to the rejuvenation of life and culture on Eigg. Tom Forsyth believed that the Trust was not only the most suitable alternative to the present land ownership system, it was also the only way to safeguard the future of what he regarded as a unique way of life, a Celtic culture integrated with the environment. Through the stewardship of the Trust, the residents of Eigg would be able to realise their full potential, an opportunity denied them under private landowners. However, the Trust was, in the end, unsuccessful in its attempt to buy the estate. Instead, in 1992 the Isle of Eigg was re-purchased by Keith Schellenberg. Yet, in 1994, Schellenberg was finally forced to sell owing to antagonism towards him from the island's residents. Police suspected arson as the reason for a fire at Schellenberg's home, while the laird himself, as reported in *The Independent* on January 28th 1994, accused islanders of attempting to burn him out, just as his predecessors had done to their ancestors during the Clearances.

Significantly, incomers and outsiders were the prime organisers of the Isle of Eigg Trust. They were making a challenge to an existing pattern of external land ownership long regarded as unjust, one that placed restrictions on communities, and indeed precipitated their decline and was one cause of emigration. There is perhaps no more emotive issue in many Highland communities than the existing pattern of land ownership, but accusations of insensitivity on the part of absentee-landlords have rarely been translated at the local level into direct action to remedy the situation. It is still the case, therefore, that for the inhabitants of the Highlands, the land to which they feel they belong does not belong to them, except symbolically and metaphorically through its appropriation in place names and as a memoryscape of the personal and collective biographies which are the realities of identity. However, as will be shown in the next chapter, local empowerment and control of the land is being realised by the Assynt Crofters Trust who have perhaps set a precedent for a new pattern of land ownership in Scotland by purchasing the North Lochinver estate. This new pattern is inspired by ideas of stewardship or custodianship. For Alan Macrae, the Assynt Crofters Trust Chairman, local acquisition of land is the only way that rural communities can benefit and thrive. Sustainabilty is the aim of the Assynt crofters, who argue that it is only though stewardship that sustainabilty is possible.

Creating a Sustainable Economy

The management and use of natural resources is a major issue in Highland communities. The Assynt Crofters Trust recognises that crofting must adapt to changing circumstances. Having acquired the land that they have always felt was theirs, the next step is to manage it in a what the chairman of the Assynt Crofters Union calls a "responsible way". One of the most important tasks is to work the land in a way that does not contribute to the neglect and decline of the last one hundred years or so and that left Assynt, like other Highland areas, impoverished. This idea of a sustainable rural land-use economy is held by many incomers who share a similar vision of a Highland future as that held by the Assynt crofters.

On the Scoraig peninsula, this vision is of natural resources managed effectively by the residents. This, it is argued, is the only way to create favourable conditions for successful diversification. There are some people who have set aside areas on their crofts so that they can revert back to 'natural conditions', and tree-planting and allowing regeneration of trees is a favoured activity. Indeed, it is tree-planting that concretely expresses the environmental ethic shared by incomers, not only in Scoraig, but elsewhere in the Highlands. In Skerray, for example, one incomer who was crofting said that he had got permission from the common grazings committee to fence off part of his share in the common grazings and "just see what happens". His intention was to "let the trees grow back", aiming in his modest way "to contribute to reversing the ecological decline of the Highlands".

There are incomers who share the ideologies of the Scottish Green Party and its rural manifesto for the Highlands. This calls primarily for sound resource management by creating a forest economy, announced as the Second Great Wood of Caledon. The manifesto argues that it is only through reforestation and the nurturing of a forest economy that the integration of ecology, economy and culture is possible. There are also spiritual and aesthetic ideals which underlie this vision The vocabulary of the Scottish Green Party is part of a wider discourse concerning notions of global responsibility, about helping to stabilise the climate and regenerate the planet. The Second Great Wood of Caledon would provide a renewable resource

> for more people than ever before to live in a new harmony with each other and the land, under new forms of land stewardship which would allow for the growth of uncompetitive, stable and non-exploitative relationships. (Scottish Green Party 1989:16)

For the Scottish Green Party, the quality and quantity of what the land can yield is a high priority, together with increased employment opportunities, and the effective management of wild animals (and even the introduction of wild animals such as elk). Central to this new forest economy is an increase in population, pointing to a positive impact of in-migration. Here it is argued that repopulation is not only desirable, it is essential for the cultural and ecological survival of the Highlands. An example of the type of land-use practice that the Scottish Green Party envisages is that found in Norway, where valleys are thickly populated, people live on small farms and where small industry thrives. Healthy forests flank the hills. This is contrasted with what the manifesto calls upside-down Highland land-use, where conifers grow along the floor of the glen and sheep graze on upland pasture. A forest economy would bring a high standard of living, an increase in public services and amenities, and a growth in the rural population. Here then, is a conservationist ethic that puts people in places, that is concerned with the survival of local economies, and looks positively upon repopulation. This contrasts with another kind of conservationist ethic that has a definite anti-people approach and that seeks to protect places by defining them as heritage areas.

Places as Heritage Areas

In 1990–91 there was considerable controversy surrounding plans by the Countryside Commission for Scotland to create up to four national parks in Scotland. What became known as the 'national park debate' represented yet another example of the tensions, and myths, surrounding environmental issues in the countryside of Britain in general. The areas singled out for designation were Loch Lomond, the Cairngorms, Ben Nevis/Glencoe, and Wester Ross. Initial public reaction in these areas was generally negative and the Commission was unsure as to whether the opposition was to the designation of these areas or to the title of national park (McGregor 1991). But because of a lack of consensus in Parliament regarding the Commission's plans, the government opposed the creation of national parks in favour of its own scheme to establish natural heritage areas.

The proposals to designate parts of Scotland as natural heritage areas were outlined by the Scottish Secretary Ian Lang in March 1991, with the Natural Heritage (Scotland) Bill subsequently going through Parliament. As a result the Countryside Commission for Scotland and the Nature Conservancy Council for Scotland, the Government's two main Scottish environmental agencies, were merged in April 1992 to form Scottish Natural Heritage. There remained considerable opposition among conservationists to natural heritage areas, however, and a lobby group (the Scottish Council for National Parks) continued to campaign for the establishment of national parks.

The scheme for the creation of national parks met with considerable local opposition. For example, in Wester Ross, at the Countryside Commission for Scotland public consultation meetings held in Lochcarron in 1989, many residents said that they wanted to be better informed about what the activities of central and local government, together with outside business interests, would mean to the area. There was concern expressed to the effect that external designations would not work without local support and that a national park would be harmful to the future of those communities within its boundaries. There is a similar suspicion about natural heritage areas.

The national park is a North American concept which developed in an attempt to preserve and protect areas of supposed pristine wilderness, together with the flora and fauna indigenous to those areas. The concept of the national park was also inspired by a belief that wilderness, as the property of the nation, should be protected by the nation. Based on similar ideals, ten national parks were established in England and Wales following the passing of the National Parks and Access to the Countryside Act of 1949. No parks were established in Scotland. There is a crucial difference between United States and U.K. patterns of national park ownership. The federal government owns around one third of the total land area of the U.S., some 10% of which is designated as national parks. In the U.K., where much land is privately owned, 9% of the total land area is designated as national parks, yet only 2% of all national park land is owned by the state. As a result most land in Britain's national parks is owned by someone else. This means that, unlike the U.S. Department of the Interior National Parks

Service, which has complete legislative and management authority over all national parks in the U.S., there is no British government agency that has comparable control over national parks in the U.K.

National parks in the U.S. are in 'wilderness' areas which are virtually free of a human population, while the parks in England and Wales are quite often densely populated, living and working landscapes. Parks in both countries are managed for the people who visit them, rather than for those who live in them. This is more pertinent to parks in England and Wales, although the designation of wildlife refuges and national parks in Alaska, while aiming to protect animals and the environment (especially from oil and gas development), restricts the rights of Native peoples to hunt and fish in those areas. While conservationists express a sincere concern for wildlife and the environment, the ways of life of those people dependent on the use of natural resources are often regarded as expendable (Brower 1988:42).

Changes in American environmental consciousness can be traced from Washington Irving's 'storied associations' of places in the landscape, and a frontier spirit (so vividly portrayed by James Fenimore Cooper), through to Emerson's philosophy about nature revealing itself through man, and on to a Thoreau- inspired back to the land quest for harmony and grace. Recent nature writing that uses the backdrop of Alaska, for example, has drawn heavily on Native American principles for living in relation to the earth, often combining elements of Zen and Taoism (e.g. Nelson 1989). The Alaskan environmental movement is also endorsed by an academic environmentalism whose discourse is about nurturing a sense of place, living comfortably and sustainably with nature, exchanging gifts with the land, and 'groping towards grace' (e.g. Weeden 1992).

In North American nature writing, generally, nature is viewed as something inherently wild and dangerous (e.g. Dillard 1974, Lopez 1989), a harsh and unforgiving environment for humans to test themselves against (such as in the novels of Jack London), or as a source of spiritual nourishment (Haines 1981), or as simply a place to live in and write about (Monaghan 1983). This kind of literature is in keeping with a tradition that considers 'American space . . . the natural environment of a race fitted for a spacious destiny' (Coetzee 1988:60). In stark contrast, British, or more specifically, English attitudes to landscape are constructed from ideals of the beautiful, the sublime and the picturesque. Although by the beginning of the nineteenth century the picturesque had been superseded by the sublime and the romantic tradition associated with Wordsworth, whose work has recently been reinterpreted as a 'romantic ecology',[2] it has been suggested that 'the cult of the picturesque made the contemplation of landscape a widespread cultural recreation' (Coetzee 1988:40).

Instead of being perceived as a place of savagery, nature was celebrated by eighteenth and nineteenth century poetry and prose as a place where man could discover his essential self and his inner life, through solitude and contemplation. The landscape was imbued with a natural harmony, a place of discovery and reawakening, untouched, unaltered by humans. Through an idealisation of rural life by writers, artists, poets and social observers, and as a powerful motif in literature, the countryside was depicted as an area of harmony and peace. Where there was natural harmony there was also social harmony; conflict and change were regarded as only taking place in the city. In this way villages and the imagined natural ease of rural life was contrasted with the suffering, squalor and unnatural life of the cities. As Williams has put it

> The 'modern world', both in its suffering and, crucially, in its protest against suffering, is mediated by reference to a lost condition which is better than both and which can place both: a condition imagined out of a landscape and a selective observation and memory (1973:180)

The British countryside, having been attributed a 'traditional' appearance has become the concern of a conservationist lobby that has assumed responsibility for preventing the further destruction of the countryside. But conservation is concerned not only with halting development and preventing the loss of wildlife habitats and landscapes of special scientific and aesthetic interest, but also with the preservation of the countryside. Such preservationist ideals aim to solidify the past and commodify the landscape, in order to underpin institutionalised notions of heritage. Conservationists may wish to preserve landscapes because of their natural beauty, but these landscapes are also considered to be cultural artefacts, symbols of a shared past and crucial contributors to a sense of national identity.

Scottish Natural Heritage was established to defend and protect what are regarded as natural Highland landscapes. The underlying philosophy is in some ways similar to that of national parks authorities. But there is then a danger that Scottish Natural Heritage will ignore the fact that these 'natural' landscapes are the result of a long process of decline, neglect and destruction. Focusing on pristine wilderness, the Scottish conservationist lobby makes a fundamental error by ignoring the human element in the landscape, while at the same time recognising the human need for the continued existence of rural landscapes. In contemporary Britain heritage is regarded figuratively as the product of an industry (Hewison 1987), something manufactured on a large scale and actually replacing real industries, including agriculture. Natural heritage areas are inextricably linked to the existing romantic and mythical representation of Scotland, a feeling articulated by observers of the Scottish scene as hegemonic in repressing Scots' own sense of identity (e.g. see McCrone 1989).

While there is concern over uncontrolled tourism, forestry, and industrial development, a significant point about natural heritage areas is that they threaten to redefine areas of Scotland in terms of their importance for the heritage of the United Kingdom as a whole. To consider this in terms of the nation's requirements is to ignore the significance of the locality. In attempting to preserve a perceived traditional landscape and the meanings attached to places, new places are imagined, created and imposed. The sense of a shared past symbolised by the landscape becomes commoditised and objectified, almost homogenised. The landscape is less one of subjective experience and multifarious meaning - a locality - and more one that is morally and aesthetically valued in wider national and naturalistic, rather than existential, terms.

Local people fear that somehow the institutionalisation of heritage areas will have severe implications for local ways of life, such as crofting. Fears are certainly not unfounded that a natural heritage area would effectively ignore local knowledge and human experience which are important for a sense of community and identity in the Highlands. Because preservation and conservation inform notions of heritage, crofters are faced with restrictions that would deny crofting any chance of growth, innovation, diversification, and adaptation which are vital for the future well-being of many settlements. The argument advanced by crofting interests is that conservation is misguided in emphasising preservation. What crofting needs is a conservation policy and an indiscriminate attitude towards crofting on the part of Scottish Natural Heritage. This means recognising that conservation can be achieved by allowing croft land to be worked, and for land that has fallen into disuse to be designated as croft land rather than fencing it off and labelling it as a natural heritage area to be protected.

For any form of environmental management to succeed, a participatory approach between environmental agencies and local communities to be affected by such management is needed, and anthropologists have described successful management programmes working to this approach which do work. As an alternative to 'rational' science-based management, a participatory approach requires the involvement of local people in the design and implementation of environmental and development projects. For example, participatory approaches to resource management have been developed most strikingly in parts of the Arctic. In the Arctic, where many Native communities rely on subsistence hunting and fishing, central government agencies responsible for resource management have, on the whole, recognised the value of the indigenous environmental knowledge of those people dependent on the use of natural resources. This has led to the integration of conventional scientific management with traditional knowledge. As a result, co-operative wildlife management programmes have been effective for several years in Canada and Alaska (e.g. Berkes 1982, Freeman 1989). Furthermore, Inuit in Greenland, Canada and Alaska have set a precedent for local control of resources and environmental management by implementing their own conservation strategies to safeguard the future of Inuit resource utilisation (Nuttall 1993b, 1993c). Here, conservation is not preservationist, but user-based.

It is somewhat surprising that, while indigenous environmental knowledge and traditional resource management strategies in the Arctic have been taken seriously by advocates of 'rational' science-based systems, communities in rural Scotland face restrictions on realising the potential use of natural resources. Environmental management is more likely to succeed if a degree of decision-making power is given to local organisations. Given the present pattern of land ownership in Scotland, it is difficult for local organisations to be effective in decision-making processes regarding resource management. In Greenland and the North American Arctic, the achievement of Native land claims settlements and aboriginal self-government, has meant that local populations, and the Native organisations that represent them, now have constitutionally protected rights and the legislative power, in some cases, to implement policies that actually control and monitor human activity in the Arctic, and allow some control over the level and extent of development.

It is important that locally specific cultural values are integrated into aspects of resource management and economic development policy in rural Scotland, and perhaps resource management programmes in the Arctic can provide models for design and implementation. Yet, Arctic communities have enjoyed a level of cultural politicisation unknown in Scotland, and indigenous knowledge in Scottish rural areas is often ignored and local people are not recognised as a valuable source of environmental knowledge and expertise. At one meeting of the Bettyhill branch of the Crofters Union in January 1992, this attitude was very much in evidence. Local crofters from the parishes of Farr and Tongue had met, not only to conduct union business, but to hear the views of a member of what was still the Nature Conservancy Council for Scotland, and two members-elect of the board of Scottish Natural Heritage, on what the new agency's policy would be for North Sutherland. One of the latter two men had failed to get off to a good start with the thirty or so people who attended, before the meeting had even commenced. Striding into the lounge of the hotel where the meeting was held, the first thing he did was examine the peats used for the fire and express abhorrence at the way they had been cut. Holding one peat aloft, he remarked how it was a fine example of the damage caused by peat-cutting machines, rather than the more 'environmentally friendly' traditional cutting of peat by hand.

The subject of peat cutting was one that was returned to as the meeting progressed. The three speakers expressed concern about ecological destruction in the Highlands, and talked of the need to preserve areas of peat bog from non-traditional cutting methods. With the aid of overhead projections, maps of the north of Sutherland were used to show areas of peat bog that were of scientific interest. When one woman asked "of scientific interest to whom?", the reply came that they were 'of interest to Scottish National Heritage'. "What about the human interest?", the woman asked. The speakers argued that the conservation of natural landscapes was necessary precisely because it was in the human interest to do so, "before we lose the diversity of animal and plant species and natural habitats in which they thrive". In the crofters' defence, it was argued that, not only were the potentially protected peat bogs essential to the crofting communities concerned, they had been cut for several generations and still attracted a variety of bird life.

The counter-argument to this defence was that peat cutting was regarded as 'ecologically sound' if traditional methods were used, but hardly acceptable if modern technology replaced these methods. This precipitated heated debate on the importance of local knowledge, and about the need for conservationists to consult with crofters before making decisions about resource management. As one crofter put it:

> Who asks us about these things? And who makes the decisions? It seems to me that outsiders and white settlers are deciding on how we live here.

Following the meeting, one man spoke of his fears that conservationists were more concerned with preserving areas of scientific interest for tourists and incomers:

> All this talk of protection of nature and the environment. It's not anything to do with people living here. They want it all to look pretty for

visitors. They'll have us living in black houses next, to make us look more traditional. I suppose we're not really worth protecting. Maybe we're not primitive enough! Put us back in black houses, and we'll make pretty pictures for the tourists, out in the fields with the beasts and cutting the hay. And then we'll be worth protecting.

Some people, such as Alan Macrae of the Assynt Crofters Union, regard the designation of heritage areas as an attempt to keep people in a position of disempowerment, and to deliberately ignore the very things that visitors to the Highlands should really see and learn about:

A natural heritage area up here would mean signposts, nature trails, fenced off areas of interest. It would be a false heritage, ignoring the real heritage of the area. The Highland Clearances, the long hard struggle for land by generations of crofters, the struggle for security of tenure. This is the real heritage!

In the views of some, then, heritage areas are restrictive and potentially hegemonic.

Heritage is not only the concern of conservationists, politicians and planners. Incomers are also regarded as protagonists of the heritage industry. When they are accused of 'changing the area', this is not only understood in terms of affecting the demographic composition of local settlements, or assuming positions of power on local councils, having an impact on language or dialect, or buying up property and contributing to out-migration by forcing young people to look for affordable property elsewhere. Rather, such change stems from a qualitatively different orientation to the environment that ignores, and contributes to the erosion of, the personal and collective experiences that make a sense of place for local people meaningful. The ease with which people move from place to place is perhaps an aspect of modernity, 'the restless spirit of the age'. But even separated from a secure place-based community, there persists a human need to impose meaning on new places, to nurture a sense of identity and feeling of belonging as an antidote to the possibility of individual estrangement and despair. But the imposition of new meanings often results in the extinguishing of what already exists. Incomers, however, would not, perhaps, see themselves as changing an area, but some would consider that they deliberately contribute to its preservation. By doing so, there is a danger that places will stagnate and decline both physically and culturally. Paradoxically, it seems, while some incomers want to preserve the areas they move to, in many cases it is local people who want change and an opportunity for growth and development. Yet, at the same time, as will be shown in the next chapter, it is a powerful argument that rural areas actually need in-migration for economic development to be successful.

In the late winter of 1992 at a meeting in Farr of the local historical society for the north of Sutherland, one incomer, a woman from Lancashire and in her early forties, outlined her plans for a network of heritage and nature trails for the area. Stressing the importance of tourism for the local economy, she proposed that the historical society should design a number of marked trails and printed guides for visitors. These trails would introduce tourists to the 'variety of flora and fauna, and the geology found in the area'. Also included would be 'significant' historical details, such as information on local estates and on the local economy. It was notable that she did not mention the importance of Gaelic place names. When it was suggested to her that visitors would find place names and their meanings of interest, she dismissed this by replying that, for the time being, she was only concerned with designing nature trails. The landscape to be covered by such proposed nature and heritage trails is one that, like many others, had been cleared of most of its human population by the mid-nineteenth century. But depopulation has also continued into the twentieth century and several crofting townships have been abandoned in the last fifty years or so. At the initial proposal stage, at least, the heritage trails were not going to point to this as a landscape emptied of people, but one that is empty of people.

The controversy over the Skye bridge also offers an insight into the contested attitudes and conflicting visions of the Scottish rural future. Already under construction at the time of writing, the bridge will link Kyle of Lochalsh on the mainland to Kyleakin on Skye when completed. Construction has been disrupted by environmental groups, and while some anti-bridge feeling may express a romantic notion that Skye should be approached from the mainland by ferry, opposition from residents on Skye has centred on the government's plan for a privately-funded toll bridge, rather than the bridge itself. Local consensus seems to be that a bridge connecting Skye to the mainland is needed, but reaction to a toll bridge is negative and has been reported widely as one of dismay (e.g. Jackman 1991). Speaking on BBC Radio Scotland News in April 1991, the Labour MP Brian Wilson called it ". . . an act of historic wrongness" to impose a toll on the people of Skye. And while there has been some debate about whether residents should be exempt from paying to use the bridge, people who work on Skye but live on the mainland are not impressed by the prospect of a Skye bridge imposing tolls on non-residents.

The building of the Skye bridge throws into relief three competing orientations. Firstly, there is the concern expressed by conservationists over the environmental impact that the bridge and its construction will have. Secondly, there is a concern that the bridge will destroy the 'magic' and 'romance' of Skye. Thirdly, there is the environmental orientation of residents who are in favour of a bridge because of the potential economic benefits which improved transport links would bring. And it is worth mentioning that the construction of a road bridge linking the island of Burra with the Shetland mainland opened up new employment opportunities for Burra's residents (Byron 1986). But, with little or no decision-making powers vested in local organisations, there is growing demand for what is referred to as a 'community-based' approach to development. As a visitor to Skye mused, 'the people of Skye ought to build their own bridge and impose a toll on others for its use!' Instead of taking an anti-people approach of the kind that underlies conservationist and preservationist environmental orientations, a community-based approach to development is one that not only places people first, but one that aspires to effective environmental management as well as addressing a situation of powerlessness. However it is not an approach without its own problems, and this is a theme that will be taken up further in chapters six and seven.

One aspect of counterstream migration which this chapter has pointed to is that there is an obvious contradiction regarding development. On the one hand there is a widespread image of incomers as agents of change and disruption, yet on the other it is the locals who desire change, improvement and development, while incomers are in favour of conservation.[3] Yet, such a contradiction should hardly be surprising and is entirely consistent with the other kinds of issues and situations discussed in this book. While the complex we have called 'incomer' is a metaphor for change and that of 'local' for stability, the reality is ambiguous and does not make for a straightforward analysis.

Notes

[1] See for example Mike Tomkies, 1984. *A Last Wild Place*. London: Jonathan Cape. According to the dust jacket this book is 'much more than the chronicle of a man who left city life in order to study the wilderness' and the author 'reveals through his quest . . . our urgent need to become retuned to natural rhythms if mankind is to regain a measure of health and sanity in a world bent on self destruction.' These are sentiments, of great antiquity, which have already been encountered in connection with the anxiety aroused by rural depopulation discussed in chapter 2.

[2] See Bate (1991) who has produced a reading of Wordsworth in the light of the recent political history of the environment or 'green' movement.

[3] For example, islanders on Lewis, both incomer and local, formed an action group in early 1994 to protest against construction of a visitor centre at Na Tursaichean, the standing stones at Callanish on the west coast of the island. The visitor centre, due to be completed by summer 1995, is the plan of the Western Isles Council and has the backing of Historic Scotland, which sees the plan '. . . as bringing the magic of Na Tursaichean . . . to a wider, more appreciative audience' (*Scotland on Sunday* 27th February 1994).

Chapter 6

Crofting, Sustainability and the Highland Future

The politics of conservation have undergone a radical transition in recent years, as images and ideas of the British countryside and agricultural practices have been re-evaluated. At one time, the farmer was a symbol of rural stability, 'the embodiment of rustic simplicity' (Lowe et al 1986:25). Above all, the farmer was considered to be the natural conservationist, tending his crops and livestock, with the farm and its patchwork pattern of fields and hedgerows giving the countryside its 'natural' appearance. But such guardians of the countryside have quickly become the target of conservationist groups who now see the real threats to rural areas as emanating from intensive agricultural practices, together with forestry expansion, rather than originating principally from urban and industrial development. Both farming and forestry have been accused of having a devastating impact on the sustainable productivity of ecosystems by destroying habitats such as hedgerows, heathland, ancient deciduous woodland, grassland, and marshland. For conservationists, far from being 'a way of life', farming has become a large-scale agribusiness, a government-managed industry subject to wider national and European decision-making processes. This has provoked a conservationist response that seeks to expose the truth about the political economy of modern farming (e.g. Shoard 1987) and aims to curtail agricultural productivity.

Yet, as was pointed out in the previous chapter, environmental protection remains preservationist in aim and practice. Human activity, it is argued, has resulted in the loss of, and damage to, wildlife and landscape, and it is therefore human activity which has to be controlled. The conservation and management of natural resources, however, cannot be possible if they are viewed in isolation from, and as independent of, the rural economy. Two things are considered crucial for the future of the countryside in Britain as a whole: the responsible and effective management of natural resources and the rejuvenation of the rural economy. Neither is possible if an anti-people approach to conservation is adopted. Rather, to ensure the health and stability of both the physical and social landscape a new conservation ethic needs to be adopted. This would recognise that ecological, cultural and psychological aspects of rural life cannot be separated from one another, and that culturally specific values should inform rural development and resource management policy. The future of rural areas is held to depend on 'thriving communities' which can absorb and benefit from economic in-vestment, that no longer suffer from continued ou-migration, and which are characterised by diversification in an integrated economy. Effective conservation of landscapes would be achievable through a user-based ap-proach, rather than a preservationist approach, and it is this argument that will be considered here by focusing on crofting in the Scottish Highlands.

Rural society in the Highlands is inextricably bound up with crofting. This chapter examines the contemporary situation of crofting with particu-lar regard to four areas of social and cultural interest. First of all there is the continuing effect of crofting in defining and characterising the distinctive quality that is the Highlands, a quality which people draw upon to sustain both individual and collective identities. Secondly, crofting is perceived to be undergoing a transformation so that its supporters argue its case now as a model for sustainable rural development for the future rather than as a relic from the past worth preserving in this modern age as an example of a way of life which has virtually disappeared. Thirdly, crofting offers an al-ternative to high input agri-business and its concomitant negative envi-ronmental impact. Finally, and crucially, crofters and the representatives of crofting interests see the crofting system as having the potential to estab-lish, through ideas of stewardship and community empowerment, an alter-native to the existing system of land ownership in Scotland. As this chapter will discuss, there are many people who firmly believe that the future sur-vival of crofting depends on 'new blood', not only from within the crofting communities themselves, but from outside. In this way, incomers are en-couraged and welcomed.

Crofting: Livelihood and Identity

A croft typically, as has already been noted in the previous chapter, comprises an area of arable and grazing land adjacent to the crofthouse and a share in a common pasture of rough hill grazing. However, it is important to appreciate the extent to which crofting is an institution as well as a practice. The grazing share in the common pasture enjoyed by each croft is defined as a fraction of the total stocking capacity of the common grazing. The crofts and their shares in the common grazing vary in size. The crofts which together share a common grazing comprise what is called a township. The herds and flocks of individual crofters run together on the common grazing and it is a requirement by Act of Parliament that all those who have a share in the common grazing must elect from among themselves a committee, which has power to raise dues in the township, to administer the grazing and the management of the flocks and herds, as well as its pens, fences, dips and other equipment. The common grazing and the statutory basis of the grazings committee endows the individual crofts with a material common interest and imparts an objective reality to the township as a community. A township is much more than families dwelling together as neighbours in a collection of houses.

Nevertheless a crofter and the township in which he has shares in the common grazing is a tenant of a landlord, though, since the Act of 1886, the crofter enjoys almost absolute security of tenure. Assignation is the main means by which croft tenancies normally change hands and are therefore the subject of considerable local interest in the rest of the township because of the likely implications for the other shareholders in the common grazings, as well as of wider interest among people who wish to acquire a croft. By law a crofter is able to assign the croft to a spouse or cognatic relative provided that the consent of the landlord is obtained[1]. If the landlord withholds consent, or there are objections to the effect that the person to whom the croft is being assigned is not a relative, then the Crofters Commission has powers to intervene and may declare the croft vacant. Many crofters believe that the Commission ought to choose a tenant from among applicants but that is still a right of the landowner. When the person to whom the croft is being assigned is not a relative then approval of the Commission must be given. In considering whether of not to grant the assignation the Commission's stated aim is to ensure that crofting communities are healthy, that the land is worked, and that the operation of the township is viable socially and economically.

The person to whom the croft is assigned will normally compensate the crofter an agreed sum for improvements to the croft which the crofter has carried out, such as rebuilding and modernising the croft house, out buildings, and the like. In cases where the assignee is not a relative the money paid over can approximate to a market price. However, whether imagined or real, the common grazing land and associated cooperative and communal practices, together with the privileges of kinship relationships as regards access to crofts, obviously preserve a link to an earlier epoch, of a kin based society of clans and communal land tenure, long before the Crofters Act of 1886 and the Clearances of the late eighteenth and nineteenth century. In this way the institution of crofting works to accommodate both the values of a market economy of freely entered contracts and the particular privileges and status which arise from identities based in kinship relationships, association with particular localities, and being part of an exclusive institution. The material reality of the obligations of cooperation and joint interests in each township as well as the cultural meaning and the ideology of crofting as an institution inherently linked and confined to a defined region (the 'Crofting Counties') are together, throughout the Highlands and Islands, a powerfully rich domain from which can be borrowed images to articulate and express the idea of community. It provides a source for individual and community identity, a symbol of a 'traditional' lifestyle, giving what Cameron (1980:14) calls 'that strong identity and continuity of family and place that passes down in an ancestral landscape'.

Moreover, crofting, which is essentially a part time occupation, means that the institution, through the crofters themselves working in a wide range of other sectors of the economy, engages directly with the rest of Highlands and Islands society.[2] As Cohen observed of an island in Shetland, crofting has 'more salience as an idea than as an economic activity' (Cohen 1987:100). The crofting community penetrates, and is penetrated by, the wider society in a way that does not apply to, for example, full time farming. There are, of course, variations from one part of the region to another as regards the objective proportion of crofts and crofters to the rest of the population and this may well have implications for the culture of the local society.. The contrast between the islands of Skye and Mull is extreme and often made, but usually informative. On Skye there are 1808 crofts and about one in six of the total population is a crofter while on Mull there are only 113 crofts and one in twenty of the population is a crofter.[3] It may well be that the reported sense of the 'Englishing' of Mull is in part at least a function of the relative attenuation of the presence of crofting on that island as a consequence of the simple dilution of crofters in the island's population.

The interpenetration of crofting as an institution with wider society has in turn consequences for the nature of crofting. With a croft on average providing employment for only two days a week, unless income generating work can be found for the remaining days of the week then the croft and the crofter face impoverishment. By the same token when the crofter can enjoy other sources of income so the croft and the crofter flourish. However, during the economic depression of the interwar years such opportunities were limited, and even in to the 1950s the Highlands and Islands did not share directly in the post war expansion of the British economy. Official policy, as expressed for example, by the Taylor Commission of Enquiry into the Condition of Crofting, took the view that crofting must become a full time occupation and therefore that crofts must be encouraged to amalgamate into fewer and larger and economically viable units, in effect small farms. Complementing this approach is the proliferation of subsidies for agricultural production.[4] However, during the last twenty years there has been a growth and diversification of the Highland economy and with it a growing confidence among crofters. Indicative of this was the establishment of a new Scottish Crofters Union in 1988. Four years later it had 4,500 members in 58 branches. Few crofters can hope to have more than several acres of arable land and a share in the common hill grazings. Survival in crofting, therefore, depends on occupational diversity and pluriactivity and, as we shall see, there is concern to ensure that rural development policy recognises this as rural areas become less dependent on agriculture. At the same time retaining a crofting population cannot be achieved by more and more complex schemes of subsidy and grants directed at the two days a week on the croft. Though even here there are indications of the new role of crofting in the environment with the addition to the list of schemes the Goose Scaring Scheme and the Corncrake Initiative.[5] More significant has been the Crofters Forestry Act 1992, initiated by the Scottish Crofters Union who negotiated with the Land Owners' Federation and the Scottish Office, which changed the law so that the crofter who plants trees is the owner of them and not the land owner as was previously the case, although the consent of the land owner is still required.

Identity and cultural continuity are recognised as central for the future of the crofting way of life by the representatives of modern crofting, the Crofters Commission (Ughdarras Nan Croitearan), and the Scottish Crofters Union (Aonadh Nan Croitearan) and its various local branches. Although crofters were given statutory rights to buy their crofts with the passing of the Crofting Reform (Scotland) Act in 1976, very few have opted to become owners and have remained as tenants. Out of 17,500 registered crofts in the Highlands and Islands, less than 2,600 are owner-occupied. Those who buy their crofts are no longer the secure tenants of a landlord, and, while they may gain the right to sell their house and land in the property market, they relinquish certain rights as crofter tenants, such as access to the valuable and valued Croft Buildings Grants and Loan Scheme, and, from the early 1950s until the introduction of the Community Charge, a fifty percent discount from rates. A discount is being reintroduced since the Community Charge was abolished because the Council Tax is partly based on the market value of houses and this does not apply to crofts. However, they do remain eligible for other subsidies such as the Crofting Counties Agricultural Grants Scheme.

But whatever might be the gains to owner occupation, and, except in some few specially favoured crofts as regards property development potential, they are at best marginal, the symbolic consequences are enormous. Throughout the nineteenth century security of tenure as holders of heritable tenancies was hard fought for and many crofters are reluctant to relinquish their rights. One crofter, a man from Lochinver in his mid-thirties, summed up this general feeling when he said 'My ancestors fought for this right. Their blood ran in rivers through the crofting landscape'. Furthermore, there are crofters who associate the 1976 Crofting Reform Act with a tradition of historical events that began with the Clearances, because they believe the main beneficiaries of individual croft ownership would really be the landowner who has sold the croft, and the government, whose fiscal position as regards the crofter is improved. The transition from tenant to landlord also disrupts the existing structure of social relationships in crofting communities. There remains a feeling prevalent in crofting circles that unless what is popularly described as the feudal nature of landownership in Scotland is altered, there will be no benefit to those crofters who, one by one, decide to buy their crofts and, in effect, take their property out of the crofting, but a cumulative loss to crofting as an institution. While the 1976 Act allows for crofts to be withdrawn from the crofting institution, in practice the removal of the croft from the Commissions list of crofts the Act specifically does not permit the creation of new crofts, that is, the addition of crofts to those already listed as such by the Commission.

One of the most difficult and sensitive issues which is associated with the loss of land to crofting is the assignation of crofts to individuals from other parts of the United Kingdom and the demand for crofts from young local people. Despite the complicated nature of crofting tenure which requires, when a croft is being assigned to a non-kinsmen, the approval of the Crofters Commission and the landlord, a number of incomers acquire crofts each year. Outside the crofting counties 'incomers' would be cited as the cause of local people being excluded from local property, but in the crofting counties the necessary intervention of the Crofters Commission in such cases means that it is this body that attracts some of the opprobrium and the blame for allowing non-local people to acquire crofts. However, as the Commission points out in its defense, it cannot choose who should be assigned a croft, that is a right which belongs to each individual crofter who must decide between a rich 'incomer' willing to pay a high level of compensation in cash, and the poor 'local' who cannot.

The Future for Crofting

Raymond O'Malley, a teacher from south west England who worked a croft in the West Highlands during World War II, in his account of his crofting experiences, wrote that 'some day the democratic notion may prevail that the individual members of the human race all have equal claim upon the most precious of the world's resources; and if that day comes the crofter and the despised peasant farmer may come back into their own.' (1947:9)

O'Malley's sentiments are echoed in the present by leading advocates of crofting such as James Hunter, the first director of the new Scottish Crofters Union. Hunter argues that crofting has a claim to be taken seriously as an ecologically-sound form of land use that achieves a balance between nature and people in the rural environment. Hunter's vision extends to new crofts spreading out beyond the conventional crofting counties to other parts of rural Scotland, some of them to be created on derelict industrial land, which would encourage a new generation of part-time and hobby farmers (Hunter 1989, 1991). Part-time farming has tended to be an urban fringe phenomenon, and in Scotland the landscape of the industrial belt of central Scotland between Glasgow and Edinburgh is the target for an official policy of small holdings and new part- time farming areas (Cramb 1991). Quite possibly, unlike the worker-peasants of the nineteenth century who combined factory and farm work, the new part-time and hobby farmers will be drawn from professional and managerial occupations given that part-time farmers must derive the greater part of their income from other forms of employment, and that substantial investment is needed if the enterprise is to succeed in having the kind of attractive environmental impact which is desired. Much of the appeal of part-time farming, however, must lie in its recreational value. It is a way of getting back to the land, but not being tied to it, an attempt, perhaps, to discover one's rural roots inspired by '. . . the comforting myth of a lost world in which mankind lived in closer harmony with nature' (Sinclair *ibid.* 15), a myth that took on greater meaning as the Industrial Revolution gathered momentum.

In other parts of the British Isles a return to small farming and cottage farming is regarded as a desirable alternative for those who aspire to a greater quality of life rather than remain unemployed in a suburban housing estate. For this reason among others, in the west of Ireland there is a slow process of rural rejuvenation, contrasting with the terminal decline of the late 1960s and 1970s chronicled so vividly by Brody (1973)[6]. Families disillusioned with rising levels of crime, drug abuse, poor housing conditions and unemployment in Dublin are taking advantage of a new scheme called Rural Resettlement, started by a man named Jim Connolly[7]. With over two thousand families on their waiting list, Rural Resettlement is able to find homes for people in such places as County Clare and County Limerick. Through the scheme, people are also able to learn, at classes in Dublin, skills that are necessary for rural living, such as turf cutting, handicrafts and some agricultural techniques. Most people who have already moved are renting homes, while some are able to buy property, and Rural Resettlement is hoping to have its financial problems eased by grants from the Irish government and from the EU. Finding employment in the west of Ireland is no easier than in urban areas and some families have to rely on welfare or casual work. As rural living throughout the British Isles is now one possible choice of 'lifestyle' among several, existing on welfare in a place of one's choice is preferable to the alternative of life on welfare in a depressed urban setting. This is a sentiment echoed throughout the Highlands and Islands of Scotland. For example, as a prawn fisherman on Skye put it, "if you're going to be unemployed, you may as well be unemployed here".

The migrants to Ireland's western seaboard are known by the established and long-term residents as 'blow-ins'. Initially, and as is probably to be expected, the 'locals' were reported to be worried about competition for jobs coming from the 'blow-ins'. However, the return of people to the deserted shores and empty cottages of Limerick, Clare, Connemara and other places has actually saved jobs, as the numbers of children in local schools has increased and more rural residents means greater demand for local services. As was noted in chapter one and chapter two, the unstated assumption in the expressions of concern about depopulation in rural Scotland is that 'locals' will return to repopulate the abandoned crofts and townships. While repopulation in the Scottish Highlands and other rural areas has been achieved by people other than 'locals' and 'exiles', the resettlement underway in Ireland's western seaboard can perhaps make claims to be the kind of 'mass resurrection' wished for by Scotland's poets, as many of the 'blow-ins' are returning to the land they or their parents had no choice but to leave. By returning to the small farms of the west, the urban Irish are making a claim to a life that is their rightful heritage.

It is forcefully argued by Hunter and others that crofting can provide the basis and the future for highly diversified rural economies in Scotland. Within a European context, given that the European Community is seeking to limit agricultural productivity, rural regeneration will be successful if other sources of income and employment can be combined with less intensive farming. Furthermore, after a long history of emigration, rural repopulation is regarded as both a sign of a vital landscape and the cause of the rejuvenation of remote rural areas of the British Isles. The extension of crofting in Scotland is now seen as one way to encourage more people to move to the countryside from urban areas and combine crofting or hobby farming with other activities.

This emphasis on crofting as having a vital role to play in shaping the future of rural Scotland contrasts sharply with attitudes that prevailed until relatively recently. As mentioned earlier in this chapter, crofting is not, and never has been, viable in an agricultural sense. Indeed, up until the 1960s, crofting was regarded as 'essentially inefficient, outmoded and generally incapable of adaptation to the requirements of a modern economy' (Hunter 1991:202). Crofting was believed to be a problem, something that hindered the economic and agricultural development of the Highlands and Islands. It was generally supposed that crofting was responsible for the 'backwardness' and destitution of the area. It was also a system that was seen to be in decline, offering nothing to the young but hardship and grinding poverty. The only option was to leave the crofting areas in the hope of finding an alternative to such a hopeless life.

In the 1930s and after the second world war, at a time when the overriding concern in agriculture was with the maximising of food production, made possible by increased technology, crofting was threatened by government agricultural policy that aimed to increase agricultural productivity and efficiency through the amalgamation of farms and small crofting units, thus creating viable holdings. Hunter relates how, in 1960, the Crofters Commission itself 'went so far as to propose that security of tenure should be widely curtailed and at least two-thirds of the crofting population persuaded to abandon those smaller holding characterised by the Commission as hopelessly uneconomic. The land thus made available, the Commission suggested, should be used to create more substantial agricultural units' (1989:9).

But, Hunter believes the notion of a viable holding is elusive and argues that 'a crofting policy geared to the creation of viable agricultural units . . . would have had the inevitable effect of settling our crofting localities on the road to the wholesale rural depopulation in those hill farming districts, such as upland Perthshire, where hirsel after hirsel has been thrown together in a ceaseless effort to keep essentially marginal agricultural enterprises in profit.' (1989:5).

Such a situation was prevented by the organising and politicisation of crofting opinion in the crofting areas themselves, strengthened in particular by the formation in the early 1960s of the Federation of Crofters Unions to defend security of tenure. Part of the crofting 'problem', however, was not crofting itself but an attitude held by governments and administrators that regarded crofting simply as an agricultural system, rather than a wider cultural system embracing many other aspects of social and economic life, and dependent on other sources of income beyond the uncertainties of farming activities. It was the paucity of other forms of employment in the Highlands and Islands necessary to supplement croft work that governments failed to consider. Those now concerned about the future of crofting argue that the potential economic viability and cultural continuity of crofting relies on a more integrated approach to rural development that encompasses non-farming initiatives as well as agricultural projects.

Despite the history of depopulation in the Highlands, crofting has still managed to keep people in rural areas, unlike full time farming which, because of amalgamations and changes in methods and technology, has actually emptied the countryside of people. Although 80% of the land area of Britain is given over to farming, 80% of the British population lives in towns and cities. Hunter believes that crofting areas are demographically healthier than farming regions elsewhere in Scotland and throughout the United Kingdom. Travelling in many areas, such as Wester Ross, Lochaber, and Skye, one can see considerable numbers of new houses, both occupied and under construction, that would seem to indicate a continued demand by a growing population. Certainly, in the Highlands and Islands region as a whole the population is expected to rise by 6.4% over the ten-year period 1988–1998, from 201,866 to 214,743 an increase of 12,900 people (Highland Regional Council Structure Plan Review 1989).

There are many factors responsible for this increase, such as in-migration, fewer people leaving, an expanding economy, and changes in the structure of employment. A rise in population puts crofters in a very strong position when advancing their claim for crofting to play a central role in rural development. Crofting not only underpins the cultural viability of many communities by, among other things, keeping people in rural areas and thus providing support for local services, it also supports more people per hectare than any other form of farming. . There is renewed confidence in crofting and it is the reason 'we still retain the thickly-peopled country-side that almost everybody else has lost' (Hunter 1989:6). A 'thickly-peo-pled' countryside is now regarded as a healthy ideal, a stark contrast to the attitudes that prompted the setting up of the Congested Districts Board, the forerunner of the Highlands and Islands Development Board, to oversee what was then considered to be a problem of overcrowding, particularly in places such as Lewis and South Uist.

The regeneration of rural economies will depend on the availability of employment and income generating possibilities necessary to retain popu-lation. Here, diversification and pluriactivity are the key ideas. With the gradual curtailment of intensive agricultural practices, agricultural produc-tion looks set to play a less dominant role in rural areas and become just one of many necessary economic activities in a highly-diversified High-land economy. The argument advanced for crofting is that crofters have, through sheer economic necessity, been successful in combining small-scale agricultural activities with other forms of employment and wage-la-bour. Hunter and others in crofting circles argue that crofting can be combined with other activities, such as fish farming, tourism, fishing, and any other flexible, or part-time employment. This in itself, it is claimed, is enough to demonstrate that crofting provides a model for a rural policy concerned with developing a sustainable local but nationally integrated economy. The Scottish Crofters Union also firmly believes that crofting can be combined with forestry, but before crofting-forestry could happen on a large scale legal reforms would be needed (Hunter *ibid.* 7).

The combination of crofting and forestry points to another of crofting's claims, that it is potentially an ecologically sound form of land manage-ment. Crofters do not wish to see agricultural practices restricted by a non-agriculturally focused rural policy. It is essential that crofting remains, in essence, tied to the land, and that crofters remain committed to working and managing the land. In the Highlands, what are generally supposed to be pristine landscapes, can also be regarded as the result of centuries of decline, neglect and destruction through extractive land use practices. For many crofters, conservation is not about preserving landscapes from human activity, 'it can only be effective if the land is worked' according to the president of the Assynt Crofters' Union. In the absence of any large-scale land reforms by central government, this is a responsibility that crofters are taking upon themselves, as we will see below. They argue

that croft land can only be worked if crofters are freed from existing restrictions that prevent them from doing so. And here, crofters are engaged
in a discourse that centres on empowerment and landownership, arguing
forcefully that, in the words of the Assynt Union's secretary, 'only if crofters are given rights in the land and the feudal system of landownership in
Scotland ended that crofting can really provide the backbone of a diversified rural economy'.

Land: Community Ownership or Individual Ownership?

Almost all countries in Western Europe have strict controls over foreign
purchasing and ownership of domestic land, especially if it is felt that it
will have a negative effect on rural life and agricultural practice. The exception, however, is the United Kingdom and as a result Scotland suffers
from an unparalleled problem of external landownership (Carty and
Ferguson 1978). As the manifesto of the Scottish Green Party puts it

> The Highland laird yet lives on as part of an anachronistic pattern of
> feudal landownership that keeps people from a true fulfilment of their
> potentials and the land from becoming the rightful equal source of possi-
> ble livelihood and pleasure to all.

Large estates and vast tracts of land are owned primarily by individuals,
both UK nationals and foreigners, although obscure offshore companies
and trusts jealous of their privacy are also common enough. In England
private land ownership had become the dominant system by the sixteenth
century (Macfarlane 1978, 1987), replacing a previous communally-ori-
ented system in which property rights were not vested in individuals, but in
kin-based groups. In Scotland, as Highland land became the property of
individuals rather than the territory of clans, that is, the space in which the
clan and its leadership dwelt, it became a commodity with economic value
that could be freely sold and bought on the market. This commoditisation of
land disinherited people from a fundamental relationship with a landscape
that, with its previous system of communal tenure, was inscribed with human experience and could be read as a map of social relations. Now Highland land is an investment, rather like a work of art, where the economic
value of estates is largely measured by changes in market value, and which
meanwhile provides the owner with some aesthetic satisfaction, and an
orientation towards conservation rather than change and development. From
the point of view of those dwelling on such land the rights of their landlord,

however attenuated they may be, are still irksome. For example, as we have seen, a crofter must have the permission of his or her landlord even to plant a tree for his own use and the crucial matter of assignation of crofts involves the landlord. Improvements to a croft or the common grazing such as new buildings, drainage, or whatever, for which grants are available will all require that the land owner be consulted. And therefore the disposition and circumstances of the land owner are very relevant. If he is in Venezuela trying to avoid the attentions of the Serious Fraud Office, this can be a cause of considerable anxiety and frustration to the tenants of his land.

The agricultural potential for generating income from Highland land is debatable. However, the issue is not so much about what the land can yield (although given the right kind of management, crofters would argue that it is productive), but about who should own the land. Opponents to private ownership include conservationists as well as the people who live under such a system, and suggested alternatives have been forms of public ownership, trusts, and community ownership. The call for public ownership is illustrated by the controversy over the Mar Lodge estate in the Cairngorms, which received regular coverage in the press on both sides of the border during the Spring of 1991. The 77,000-acre estate had been put on the market by its owner, John Kluge, an American billionaire, for £7m. Conservationists called on the government to purchase the estate for the nation, or to give financial support to a voluntary trust, citing its importance as an area of mountain wilderness with ancient Caledonian pine forest, and as a habitat for rare birds such as golden eagles and ptarmigan. Supporters of public ownership said the estate was too important and too valuable to remain a 'private playground' (Edwards 1991), and should be managed by Scottish Natural Heritage, although in the House of Commons the Under Secretary of State for Scotland was reported to have emphasised 'the tradition of private ownership' in a positive way (Goodwin 1991), confirming a reluctance on the part of Conservative governments to interfere with the rights of private property and ownership.

Although the Crofting Reform (Scotland) Act of 1976 and the Crofting Forestry Act of 1992 make some important detailed changes among the bundle of rights and obligations linking crofters, land owners and the state, there has been no recent fundamental land reform in Scotland since the nineteenth century. So it is perhaps appropriate that in parts of the Highlands crofters are campaigning to change the existing pattern of landownership within the framework of present land law and the law of trusts. Of historical significance has been the achievement of the members of the Assynt Crofters' Union in northwest Sutherland who, like many others, believe that the problems currently experienced in the Highlands cannot be resolved until land is in the hands of local people rather than private individuals and anonymous consortiums. They recently took the initiative to challenge the pattern of Highland landownership and have perhaps heralded the beginnings of a new period of land use.

The crofters in Assynt set up what they call a co-operative, the Assynt Crofters Trust, to raise funds to buy the 21,000 acre (8,498 hectare) North Lochinver Estate owned by a Scandinavian property company which became bankrupt. In attempting to meet the £460, 000 asking price, the Trust appealed to expatriate Scots from around the world. Besides backing from individuals in Scotland and abroad, public bodies such as Highland Regional Council, Caithness and Sutherland Enterprise, Highlands and Islands Enterprise, and Scottish Natural Heritage all pledged assistance in the form of grants and loans amounting to £160,000. They even had the sympathy of a Conservative Government Minister, Sir Hector Munro. The Trust was eventually able to buy the estate for £300,000 in December 1992 and took possession in February 1993. Their success in persuading the London liquidators acting on behalf of the Stockholm creditors of the bankrupt company to accept their offer was a threat by the crofters to purchase their crofts under the terms of the Crofters Reform (Scotland) Act 1976. Especially significant was a decision by the Scotttish Land Court on 14th November 1991 in the case between Whitbread, a member of the rich brewing family and Donald MacDonald of Kinlochewe, one of his crofting tenants, which in effect means that crofters can nominate a new landlord and insist that the landowner conveys the croft land to that person. Moreover by the same ruling a landlord can no longer claim the conventional fifty per cent of the proceeds of the sale of 'decrofted' land and is entitled to only fifteen times the rent, perhaps as little as fifteen pounds instead of fifteen thousand pounds. The effect on the value of land with a considerable crofting population was predictable.[8]

For the crofters of Assynt, who have now, in a sense, become landlords while curiously enough remaining tenants (they have not bought their crofts but individually pay rent to themselves as a cooperative), their powerlessness through not owning the land they work is longer an issue. They have set a precedent which has quickly been followed. In May 1993 the crofting township of Borve and Annishadder in Skye agreed a price with their landlord for the township land. The Assynt crofters, who have purchased not only their tenancies but the whole estate, have brought to an end a long history of ownership by individuals or obscure companies whose interests diverged completely from those dwelling on the land, 'the community'.

Inclusion or Exclusion: The Preservation of 'Crofting Stock'?

The Assynt crofters took a decisive step towards common ownership and community empowerment, and, among other matters, are now turning to address the demand for crofts. However, this cannot be done by creating new crofts, defined as those registered with the Crofters Commission, unless there is a change in the law. The Assynt Crofters Union has started to collect information systematically as evidence of pressure on crofting land and of the demand for crofts in Assynt. At present evidence tends to be anecdotal, such as the story of a man in the Lochinver area, who is regarded as one of the hardest working crofters, but who is only able to sublet a croft and wishes to have tenancy of his own croft. The Assynt crofters cite this as an example of the circumstances many people experience. It is regarded as particularly insidious that they should be excluded, however, because many of them come from what is described as 'crofting stock'. The counterpart of such particular cases are generalised complaints about crofts which are not worked by the tenant and even where the tenant does not reside in the croft house, and which are referred to as 'the problem of absentee tenancies'. This is a particularly vexed issue and one which the Scottish Crofters Union, whose purpose is to defend crofters' rights, has to be cautious about since what is darkly referred to as the 'the ultimate sanction', in effect the absentee crofter being cleared off the croft, has, too many unacceptable symbolic overtones. After all, migrant labour which has a long tradition in the Highlands, when crofters had to leave home in search of work, is not easy to distinguish from 'the problem of absenteeism'. And in many cases the 'absentee' is also a 'local', while the local resident looking for a croft may be an 'incomer'. Some contradictions need to be explored here.

While there is a need, a desire for 'new blood' to ensure the survival of crofting, there is concern that this 'new blood' should not be allowed to contaminate the 'purity' of the Highland 'crofting stock'. Do the Assynt crofters wish to exclude outsiders, i.e. non-'locals', from entering crofting? Would it be politically possible to change crofting legislation in such a way as to exclude those who cannot trace a connection with the existing 'crofting stock'? Local opinion is not unanimous. One retired crofter from Stoer, a few miles north of Lochinver, thought that crofting 'has no future with all these incomers living here now. The old people have gone.' On the other hand a neighbour offered a positive view by welcoming incomers: 'We'd just be sitting up here on our own, looking out at the bay and a township of deserted crofts.'

This aspect of the relationship between locals and incomers involved in modern crofting is illustrated in the following incident which concerns the election of a new chair and secretary of a local Crofters Union branch in northern Sutherland in early 1992. Towards the end of the meeting the then incumbent chair and secretary announced that they were now stepping down and would like the members present to nominate candidates to succeed them in office. With no nominations forthcoming, the retiring chairman himself then nominated a man in his early twenties who had entered croft- ing only two years previously. There was some whispering and a sense of unease among the members present , but as no other nominations were forthcoming, the young man was duly elected unopposed. Similarly, the only person nominated for the post of secretary was elected unopposed, yet there was a sense of disquiet about the choice, an Englishwoman. The fol- lowing morning, critical discussion of the choice of new office bearers was far from muted, as people spoke over the telephone and visited one another at their crofts to discuss the matter. In conversation, the criticism initially concentrated on the new chairman's relative inexperience, but ultimately came around to, and terminated with, the observation that he was an 'out- sider'. The new chairman had been born in England, although his parents had moved to Sutherland when he was a child. Unable to agree among themselves which one of them stood out as suitable for elected office be- cause of the possibility of causing offense or perhaps aggravating latent differences, they could agree that those who did assume office by default were less than adequate, certainly by comparison with anybody else and would therefore need their support, and in such expressions of agreement thereby repaired their solidarity and sense of 'community'.

By ending an external and distant ownership, the achievement of com- mon ownership of the North Lochinver estate also makes a statement about feelings towards outsiders generally, and about the kinds of values and types of agency that outsiders represent. In a sense, community ownership rejects market oriented, individualist claims to property rights, opting in- stead for a return to communal property rights that are embedded in struc- tures of mutual obligation, kin-based relations, and patrimony. Some eighteen months before the purchase, one man from Achmelvich commented that, 'Once we've kicked the landowners out we'll have taken a step to- wards stopping all these incomers buying up our houses and land.'

Alan Macrae, president of the Assynt Crofters Union, is someone who speaks elegantly and forcefully about the symbolic importance of crofting land, about it being land that 'Our forbears fought for, and as such he believes its future depends on the willingness of 'local people' to work the land. While acknowledging that incomers are successful at crofting in the Assynt area, he believes that no incomer can ever feel the same sense of attachment to the land as he himself feels, as someone born in the area feels. He believes a strong bond to the land, the intensity of emotional attachment to the croft, can only be experienced by 'someone who is of true crofting stock'. Incomers who wish to enter crofting should not be denied the opportunity to do so, however, providing they can work the land. Indeed, they too are regarded as necessary to ensure the continuity of crofting. For Alan Macrae and others who share a similar view, what is lost, however, is a profound relationship with the land. Crofting will continue if incomers enter the institution, but at a cost of losing an intricate relationship and delicate balance between people and the land, something that underpins a sense of identity and continuity with the past. The rejuvenation of the North Lochinver estate is now possible because the land is 'in the hands of the people'. Assynt was considered by those who live and croft there as a dying landscape. But now the people, the true inheritors of the land, are in possession of it and implicit in much of what is said about the estate's future is that rejuvenation will primarily be by and for local people.

Some of Alan Macrae's sentiments are shared by his father, John, a retired crofter in his late 80s. For John, however, the relationship between people and the land has already been transformed. For him crofting meant a life of drudgery, so much so that 'the sensible people left the land in search of a better life'. The contemporary situation is different, he believes, as the future for crofting lies in an association with tourism. As he put it, 'scenery is the most valuable commodity in the Highlands. Crofters need to make ends meet through "two-legged" animals now'. John Macrae spends much of his time writing his memoirs, but while he would not wish to see a return to the crofting past, he does believe that with the old 'crofting stock' gone there is a loss of memories, a disassociation with the land.

The Crofters Commission Annual Report for 1991 showed that more than half of all crofts which changed hands during that year went to people who were new to crofting, which we can perhaps take to mean something the same as people who are not of 'crofting stock'. The Commission deals on average with around 110 assignations to non-family members per year of which about 103 are approved. Not all them would be regarded as 'incomers' and the figure would of course include a number of 'locals'. In the same way, though, about 15% of family assignations were to cousins and there are regular demands of the Crofters Commission that 'family' should be redefined to exclude first cousins and other distant relatives which suggests that even among 'family' assignations there is a feeling that 'incomers' are taking over crofts to the exclusion of 'locals' (*The Crofter* February 1991:2). Defining 'locals' and 'incomers' is clearly a highly charged subject.

The Commission's 1991 report pointed to a trend of younger people attracted to crofting primarily because of a belief that it is not only 'green' and ecologically-sound, but also because it is seen as the way land use will progress in the future. This will probably do much to strengthen European Community commitment towards the expansion of crofting, which is currently supported by an EC Integrated Development Programme and Rural Enterprise scheme. The two most significant reasons for supporting and encouraging the expansion of crofting are that the rural population is maintained (and, as a result, will hopefully increase) and that, as a system of land use, crofting has a low environmental impact. Perhaps more significant to them than maintaining a 'crofting stock', the EC and the Crofters Commission are instead focusing on the importance of crofting for integrating culture, economy and the environment in rural Scotland. With growing emphasis on the need to understand how we can live sustainably with the environment, the argument is that valuable lessons are to be learned from crofting. In crofting communities, the crofter is now seen to be elevated to his rightful role as steward of the landscape, and as an environmentally-friendly diversified farmer.

Many of those now entering crofting for the first time are inspired more by a green idealism underpinned by a philosophy of sustainable livelihoods than by a simple desire to escape from urban life and live a rural idyll. This is related to a new environmental ethic increasingly endorsed by government and European Community policy. Not only does the European Commission see rural societies as a natural framework for the creation and development of small and medium-sized enterprises (what it calls SMEs), for Jacques Delors there is 'no better example of collective wealth' than rural development.[9] Yet, perhaps more than any other issue, this is where conflict between 'locals' and 'incomers' is apparent. Rural regeneration may aim to repopulate those areas of Scotland that have been emptied of people, and rural enterprise schemes and integrated development policies may hold a promise of future prosperity, but as was discussed in the previous chapter, the revitalising of rural areas involves the redefinition of landscape.

The cultural impact of counterstream migration is about more than conflicts between people, for example over house prices, and conflicting personalities. The repopulating of the landscape with organic crofters, tree planters, retired people and so on must be seen within a wider context of the appropriation and commoditisation of the landscape. As we saw in the previous chapter, this is most apparent when highly personalised local landscapes are redefined as heritage areas. Rural areas in Scotland and throughout the British Isles and Europe are held to be vital for not only those people who live there, and who intend to move there, but for the urban population at large who depend on the countryside for recreation. This causes conflict over resources, which is the subject of the final chapter.

Notes

[1] If a crofter dies intestate then his property is shared among his relatives according to Scots Law. This applies to a croft tenancy. However only one person can succeed a crofter as the tenant. As a consequence 'few of the many problems which the Scottish Crofters Union has to deal with have caused so much heartbreak as those which have arisen from the still common failure of crofters to make wills arranging for the disposal of their croft.' (*The Crofter,* February 1992:6).

[2] Occupations off the croft vary widely but include general practitioners, teachers, local government officials and employees, laboratory technicians, police officers, students, off shore workers, social workers, potters, yacht charterers, overseas development consultants, fish farmers, publishers, financial consultants, expedition guides, journalists, shopkeepers, mechanics, lawyers, the list is endless. The old stereotype of the crofter as road worker with wheel barrow, pick, and shovel is being joined by others such as 'the highly paid local government official', and the 'new crofter' (Barbour jacket and Hunter wellies, instead of dungarees and tackety boots).

[3] This information is taken from a very useful study of Skye; J. Graeme Robertson, 1988. *Rural Land Use of Skye.* Portree: Habitat Scotland, and the Highlands and Islands Development Board, 1973. *Island of Mull: survey and proposals for development.* (Special Report No 10) Inverness: HIDB.

[4] These are; Hill Livestock Compensation Allowance, Suckler Cow Premium, Sheep Annual Premium Scheme, Crofter Building Grants and Loans Scheme, Crofting Counties Agricultural Grants Scheme, Farm woodlands scheme, Livestock Purchase Loans Scheme, Rural Enterprise Scheme, Agricultural Development Programme, ESA Scheme, Farm Business Non-capital Grants Scheme, Bull and Ram Supply Scheme, Artificial Insemination Scheme, Highlands and Islands Sheep Health Scheme. This is not intended as a definitive list but merely an indication of the kind of government support that is available.

[5] The Corncrake Scheme is funded by the RSPB and Scottish National Heritage and compensates crofters where corncrakes breed for late cutting of grass fields. The scheme was introduced in 1992 is based on one which has been operating in Northern Ireland.

[6] In his introduction to the second edition of *Inishkillane* (London: Faber and Faber 1986), Hugh Brody remarks that, as of the early 1980s, people were beginning to return to the farms of the west of Ireland, after years of exile in Dublin, London, the United States and elsewhere.

[7] This information on Rural Resettlement is taken from an article by Maggie O'Kane, 'Welfare wagon-train to the west', published in *The Guardian*, July 2nd 1994.

[8] See the valuable, and award winning, report on this case and its implications by Torcuil Crichton in *The West Highland Free Press*, 26th June, 1992.

[9] Commission for the European Communities 1992, *New Vitality for the Countryside*.

Chapter 7

In-Migration and Community Empowerment

In-Migration and Conflicts Over Resources

Throughout this book we have drawn attention to the complexity of meaning in the terms 'local' and 'incomer' and have demonstrated the difficulties of assessing the impact of counterstream migration in rural areas of Scotland. In this final chapter we illustrate this aspect further with reference to resource conflict and community empowerment. These are two areas where, for purposes of restricting access to local resources, definitions of 'local' and 'incomer' are contested no less than in other situations. To contextualise the Scottish situation this chapter considers cases from elsewhere in the British Isles, Europe and North America.

Some of the social and political implications of in-migration are evident in conflict over access to resources, however broadly defined, and their exploitation and use. Newcomers may be seen by the established residents of a place as competitors for jobs (see Elias and Scotson 1965) and housing (e.g. Newby 1980), or an area may experience an influx of migrant labourers who benefit from development, while local people are excluded from the employment opportunities such development brings. Local people may also feel resentment towards incomers who involve themselves in tourism development and are therefore perceived to be exploiting a locality. For example, Gilligan (1987) has noted the negative local reaction to incomers in Cornwall who buy property for conversion to guest houses and holiday homes, thereby contributing to the commercialisation of the area, and in chapter three we discussed how the development of tourism in Wester Ross (with incomers as key protagonists) sensitises people to the presence of

167

incomers. The purchase of estates in Scotland for the sole purpose of making a profit from '. . . the sporting potential . . . stalking, grouse shooting and salmon fishing' (Carty and Ferguson 1978:69) is also an emotive issue. Estates are often bought as investments in tourism, although activities are intended for the upper end of an exclusive and largely foreign market. If tourism involves the exploitation of local resources, such as fish and wildlife, there is often a direct threat posed to local residents who depend on them. An example is the controversy over haaf-net fishing on stretches of the Solway near the mouth of the River Annan in south-west Scotland. This pitted local fishermen, with rights granted by ancient Royal Charter, against a time share organisation that had bought up fishing rights on stretches of the Annan. As in so many other similar cases, an 'ancient tradition' was perceived to be under threat by outside developers. [1]

In such situations, incomers and outsiders are seen to be encouraging, and making a living from, other transitory and seasonal outsiders. By doing so they help transform areas into objects of the tourist gaze (Urry 1990) and come to occupy economically powerful positions in communities, while local people are often in subordinate dependency relationships and may experience their situation as one of dispossession (Gilligan ibid.). With local culture appropriated and cultivated by outsiders and then exploited as a resource for economic and commercial gain (especially if the income earned from tourism goes outside the local area), for some local people tourism development and the presence of incomers can only nurture or intensify a sense of alienation and of imminent social change. Local people may also become dependent on incomers and outsiders for seasonal or long-term employment when primary industries, such as fishing, decline. Rather, tourism often develops in areas at the same time as they are experiencing rapid social change, and while it contributes to social and economic transition, as Gilligan (1987) observes, the success of tourism can become necessary for the economic survival of some areas. Local discourse about the real or imagined impact of in-migration is important for making sense of this inherent contradiction.

As we have seen for Scotland and Wales, employment and housing are two matters most often cited as perceived common problems resulting from in-migration, although it is easy to attribute the cause to incomers without considering changes in the wider economy. Nonetheless, these issues are high on the Scottish and Welsh nationalist agenda. Although, violent expressions of hostility towards property owned by incomers in Wales are a constant threat, Davies (1989) has noted the absence of everyday talk legitimising violence. In some parts of the world, however, established and indigenous residents of areas that have experienced an influx of migrants and settlers sometimes resort to extreme violent tactics in an attempt to force them to leave. A recent example of this concerns resentment of so-called 'foreigners' in the north-east Indian state of Arunachal Pradesh. During the summer of 1994 anti-foreigner feeling came to a head when the All-Arunachal Pradesh Students Association called for all foreigners to leave the state, or a shoot-on-sight policy would prevail.[2] Migrants were considered to be placing too much pressure on local resources by cultivating agricultural land and dominating the labour market, and the indigenous response is indicative of an emergent nationalism and political hopes for autonomy.

While small numbers of incomers who move to an area and then look for employment may be competing for jobs that are few and far between, the changing geography of production and employment means jobs are often created in rural areas and incomers are then attracted to them. Recent population growth in rural areas of some European countries illustrates this. For instance, in Denmark since the 1960s a steady decline in (and decentralisation of) manufacturing industries based in the Copenhagen metropolitan area has been countered by the growth of such industry in rural areas of the west, such as Jutland (Court 1989). Although metropolitan population deconcentration has continued, employment opportunities in rural areas and small towns have increased thus attracting incomers, or commuters who still retain social and economic connections to urban areas. Similarly, employment opportunities have increased in rural Germany (Kontuly and Vogelsang 1989), although Winchester and Ogden (1989:184) have argued that in France '. . . evidence for movements of jobs into the rural periphery at the behest of big business is extremely flimsy'. Migrants from urban to rural areas of France tend, on the whole, to retain their existing jobs because of good transport links, which make commuting possible, and because decentralisation of manufacturing industry has been to the hinterland of large cities and towns, rather than to the remote periphery. Those who do move to remote rural regions of France include migrants from Britain and other European countries, who like their counterparts in Scotland, are attracted to rural occupations, such as small scale agriculture and wine-making (e.g. see Buller and Hoggart 1994).

But economic opportunity in rural areas is not always guaranteed for the long-term as it may be based on exploitation of non-renewable resources. Striking examples of the social impact of short-term migrant labour on communities include the Canadian North and Alaska, where oil and gas development brings its own special problems and follows a familiar pattern of 'boom and bust' (Berger 1977). The boom and bust nature of much northern development means large numbers of newcomers are attracted to rural areas, where they may be resident for several years (e.g. Norris and Pryor 1984), but who then may depart abruptly once the boom is over, only to leave behind a disrupted and demoralised local population. This is especially the case with the construction of oil and gas pipelines and drilling platforms. For a short period, rural areas may enjoy unprecedented prosperity, but this kind of industrial development may do little to stem an overall trend of depopulation. For example, in Norway the boom and bust cycle experienced by the oil industry in the 1970s and 1980s, together with increased migration away from rural areas to urban centres, contributed to an '. . . increasing growth of the major cities, a stagnation of many medium-sized towns in less central parts of the country, and serious decline in most peripheral rural areas (Hansen 1989:119). Similarly, mining (another rural industry) may attract incomers to an area, although the exhaustion of mineral deposits and fluctuations in the world economy can result in rapid depopulation, leaving only ghost towns as has been the case in Australia (see Hugo 1989:73).

As a result of oil development in Scotland, small towns and rural communities have not been exempt from the impact of short-term migrant labour. Moore (1982) has examined the situation in Peterhead, in North East Scotland, while Giarchi (1984) has shown how the impact of (mainly male) incomers to the oil platform construction yards of the west coast resulted in hostility between them and established male residents arising from a competition for local resources (and, in some cases, a competition for local women) and a heightened sense of cultural differences.[3] Resentment may also arise because local people often have no opportunity to participate in the development process as equals to incomers. For example, on the Shetland island of Burra the early days of oil-related development guaranteed high wages for professional incomers with technical skills, while most local people could only obtain short-term, unskilled work (Byron 1986). Furthermore, local people are rarely able to control the level and extent of development. Moore's study of Peterhead illustrated how in-migration highlighted the powerlessness of local people when faced with decision-making processes at the national level that concerned the future of the town.

In relation to this, in-migration becomes a political issue with respect to the continued out-migration of local people from those rural communities where there is a lack of educational or employment opportunities, while incomers to those same communities enjoy salaried employment. This is the case in various parts of the Arctic and sub-Arctic, such as Alaska, Greenland and northern Canada, where Native peoples like the Inuit often come into conflict with predominantly white, Euro-American newcomers. These people are often representatives of government agencies and institutions who go north to work as doctors, nurses, administrators, teachers, national park wardens, wildlife officers, and so on. They are given good housing and benefits and Native peoples are often made to feel that they are wards of a paternalistic state (Paine 1977). Brody (1975) has described the situation of powerlessness experienced by Inuit in the eastern Canadian Arctic in relation to the whites who move there, while Riches has remarked that 'conspicuous among whites in northern communities is their tendency to group into cliques' (1977:166). Not only are they demarcated socially from the indigenous residents, but divisions arise between different categories of whites, especially between 'old-timers' and newcomers (Plaice 1990, Riches ibid.).

Part of the problem of newcomers to Arctic and sub-Arctic settlements is their relatively short stay and they are seen as strangers who leave only to be replaced by other strangers. In Greenland, which has a long history of ethnic and ideological conflict between Greenlanders and Danes, where, despite Home Rule, the continued presence of Danes causes occasional friction and discontent in many settlements.[4] Most Danes go to Greenland on two-year contracts as teachers, doctors and administrators. While many of them return to Denmark, and quite often have no further association with Greenland, others choose to stay in Greenland, settling and marrying Greenlandic women. The majority of Danes in Greenlandic settlements, however, do not interact with Greenlanders on a social or casual basis. To the native population they remain strangers (Greenlandic: *takornartat*) and are regarded as belonging elsewhere. Danes on contract work know they will return to Denmark, and Greenlanders are usually critical of the fact that they come to Greenland to earn high salaries and make no attempt to learn the Greenlandic language. The Danes tend to be self-contained, spatially distant from their close social associates in Denmark yet retaining a set of values and interests that maintains the social distance between themselves and the Greenlandic community. Often, resentment towards Danes is intensified because the number of Danes in Greenland increases during the summer months when skilled and unskilled workers arrive to work on construction projects (Nuttall 1992:103).

Greenlanders tend to regard Danes as sojourners who have little incentive to assimilate into the host community. Their stay is brief and they usually explain their reasons for being in Greenland as a wish to combine work experience with travel and adventure. Like expatriates throughout the world, they regard their jobs as a means to an end rather than an act of benevolence for the future well-being of the native population (although contrast this with Paine (1977)). While working publicly with Greenlanders in schools, hospitals and administration, Danes live intensely private lives shared only with other Danes. As sojourners who interact with other sojourners, Danes enjoy constant reminders of home in the form of Danish food, TV, music, annual holidays back to Denmark, the Danish language and good housing. By not aspiring to membership of the host community, Danes remain strangers to the majority of Greenlanders (Nuttall 1992:104). Yet, they are strangers who are both inside and outside the host community; inside as short or long term residents, outside due to ethnic and cultural differences.

The lifestyles of newcomers to Arctic settlements contrast sharply with the situation of Native peoples who migrate from rural to urban centres. For example, in a study of the migration of Alaskan Natives from rural to urban areas, Noss (1987) has shown how these migrants suffer from severe health problems and have higher mortality rates than non-Natives. In an attempt to remedy this and other problems, Native organisations throughout the circumpolar north are campaigning for equal rights. In Greenland, for example, the Home Rule Authorities have embarked on a process of 'Greenlandisation' (Nuttall 1992), thereby aiming to replace Danes with Greenlanders in all areas of employment. The result of these kinds of political developments is that definitions of Native and non-Native, or local and incomer, are becoming formalised. Just as Highland Regional Council has arrived at a definition of 'local' for the purposes of planning policy in the part of rural Scotland for which they are responsible, so small communities in the Arctic are defining the categories of 'Native', 'indigenous', and 'local' people in contrast to 'newcomers', 'outsiders' and 'non-Natives'. Yet, as the next section shows, in practice such definitions are not at all clear cut.

The Problem of Restricting Access

Increasing competition for resources may result in communities attempting to restrict rights to access and use, either through a system of issuing licences or by campaigning for other forms of government legislation, such as, in Scotland, land reform to restrict the sale and purchase of estates. This usually entails defining 'local' and 'incomer' and arguing that incomers and outsiders should be excluded from engaging in customary resource use or development, precisely because communities often claim that the local use of resources is based on exclusive rights and centuries of use. For example, Bjørklund noted that the persistent demand of the Sami fishing population of the north Norwegian fiords, that access to the area be restricted, is well documented by the protests which they have on several occasions voiced against external intruders.

> In the 1750s they complained to the authorities that Sami reindeer herders were fishing in the fiords. A hundred years later, new complaints were sent to the king regarding Norwegian settlers occupying important grazing grounds used in common by the Sami. And from the 1950s they protested strongly against the trawlers which by then had begun fishing in the fiords (1991:43).

But definitions of 'local' and 'incomer' are often contested precisely because it is far from easy to reach agreement on who is a local and who is an incomer, and this may even extend to ethnic identity as in the case of the Sami already mentioned (Stordahl 1991). If 'local' and 'incomer' are paired opposites, then we must also consider that there are intermediate categories of people between these two extremes whose status is ambiguous. As a result their status in the community and their rights over and access to resources are also ambiguous, uncertain and disputed. As we discussed in chapter six, this creates problems for imposing limitations on the assignation of crofts. People themselves recognise the ambiguous nature of these categories and use them to represent themselves and others in various contexts and situations. In his study of Muker, a Yorkshire Dales parish, Phillips illustrates how identity may move along a scale of localness,

> ranging from 'real Yorkshire Dalesfolk' at one pole to 'people from away' at the other. Such *scalar* qualifications usually entail temporal distinctions. There is, for example, a difference between the 'real' Muker families (of three or more generations in Muker) and other local families who have been in Muker for only two generations. There is also a distinction made between a 'new incomer' and an 'old incomer' who, after many years' residence in the parish, is counted as 'a local now'. It is the 'now' which is significant: it suggested that continuous and contiguous residence in the locality is as important a character of local identity as is descent (1986:144).

Similarly, Gilligan (1987:80) shows how incomers in the Cornish town of Padstow are located on a 'sliding scale of exclusiveness' and definitions of local and incomer/outsider are worked out in diverse contexts. While not all incomers in Padstow are recognised by locals (i.e. those who define themselves as 'Padsta people' based on descent from several generations) as being 'local' if they are long-term residents, some established incomers are considered to be 'naturalised' in comparison to recent migrants. And this distinction is sharpened when Padsta people' compare 'naturalised' locals, who set out to fit in, with recent incomers involved in the tourist industry, who arrive and then exploit the area for commercial gain.

Disagreements over who can be considered a 'local' and who an 'incomer' are especially evident in areas that have a long history of in-migration, or indeed where migration has shaped and defined cultural identity. Alaska is a fine example of this. At opposite ends of the social and cultural spectrum of the state are categories of 'Native Alaskans', who are usually, and for official purposes, defined as the indigenous peoples such as Eskimos, Aleuts and Athapaskans, and 'non-Alaskans', who are either recent arrivals and transient residents (known as Cheechakos), and tourists and visitors. However, in between there are categories of people who define themselves and are defined by others as native Alaskans because they were born in Alaska of Euro-American or other parentage, and Alaskans of long-term residence, often called 'sourdoughs'. The history of Alaska is also one of migration and residential mobility. What newcomers to Alaska have in common is the fact that they are migrants and this contributes to the defining and working out of a sense of community and identity amongst them (Cuba 1987). The complications of defining Alaskan identity, however, become apparent when such issues as subsistence hunting rights dominate the legislative agenda of the state. A continuing and controversial issue regarding subsistence hunting concerns disagreement over giving preference to rural residents, thereby excluding people living in urban areas from opportunities to hunt and fish for their own use (Caulfield 1992). Ultimately, rather than discriminating between rural and urban residents, the subsistence hunting controversy crystallises around differences between Native peoples and in-migrants, or between indigenous and non-indigenous, without recognising that distinctions are blurred in many instances.

With respect to land claims and community empowerment in other parts of North America, it is often the case that identities of indigenous and non-indigenous people are confused and negotiated in individual cases. For example, Plaice (1990) shows how in a south Labrador community the population of Settlers (descendants of mixed Indian or Inuit and European blood) constantly negotiates its position to suit particular contexts, with individuals moving from constituting for themselves a secure identity as white Canadians, to identifying themselves as Native people. As the next section shows, this hardly makes the debate about, and the implementation of, community empowerment an easy one.

Community Empowerment in the Scottish Highlands

In many Highland areas, local empowerment is seen as the only way to ensure continuity in resource management and in rural life. 'Bottom up' community development is the approach favoured for the future of the Highlands, and indeed rural Scotland generally, by those people living and working there (or at least by those who claim to represent their interests). It is a reaction and response to 'top down' development imposed from outwith rural townships and communities, which is unambigously identified with the dominant society ('outsiders'). As such, recent developments in the Scottish Highlands are similar to the emergence of grassroots movements elsewhere.

Planners, it is argued, have no sense of what it is like to live in rural Scotland. Like landowners, they are considered to have no emotional attachment to the localities they make decisions about that affect the lives of people living there. This situation has parallels elsewhere in Europe with regard to resources. For example, in northern Norway, traditional Sami fishing activities come into conflict with the marine management ideologies of the Norwegian state. Whereas Sami regard marine resources in the fiords of the north Norwegian coast as property in common for the local population, 'the Norwegian authorities based their fisheries management upon the view of these resources as *common property*. Thus the implications of this policy were destruction of the very same resources because access was open to everybody' (Bjørklund 1991:45).

The discourse about 'community empowerment' in Scotland finds expression, most visibly and publicly, in 'community conferences' organised by Highlands and Islands Forum. Highlands and Islands Forum (formerly Highland Forum) acts as co-ordinator for a network of local groups throughout the Highlands and Islands. Its first two conferences, held in the late 1980s took as their themes 'local decision-making', the 'management of local resources' and 'community sustainability'. The third conference, held in Inverness in November 1991, was designed to advise communities how best to respond to agency led developments and local and national government policy which is often irrelevant to, or in conflict with, local needs. It aimed to demonstrate that communities can take the initiative in determining their futures at a time when European Community talk of 'subsidiarity' and devolving power to local levels of administration was beginning to influence policy agendas (Bryden 1991). The fourth conference, held in 1994, was about communities and the land. Beginning from the local perspective of the strong relationship between communities and the land, the conference addressed issues of land reform and the Assynt crofters purchase of the North Lochinver estate was of central importance to discussion and conference debate.

Highlands and Islands Forum does not question or define what constitutes 'a community' which is hardly surprising. It is taken for granted that 'communities' exist and out there that they have valuable but fragile qualities which are vulnerable to threats to their continued existence which emanate from distant and powerful outside interests and general forces such as 'depopulation', and even 'repopulation'. And it is perhaps assumed that communities are populated predominantly by local people who can trace genealogical and affinal connection over several generations, but that their traditions are disappearing and their sense of identity is being undermined. The embodiment of the threat from beyond the pass, or across the water, is the 'incomer'. While most people seem to be agreed that in-migration constitutes a 'problem', and is cited as the cause of changes experienced in a particular way of life, it is not something that can be placed explicitly on the agenda at Highlands and Islands Forum conferences. But is it implied in community empowerment discourse? Exactly who is to be empowered, and what are people expected to be able to do once they are empowered? Will empowerment amplify a sense of local-incomer distinctions?

When people talk about problems experienced by local communities, they tend to articulate this in terms of rural- urban relations. The 'bottom-up' response is a rural solution to urban 'top-down' policy, legislation, and development initiatives. As such, it makes statements about 'us making the decisions', and promising that 'we can make changes' because 'we are not powerless'. The reaction is to outsiders 'who never listen to us', representatives of a different value system, a different culture even, that impinges increasingly upon 'our way of life'. Local empowerment will ensure that the influence of outsiders can be kept at a distance, or if need be can be worked with, and consulted with, in situations that demand a participatory approach to development. But somewhere between the rural and the urban, 'outsiders' become 'incomers' when they reside in the same locality and count themselves as among those who wish to be empowered and assume some control over decision-making which affects their lives.

Empowerment at local level may have consequences for housing policy, for example. Already, it seems to be accepted that problems of local housing demand are partly attributable to the large numbers of second homes and holiday homes, and to incomers driving up house prices (Scottish Homes 1990), while trends and changes in the wider economy are hardly considered. If community empowerment means that local communities will establish pressure groups as powerful players to place restrictions on housing, then who decides on the definition of what and who is 'local'? And what exactly is the significance of 'community'? At a 'community action group' meeting in Gairloch in March 1991, in response to talk about the need for measures to prevent incomers from taking jobs and setting up in business in the Highlands, a participant at the meeting, later identified as an 'English incomer', asked those present,

> 'That's all very well but, what do you do? If the community needs a new doctor, are you going to give the job to, someone who normally works as a dustman? You don't give a job to someone just because they happen to be local. You give a job to someone who is qualified regardless of where they're from. That goes for whether the job is for a doctor or a bricklayer.'

This is quite a complicated intervention with layers of significance. At one level the intervention is countering the appeal to the model of a bounded and undifferentiated group of people with interests and abilities held in common as representative of normal human relations with a model of human relations as an unbounded network of people who have different attributes and abilities. By doing so he reminds the audience that the community model is only an abstraction, in other words, he threatens by implication the perceived reality of community. But at the same time the use of the self-excluding second person plural 'you' rather than the including first person plural 'we', he reinstates the reality of the homogenous community of locals from which the speaker excludes himself. And the choice of the unskilled hand 'a dustman' to typify a 'local' is not only a nice example of the, probably unintended, reproduction of a stereotype of the 'local', but also endorses the sense of a group of people sharing in a common attribute even if it is reduced to a lowest common denominator, unskilled labouring.

The salience of the categories 'local' and 'incomer' as regards 'community action' is strikingly evident at meetings where this matter is prominent. A participant at the third Highlands and Islands Forum Community Conference who identified himself as 'originally coming from England' said:

> 'You try to sit on the sidelines at meetings, but you get pushed into a leadership role because no-one wants to take the initiative. Local people just tend to sit there and say nothing, so in the end it was getting difficult

for me to keep quiet at all these community action group meetings. People didn't seem to object, in fact they seemed happy for me to start organising things and put ideas forward. But it puts you in a difficult position. You think you're doing something for the community, but you just end up being criticised and put down all the time.

This man's ironic experience of being cast in the role of an interfering outsider is well understood (Frankenberg's 1957). At the same conference, a man living in rural Perthshire explained that he could not put forward too many ideas about conservation in his area 'because I'm a white settler, I come from Glasgow!'. And this comment from a twenty year old man from Gairloch is revealing:

'All our local societies are dominated by white settlers. There aren't any local people making decisions and no-one wants to attend meetings anyway. Look at our heritage society - I'm the only one who goes to the meetings who isn't a white settler, and most of them are old'.

Sometimes the congruence of 'locals' and 'community' can be turned inside out, and then locals can feel like outsiders. This situation is indicated by talk which criticises incomers as 'not attempting to integrate', and forming 'their own cliques'. One woman from South Erradale said that she felt intimated by incomers, especially 'by the educated language they use'.

But such people often have a function, as a woman from Foula in Shetland at the same conference put it:

'Having incomers on the island and letting them make decisions was a good thing. It really united all the different factions on the island and put an end to a lot of nonsense and bickering. People have someone else to blame. I suppose some incomers are kind of scapegoats, really, and we can focus the attention surrounding conflicts on them.'

Like Moore (1982), who exploded the myth of Peterhead being a homogenous community before the days of the oil boom, this woman's statement is a striking admission that incomers do not always intrude into a well-established community of stable relationships. While the residents of Peterhead expressed their own sense of identity in terms of being members of a distinctive fishing community, Moore demonstrated that the community was differentiated, and in some cases structured quite rigidly, in terms of religious affiliation, categories of 'fishing folk' and 'non-fishing folk', social class and so on. However, while incomers on Foula seem to have united the community, in Peterhead in-migration had the effect of accentuating these already existing divisions and highlighted tensions in local politics. As has been noted, in-migration also emphasised local feelings of powerlessness.

An 'empowered community' has taken a step towards a form of self-determination, and therefore stresses the boundary which is implied in the notion of community. Such an amplification may in turn heighten the sense of the presence of 'outsiders'. The idea of 'community' is something that has become virtually synonymous with 'local' and is fundamentally anti-centrist. But can it be supposed that empowerment and development will contribute to reversing the experience of decline of those special qualities and social relationships that are associated with community life?

The discourse on community empowerment as described in this chapter is essentially one in which locals, or those who are defined by themselves or others as long-term residents of a locality, are key participants. Yet, the extent to which locals and incomers have different concepts and discourses of community empowerment is not clear cut. In some situations it is undoubtable that community empowerment challenges what Touraine (1981) has seen as the production of symbolic goods by a dominant culture, and in the process rediscovers or reinvents cultural history and tradition. But if, following Habermas (1981), we are to see groups involved with furthering the cause of community empowerment as new social movements concerned not with fighting for the redistribution of property and wealth, but only for a defence of threatened lifestyles and cultures, then we run the risk of ignoring the desire at local level for the benefits of economic growth. The local communal politics of empowerment, rather than starting from a position of divisiveness within communities, enables people to articulate demands for local, rather than outside control of resources and development initiatives. The beginnings of a new form of communal land use in the Highlands and the collective discussion of problems and issues facing rural areas can be seen within the context of the politics of protest, which is about 'us and them', the 'local' and the 'outside', and makes statements about exploitation.

The assumption of power at lower levels of local administration, and even at the level of crofting townships, together with the increased participation of people in voluntary associations may enhance prospects for rural development, but it is not so much the local community, in the romanticised or historical sense, that is likely to be 'rejuvenated', as the local economy. Talk about a diverse but locally and nationally integrated economy should not be taken to mean an integrated and harmonious community. Such language may prevent recognition of the emergence of a rural society that is becoming increasingly fragmented in terms of social differentiation (if indeed, it was anything other than socially differentiated in the past). Highland communities are being constructed, and elements of Highland cultural history are being appropriated and used to define symbolic boundaries against some threatening, and dominant other. But it is precisely at the point where it becomes difficult to define the community and identify its specific features and qualities that this symbolic construction occurs. There is genuine feeling that Highland localities are beginning to thrive, and there is a self confidence about which contrasts with what was reported twenty years ago when depopulation and decline were still dominant themes in sociological studies and social and economic surveys. This feeling finds expression in such things as the optimism of Highlands and Islands Forum and the success of the Assynt crofters in acquiring the North Lochinver estate.

But while there may be grounds for optimism that communities as places to live can develop and prosper, community rejuvenation is not necessarily felt to be happening in cultural terms. The overall impact of counterstream migration is as much one of contributing to a sense of loss as of regeneration. Highland landscapes and Highland communities are not being repopulated and rejuvenated by 'local' people, those who were disinherited from the land. Counterstream migration is paradoxical in that, while it seems to be accepted that repopulation is essential for the future of Scottish rural areas, it is the wrong kind of repopulation and, in its various forms, amplifies the experience of population loss. The strong and vibrant traditional community that is supposed to have characterised the recent past is, by implication, without incomers. To the extent that restoring the vibrancy of communities is another way of describing 'community empowerment', then it will do nothing to reduce the essential ambivalence in the structure of feeling associated with the presence of incomers.

But the 'local-incomer' dichotomy, or more accurately here, the 'local-outsider' dichotomy, does not so much identify categories of person as indicate types of agency, the way things are done rather than who does them. Yet this is hardly recognised in the discourse of community empowerment which regards communities as discrete entities with distinctive traditions and common interests expressed in such shared values as kinship, lineage, livelihood, language and dialect, and so on. This is what community empowerment protects and develops. Community initiatives and attempts to achieve and bolster local control are perhaps reactions to the integrative aspects of the modern state. That such reaction is manifest in the anxiety felt towards incomers and their presence is an expression of how aware people are to what they see as the forces of cultural homogenisation. For this reason, among others, it is likely that the social and cultural impact of migration into rural Scotland will continue to influence vigorous debate about social change and the future of small communities.

Notes

[1] Haaf-netting for salmon on the River Annan and River Nith dates back over four hundred years. Fishermen have heritable rights, although in 1991 Salar Properties (UK) Limited attempted to prevent Annandale and Eskdale Council from granting licences to the haaf-netters, on the basis that local fishing at the mouth of the Annan was illegal and salmon were caught before they could swim upriver. Salar sold fishing rights to sports fishermen and claimed haaf-netting was illegal because the haaf-net constituted a 'fixed engine'. The local fishermen won the support of Annandale and Eskdale councillors (*Dumfries Courier* 22nd February 1991).

[2] This issue concerned the reaction of the representatives of indigenous tribes in Arunachal Pradash towards Chakmas resident in the state. The Chakmas were refugees from Bangladesh and were resettled by the Indian government in Arunachal Pradesh between 1964–1971. The Calcutta daily newspaper *The Statesman* reported that the indigenous tribes perceived the Chakmas (who make a living as cultivators and traders) as posing a threat to their distinct way of life (*The Statesman* 29th September 1994, p.16).

[3] For a good description of negative attitudes and prejudices of incomers towards an indigenous population, see B. Prokhorov (1992) 'Indigenes et population fluide', *Questions Siberiennes* 2:20–24. Prokhorov focuses on the situation in Yamal in the Russian North, illustrating the impact of Russians living in Siberian villages.

[4] Greenland was a Danish colony between 1721 and 1953, when colonial status was abolished and Greenland became an integral part of the Kingdom of Denmark. Greenland achieved Home Rule in 1979, and with around 10,000 Danes living in Greenland, making up almost one-fifth of the total population of 55,000, this is a striking figure compared with the fact that Danes only made up a few per cent of the population during the final years of colonial rule.

References

Aikman, Christian (nd). *Castle Tioram in Moidart*. Oban: Printed at the Oban Times.

Anon, 1920. *Romantic Badenoch: a guide book compiled for the benefit of visitors to the district*. Kingussie: Printed at The Badenoch Record.

Ardener, E. 1987. 'Remote areas'; some theoretical considerations. In A. Jackson (ed) *Anthropologists at Home*. London: Tavistock.

Argyll, Duke of, 1887. *Scotland as it was and as it is*. Edinburgh: David Douglas.

Asherson, N. 1993. The warnings that Scotland's patient nationalism could turn nasty. *The Independent*, 21 November 1993.

Bate, J. 1991. *Romantic Ecology: Wordsworth and the environmental tradition*. London: Routledge.

Baxter, C. and J. Crumley, 1989. *West Highland Landscape*. Lanark: Colin Baxter Photography Ltd.

Berger, T. 1977. *Northern Frontier, Northern Homeland: the report of the Mackenzie Valley Gas Pipeline Enquiry*. Ottawa: Department of Supply and Services.

Berkes, F. 1989. *Common Property and Resources: ecology and community based sustainable development*. London: Belhaven Press.

Bjørklund, I. 1991. Property in common, common property or private property: Norwegian fishery management in a Sami coastal area *North Atlantic Studies* 3(1): 41–45.

Black, R. 1992. *Orkney: a place of safety?* Edinburgh: Canongate.

Blackie, J. S. 1880. *Gaelic Societies, Highland Depopulation and Land Law Reform. Inaugural address to the Gaelic Society of Perth*. Edinburgh: David Douglas.

Board of Agriculture and Fisheries, 1906. *Report of the Decline in the Agricultural Population of Great Britain 1881–1906*. London: HMSO Cd 3273.

Board of Agriculture and Fisheries, 1906. *Report of the Departmental Committee of the Board of Agriculture and Fish to inquire into and report upon the subject of small holdings in Great Britain*. London: HMSO Cd 3277.

Board of Agriculture and Fisheries, 1913. *Report on Migration from Rural Districts in England and Wales*. London: HMSO.

Board of Agriculture and Fisheries, 1916. *Final Report of the Departmental Committee on Land Settlement for Soldiers and Sailors*. London: HMSO Cd8182.

Board of Agriculture for Scotland, 1920. *Report of the Committee on Women in Agriculture in Scotland*. Edinburgh: HMSO.

Bolton, N. and B. Chalkley, 1990. The rural population turnaround; a case study of North Devon. *Journal of Rural Studies* 6:29–43.

Breeze, D. J. 1992. The great myth of Caledon. *Scottish Forestry* 46: 331–335.

Brody, H. 1973. Inishkillane: change and decline in the west of Ireland. Harmondsworth: Penguin.

Brody, H. 1975. *The Peoples' Land: Eskimos and whites in the Eastern Arctic.* Harmondsworth: Penguin.

Brower, W. 1988. The conflict between environmental orientations in Arctic Alaska. *Musk-Ox* 36: 40–43.

Brown, G.M. 1983. *Hawkfall.* London: Triad Granada.

Brown, D.L. and J.M. Wardell (eds.) 1980. *New Directions in Urban-Rural Migration.* New York: Academic Press.

Bryden, J. 1991. Development from below: the changing agenda. Introductory address, the Third Highlands and Islands Forum Community Conference, Inverness, November.

Buller, H. and K. Hoggart. 1994. *British Migrants in Rural France.* Avebury: Aldershot.

Burt, Edward. 1818. *Letters from a gentlemen in the North of Scotland.* London (5th Edition) Volume 1.

Byron, R. 1986. Oil-related development in Burra Isle, Shetland. In D. House (ed.) *Fish vs. Oil: resources and rural development in North Atlantic Societies.* St. John's: ISER.

Caird, J.B. 1987. The creation of crofts and new settlement patterns in the Highlands and Islands of Scotland. *Scottish Geographical Magazine* 103: 67–75.

Cameron, D.K. 1980. *Willie Gavin, Crofter Man.* London: Book Guild.

Campbell, Alexander. 1804. *The Grampians Desolate.* Edinburgh.

Campbell, J. F. 1983 (1st published 1860). *Popular Tales of the West Highlands.* Vol. 1. Hounslow: Wildwood House Ltd.

Campbell, R. R. and D. Johnson. 1976. Propositions on counterstream migration. *Rural Sociology* 41:127–145.

Carmichael, A. 1900. *Carmina gadelica.* Edinburgh: T&A Constable.

Carter, I. 1979. *Farm Life in Northeast Scotland, 1840–1914.* Edinburgh: John Donald.

Carty, T. and J. Ferguson. 1978. Land. In T. Carty and A. McCall Smith (eds) *Power and Manoeuvrability.* Edinburgh: Q Press.

Caulfield, R. 1992. Alaska's subsistence management regimes. *Polar Record* 28 (164):23–32.

Chambers, Robert. 1874. *Domestic Annals of Scotland,* (Vol 3). Edinburgh and London: Chambers.

Chamboredon, Jean-Claud. 1985. Nouvelles formes de l'opposition ville-campagne. In G. Duby (ed) *Histoire de la France urbaine* (vol 5). Paris: Editions Seul.

Champion, A.G. 1981. Population trends in rural Britain. *Population Trends.* 26:20–23.

Champion, A.G. 1987. Recent changes in the pace of population deconcentration in Britain. *Geoforum* 18:379:401.

Champion, A.G. (ed.) 1989. *Counterubanization: the changing pace and nature of population deconcentration.* London: Edward Arnold.

Channel 4, 1991. *Game Wars.* 5 May.

Chapman, M. 1978. *The Gaelic Vision in Scottish Culture.* London: Croom Helm.

Clive, E. 1992. *Law of Husband and Wife in Scotland.*(3rd ed.) Edinburgh: Sweet & Maxwell.

Cockburn, Claud. 1967. *I, Claud, an autobiography.* Harmondsworth: Penguin.

Coetzee, J.M. 1988. *White Writing: on the culture of letters in South Africa.* New Haven and London: Yale University Press.

Coffre, Nathalie. 1992. *La conception de l'"etranger' a l'ile de Skye*. Universite ParisX-Nanterre, Maitrise d'ethnologie dissertation.

Cohen, A. (ed). 1982. *Belonging, identity and social organisation in British rural cultures*. Manchester: Manchester University Press.

Cohen, A.P. 1987. *Whalsay: symbol, segment and boundary in a Shetland Island community*. Manchester: Manchester University Press.

Cooper, Derek. 1985. *The Road to Mingulay*. London: Futura.

Court, Y. 1989. Denmark: towards a more deconcentrated settlement system. In A.G. Champion (ed.) *Counterurbanization: the changing pace and nature of population deconcentration*. London: Edward Arnold.

Cramb, A. 1991a. Crofting comes down from the hills to Lowlands. *The Scotsman*, 4 June.

Cramb, A. 1991b. Countess to lead new national parks lobby. *The Scotsman*, 10 April.

Cuba, L. 1987. Identity and Community on the Alaskan Frontier. Philadelphia: Temple University Press.

Darling, Frank Fraser. 1968. Ecology of land use in the Highlands and Islands. In D. S. Thomson and I. Grimble (eds) *The Future of the Highlands*.

Darling, Frank Fraser (ed). 1955. *West Highland Survey, an essay in human ecology*. Oxford: Oxford University Press.

Davies, C.A. 1989. Welsh Nationalism *in the Twentieth Century: the ethnic option and the modern state*. New York: Praeger.

Day, G. 1989. A million on the move?: population change and rural Wales. *Contemporary Wales* 3: 137–159.

Department of Agriculture for Scotland, 1944. *Land settlement in Scotland: report of the Scottish Land Settlement Committee*. Cmd 6577.

Department of Agriculture for Scotland, 1949. *Knoydart Estate*. Report by Mr John A. Cameron. Edinburgh: Government Printer.

Department of Health for Scotland, 1951. *Depopulation in Rural Scotland*. Edinburgh: Government Printer.

Department of Health for Scotland (DHS) Circular 40/1960.

Dickson, Malcolm. 1994. 'Should auld acquantaince be forget? A comparison of the Scots and English in Scotland' *Scottish Affairs* 7 pp. 112–34.

Dillard, A. 1974. *Pilgrim at Tinker Creek*. New York: Harper's Magazine Press.

Dixon, J. 1886. *Gairloch and Guide to Loch Maree*. Gairloch: Gairloch Heritage Society.

Durkheim, E. 1964. *The Division of Labour*. New York: Free Press.

Edwards, R. 1991. Anger at feeble heritage plan for mountains. *Scotland on Sunday*, 17 March.

Elias, N. and J. L.Scotston, 1965. *The Established and the Outsiders*. London: Cass.

Entrikin, J. 1991. *The Betweenness of Place*. London: Macmillan.

Forsythe, D. 1974. *Escape to Fulfilment*. PhD thesis, Cornell University.

Forsythe, D. 1980. Urban incomers and rural change: the impact of migrants from the city on life in an Orkney community. *Sociolgia Ruralis* 20: 16–31.

Fraser, Christine Marion. 1978. *Rhanna*. London: Collins.

Freeman, M. M. R. 1989. The Alaska Eskimo whaling commission: successful com-management under extreme conditions. In *Co-operative Management of Local Fisheries* (ed) E. Pinkerton. Vancouver: University of British Columbia Press.

Gaffin, D. 1993. Landscape, personhood and culture: names of places and people in the Faeroe Islands. *Ethnos* 58(1–2):53–72.

Giarchi, G. 1984. *Between McAlpine and Polaris*. London: Routledge and Kegan Paul.

Gilligan, J.H. 1987. Visitors, outsiders and tourists in a Cornish town. In M. Bouquet and M. Winter (eds.) *Who from their Labours Rest? Conflict and practice in rural tourism.* Aldershot: Avebury.

The Glasgow Herald, 7,8 March 1989; 11, 23 May 1991.

Glasser, Ralph. 1981. *Scenes from a Highland Life.* London: Hodder and Stoughton.

Gray, Peter. 1894. *Dumfriess-shire Illustrated.* Dumfries: Maxwell.

Gunn, Neil. 1932. *The Lost Glen.* Edinburgh: Porpoise Press.

Gunn, Neil. 1946. *The Drinking Well.* London: Faber.

Gunn, Neil. 1954. *The Other Landscape.* London: Faber and Faber.

Gunn, Neil. 1969. *The Silver Darlings.* London: Faber and Faber.

Gunn, Neil. 1987. *Landscape And Light.* Aberdeen: Aberdeen University Press.

Gunn, Neil. 1988, *The Other Landscape.* Glasgow: Richard Drew.

Gunn, Neil. 1991 *Highland River.* Edinburgh: Canongate Classics.

Gunn, Neil. 1992. *The Man Who Came Back: short stories and other essays.* Edinburgh: Polygon.

Habermas, J. 1981. New social movements. *Telos* 49.

Haggard, Rider. 1906. *Rural England: being an account of agricultural and social researches carried out in the years 1901 and 1902.* 2 vols. London: Longmans Green & Co.

Haines, J. 1981. *Living off the Country: essays on poetry and place.* Ann Arbor: University of Michigan Press.

Hancox, J. 1993. A quiet rising of the clans. *The Guardian,* 5 November 1993.

Hansen, J.C. 1989. Norway: the turnaround which turned around. In A.G. Champion (ed.) *Counterurbanization: the changing pace and nature of population deconcentration.* London: Edward Arnold.

H. M. Treasury, 1976. *Rural depopulation; a report by an interdepartmental group.* London: Government Printer.

Hewison, R. 1987. *The Heritage Industry.* London: Methuen.

Highland Regional Council. 1985. *Applecross, Gairloch and Lochcarron Local Plan.* Inverness: Highland Regional Council.

Highland Regional Council. 1989. *Structure Plan Review 1989.* Inverness: Highland Regional Council.

Holbourn, I. 1991. What makes it work — or not: Foula. Talk given at the Third Highlands and Islands Community Conference, Inverness, November.

Hugo, G.J. 1989. Australia: the spatial concentration of the turnaround. In A.G. Champion (ed.) *Counterurbanization: the changing pace and nature of population deconcentration.* London: Edward Arnold.

Hunter, James. 1992. *Scottish Highlanders, a People and their Place.* Edinburgh and London: Mainstream.

Hunter, James. 1976. *The Making of the Crofting Community.* Edinburgh: John Donald.

Hunter, J. 1989. The crofting future. Address to the Third Annual Conference of the Scottish Crofters Union, Broadford, Skye, 16 March.

Hunter, J. 1991. *The Claim of Crofting.* Edinburgh: Mainstream Publishing.

Hutchinson, B. 1949. *Depopulation and Rural Life in the Solway Counties.* (First Report of an Inquiry for the Department of Health for Scotland). London: Central Office of Information, The Social Survey.

Jackman, B. 1991. Over the Bridge to Skye. *The Sunday Times,* January 6th.

Jenkins, R. 1991. Violence, language and politics: nationalism in Northern Ireland and Wales. *North Atlantic Studies* 3: 31–40.

Johnson, Samuel, 1984. *A Journey to the Western Islands of Scotland*. Harmondsworth: Penguin (first published in 1775).

Jones, H., N. Ford, J. Caird and W. Berry, 1984. Counterurbanization in societal context: long distance migration to the Highlands and Islands of Scotland. *Professional Geographer* 36:437–444.

Jones, H., J. Caird, W. Berry and J. Dewhurst. 1986. Peripheral counterurbanisation: findings from an investigation of census and survey data in northern Scotland. *Regional Studies* 20:15–26.

Jones, Keith. 1992. The Battle for Glen Dye. *Scottish Forestry* 46:130–135.

Kayser, Bernard. 1988. Permanence et perversion de la ruralite. *Etudes Rurales* 109:75–108.

Kenna, M. 1993. Return migrants and tourism development: an example from the Greek Cyclades. *Journal of Modern Greek Studies* 11:75–95.

Kontuly, T. and R. Vogelsang. 1989. Federal Republic of Germany: the intensification of the migration turnaround. In A.G. Champion (ed.) *Counterurbanization: the changing pace and nature of population deconcentration*. London: Edward Arnold.

Leneman, Leah. 1989. *Fit for Heroes: land settlement in Scotland after World War I*. Aberdeen: Aberdeen University Press.

Littlejohn, James. 1964. *Westrigg; the sociology of a Cheviot parish*. London: Routledge and Kegan Paul.

Lopez, B. 1989. *Crossing Open Ground*. New York: Vintage Books.

Lowe, P et al. 1986. *Countryside Conflicts*. Aldershot: Gower.

Lumb, R. 1980. Integration and immigration: some demographic aspects of Highland communities. In A. Jackson (ed.) *Way of Life: integration and immigration*. London: Social Science Research Council.

Lumb, R. 1982. The demography of small communities: stable numbers and fragile structures. In H. Jones (ed.) *Recent Migration in Northern Scotland: pattern, process, change*. London: Social Science Research Council.

Mac a' Ghobhain, Iain. Co sgriobh mi? In D. Macaulay (ed) *Nua-Bhardachd Ghaidhlig (Modern Scottish Gaelic Poems)*. Edinburgh: Southside.

MacCaig, Norman. 1985. *Collected Poems*. London: Chatto & Windus.

MacColla, F. 1984. *The Albannach*. Glasgow: Richard Drew.

McCrone, D. et al. (eds). 1989. *The Making of Scotland*. Edinburgh: Edinburgh University Press.

Macdiarmid, Hugh and Lewis Grassic Gibbon. 1934. *Scottish Scene or The Intelligent Man's Guide to Albyn*. London: Hutchison.

Macdonald, Colin. 1943. *Highland Journey*. Edinburgh: Moray Press.

MacDonald, Jonathan (nd). *Discovering Skye, a Handbook of the Island's History and Legend*. Fort William: Printed by Nevis Print.

Macfarlane, A. 1978. *The Origins of English Individualism*. Oxford: Blackwell.

Macfarlane, A. 1978. *The Culture of Capitalism*. Oxford: Blackwell.

MaGregor, S. 1991. MPs evenly split on national parks plan. *The Glasgow Herald*, 27 February.

Maclean, Alasdair. 1986. *Night Falls on Ardnamurchan*. Harmondsworth: Penguin.

MacLean, Calum. 1990. *The Highlands*. Edinburgh: Mainstream (First published in 1947).

Macleod, Donald. 1856. *The Sutherlandshire Clearances*. Greenock.

Macleod, Fiona (William Sharp). 1919. *The Divine Adventure. Iona. Studies in Spiritual History*. London: Heineman.

Macleod, Fiona (William Sharp). 1910. *Pharais*. London: Heineman.

MacNeill, J. 1991. What makes it work — or not: Barra. Talk given at the Third Highlands and Islands Community Conference, Inverness, November.

Marshall, T. H. 1950. *Citizenship and social class*. Cambridge: Cambridge University Press.

McPhun, W. R. 1840. *The Scottish Tourist's Steam Boat Pocket Guide*. Glasgow.

Mendras, Henri. 1984. *La fin du paysans* (2me edition). Le Paradou: Actes-sud.

Mewett, Peter. 1982. Exiles, nicknames, social identitiies and the production of local consciousness in a Lewis crofting community. In A. Cohen (ed), *Belonging: identity and social organisation in British rural cultures*. Manchester: Manchester University Press.

Millman, Roger. 1970. *Outdoor Recreation in the Highland Countryside*. Aberdeen: Department of Geography, University of Aberdeen.

Ministry of Works and Planning. 1942. *Report of the Committee on Land Utilisation in Rural Areas*. London:HMSO Cmd 6378.

Monaghan, P. 1983. *Hunger and Dreams*. Fairbanks: Fireweed Press.

Moore, R. 1992. *The Social Impact of Oil: the case of Peterhead*. London: Routledge and Kegan Paul.

Nadel-Klein, J. 1991. Reweaving the fringe: localism, tradition, and representation in British ethnography. *American Ethnologist* 18:500–17.

Nairn, T. 1977. *The Break-Up of Britain: crisis and neo-nationalism*. London: New Left Books.

Nelson, R. 1989 *The Island Within*. San Francisco: North Point Press.

Newby, H. 1977 *The Deferential Worker: A study of farm workers in East Anglia*. London: Allen Lane.

Newby, H. 1980 *Green and Pleasant Land? Social change in rural England*. Harmondsworth: Penguin.

Norris, D.A. and E.T. Pryor. 1985. Demographic change in Canada's North. In K. De La Barre (ed.) *Proceedings: International Workshop on Population Issues in Arctic Societies*. Universite de Montreal: Departement de Demographie.

Noss, J.F. 1987. A preliminary analysis of Alaskan demographic patterns in 1980. *Anthropological Papers of the University of Alaska* 21(1–2):81–87.

Nuttall, M. 1992. *Arctic Homeland: kinship, community and development in northwest Greenland*. London: Belhaven Press.

Nuttall, M. 1993a. Place, identity and landscape in northwest Greenland in G. Flood (ed.) *Mapping Invisible Worlds*. Edinburgh: Edinburgh University Press.

Nuttall, M. 1993b. Environmental policy and indigenous values in the Arctic: Inuit conservation strategies. In Values and the Environment. Proceedings of the conference, University of Surrey, September 1993. pp. 194–199.

Nuttall, M. 1993c. Inuit subsistence whaling: indigenous resource management in the Arctic. *Anthropology in Action* 16: 9–11.

The Observer, 23 June 1988.

O'Malley, R. 1948. *One-Horse Farm: crofting in the West Highlands*. London: Frederick Muller Ltd.

Paine, R. (ed.) The White Arctic. St. John's: ISER.

Palmer, C. J., M. E. Robinson and R. W. Thomas, 1977. The countryside image: an investigation of structure and meaning. *Environment and Planning* A9: 739–50.

Parman, S. 1990. *Scottish Crofters*. Chicago: Holt, Rhinehart and Winston.

Paterson, J. W. 1897. Rural depopulation in Scotland, being an analysis of its causes and consequences. *Transactions of the Highland and Agricultural Society of Scotland* 9: 236–278.

Phillips, S. K. 1986. Natives and incomers: the symbolism of belonging in Muker parish, North Yorkshire. In *Symbolising Boundaries: identity and diversity in British cultures,* (ed) A. P. Cohen. Manchester: Manchester University Press.

Plaice, E. 1990. *The Native Game. St. John's: ISER.*

Planterose, Bernard. 1992. Reforesting Scotland: beyond conservation. In Denis Mollison (ed) *Wilderness with People: the management of wild land.* Musselburgh, Midlothian: The John Muir Trust.

Riches, D. 1977. Neighbours in the 'Bush': White Cliques. In R. Paine (ed.) *The White Arctic.* St. John's: ISER.

Robinson, G. 1990. *Conflict and Change in the Countryside.* London: Belhaven Press.

Robinson, T. 1986. *Stones of Arran.* Gigginstown/Dublin: The Lilliput Press.

Rosie, G. 1991. Clans, kilts and Celtic kitsch. *The Scotsman,* 6 April.

Royal Commission on Agriculture, 1882. *Reports from the Assistant Commissioners.* London: HMSO Cd.3375.

Said, E. 1978. Orientalism. London: Routledge and Kegan Paul.

Salvesen, Christopher. 1965. *The Landscape of Memory; a study of Wordsworth's poetry.* London: Edward Arnold.

Scenes Scottish Environment News April 1993.

The Scotsman (Weekend Supplement), 2 February 1991.

The Scots Magazine, September 1975.

Scottish Development Department (SDD) Circular 24/1985.

Scottish Economic Committee. 1938. *The Highlands and Islands of Scotland: a review of the economic conditions with recommendations for improvement* (The Hilleary Report). Edinburgh: Government Printer.

Scottish Green Party. 1989. *A Rural Manifesto for the Highlands.* Inverness: Printed at Highland Printers.

Scottish Homes. 1990. *Local Market Analyis; studies of Rural Areas — North West Sutherland.* (Research Report No. 9). Edinburgh: Scottish Homes.

Scottish Homes. 1990. *Rural Housing Consultation: a report on Meetings* (Research Report No 12). Edinburgh: Scottish Homes.

Scottish Homes. 1991. *Planning agreements and low cost housing in Scotland's rural areas.* (Consultancy exercise prepared for Scottish Homes by Baxter Clark and Paul).

Scottish Office. 1943. *Utilisation of land in rural areas of Scotland.* Edinburgh: HMSO. Cd 6440.

Scottish Office. 1991. *Siting and Design of New Housing in the Countryside.* (Planning Advice Note 36). Edinburgh: HMSO.

Scottish Office. 1992. *Scottish Rural Life.* Edinburgh: Scottish Office.

Scottish Television, 10th May 1992.

Scottish Watch. 1994. *The New Scottish Clearances.*

Searle, G. R. 1976. *Eugenics and Politics.* Leyden: Noordhoof.

Shoard, M. 1987. *This Land is Our Land.* London: Grafton Paladin Books.

Simmel, Georg. 1950. *The Sociology of Georg Simmel* (trans. Kurt Wolff) Glecoe, Illinois: The Free Press.

Sinclair, D. 1990. *Shades of Green: myth and muddle in the countryside.* London: Paladin

Skye Forum, 1991. *Proceedings of the Skye Forum Tourism Seminar, 13 April 1991.* Portree: Skye Forum.

Smout, T. C. 1991. Highland land use before 1800: misconceptions, evidence and realities. In A. Bachall (ed) *Highland Land Use: four historical and conservation perspectives.* Inverness: Nature Conservancy Council Scotland.

Stalybrass, P. and D. White. 1986. *Poetics and Politics of Transgression.* London: Methuen.

Stead, Joan. 1990. *Orcadians and Incomers: relationships on a small Scottish Island.* MA dissertation, social anthropology, Edinburgh University.

Stephenson, J. B. 1984. *Ford: a village in the West Highlands.* Lexington: University of Kentucky Press.

Stevenson, R. L. 1989. *Kidnapped.* Edinburgh: Canongate Classics.

Stordahl, V. 1991. Ethnic integration and identity management: discourses of Sami self-awareness. *North Atlantic Studies* 3(1): 25–30.

Strathern, M. 1982. The village as an idea: constructs of village-ness in Elmdon, Essex. In A. Cohen (ed) *Belonging; identity and social organisation in British rural cultures.* Manchester: Manchester University Press.

Symonds, A. 1990. Migration, communities and social change. In R. Jenkins and A. Edwards (eds.) *One Step Forward? South and West Wales towards the Year 2000.* Llandysul: Gomer.

Taylor, R. 1981. Doctors, paupers and landowners: the evolution of primary medical care in Orkney. *Northern Scotland* 4: 113–120.

Toal, J. 1993. December 8th, 1992 — A day to remember. *The Crofter.* February.

Tomkies, Mike. 1984. *A Last Wild Place.* London: Jonathsan Cape.

Tonnies, F. 1955. *Community and Association.* London: Routledge and Kegan Paul.

Touraine, A. 1981. *The Voice and the Eye.* Cambridge: Cambridge University Press.

Trevor-Roper, H. 1983. The Invention of Tradition: The Highland Tradition of Scotland. In E. Hobsbawm and T. Ranger, *The Invention of Tradition.* Cambridge: Cambridge University Press.

Tuan, Y.F. 1974. *Topophilia: a study of environment, perception, attitudes, and values.* London: Prentice Hall.

Tylor, E. 1929. *Primitive Culture.* London: John Murray.

Urry, J. 1990. *The Tourist Gaze.* London: Sage.

Vining, D and T. Kontuly. 1978. Population dispersal from major metropolitan regions: an international comparison. *International Regional Science Review* 3:49–73.

Weeden, R. 1992. *Messages from Earth: nature and the human prosect in Alaska.* Fairbanks: University of Alaska Press.

West Highland Free Press, 12 February 1993.

Wester Ross Life. 1994. Editorial. Issue No. 1, Spring 1994.

Wigan, Michael. 1991. Fishy side to time share. *The Field,* August, pp. 66–68.

Wilkie, Moya. 1991. *Penpont, a haven of tranquility?* MA dissertation, social anthropology, Edinburgh University.

Williams, Raymond. 1973. *The Country and The City.* London: Chatto & Windus.

Wilson, Professor J. 1875. Remarks on the Scenery of the Highlands. In J. S. Keltie (ed) *A History of the Scottish Highlands.* Edinburgh and London: Fullarton.

Winchester, H. and P.E. Ogden. 1989. France: decentralization and deconcentration in the wake of late urbanization. In A.G. Champion (ed.) *Counterurbanization: the changing pace and nature of population deconcentration.* London: Edward Arnold.

Woodrow, Rev. R. 1843. *Analecta.* Vol 3. Edinburgh: Maitland Club.

Zelinsky, W. 1977. Coping with the migration turnaround: the theoretical challenge. *International Regional Science Review* 2:175–178.

Index